LINCOLN, MARX, AND THE GOP

LINCOLN, MARX, AND THE GOP

Walter D. Kennedy
and
Al Benson, Jr.

Produced in the Republic of South Carolina by

SHOTWELL PUBLISHING LLC
Post Office Box 2592
Columbia, So. Carolina 29202
www.ShotwellPublishing.com

Cover Design by Boo Jackson

ISBN   978-1-947660-91-5

FIRST EDITION

10 9 8 7 6 5 4 3 2 1

CONTENTS

General Joseph Weydemeyer

Karl Marx described this Union General as "My friend Joseph Weydemeyer." Weydemeyer was a fellow member with Marx and Engels in the London Communist League. With assistance from Marx, Weydemeyer was introduced to Charles A. Dana, the secretary of war in Abraham Lincoln's administration. Dana, a close friend of Marx, assisted Weydemeyer in publishing various communist journals in the United States including the first copies of the Communist Manifesto. Weydemeyer was active in Republican Party politics, supporting both Fremont in 1856 and Lincoln in 1860. (Drawing by Aubrey Haden, courtesy of Walter D. Kennedy.)

Chapter 1

AMERICA, THE 1848 SANCTUARY FOR MARXISM

MOST AMERICANS find it very difficult to think of Marxism, socialism, or communism other than within the context of their lifetime. Beyond a few early twentieth-century labor movements, most Americans have no concept of the various communistic communities and socialistic propaganda organs active in the United States in the early nineteenth century. Yet, most people have some knowledge, although very limited, of places such as Brook Farm in Massachusetts, the Oneida community in New York, or the Shaker community in Ohio. The names of men such as Horace Greeley or Ralph Waldo Emerson do sound a little more than just familiar to these and other Americans, and yet these places and names are associated with early American communistic communities.

All three named communes, as well as many others, were experimental cooperative communities based upon a communist model. Brook Farm became famous, or if you rather, infamous, as the home of the Transcendentalist Club. A prime objective of Brook Farm was "to substitute a system of brotherly love [and] cooperation for one of selfish competition."[1] Like all communist propaganda, what sounds good, "brotherly love [and] cooperation," has a darker component. The twentieth century abounds with evidence of what

---

1 Morris Hillquit, *History of Socialism in the United States* (Funk and Wagnalls Company, New York and London: 1910) 97.

9

communist "brotherly love [and] cooperation" can do. John H. Noyes of Vermont founded the Oneida community in 1848. Noyes has been described by socialist historian Morris Hillquit as "the first historian of communism in the United States."[2] Although known today for their fine furniture, the Shakers were also part of America's embryonic socialist movement. Following the logic of all socialist societies, within these communes the ownership of private property is attenuated if not denied altogether to members. For a socialist, private property is considered an evil because it noticeably demonstrates inequality—perfect equality being the cornerstone of most socialist societies. According to socialist logic, competition (i.e., the free exchange of goods and services in a free market) is the source of greed and selfishness. With these presuppositions firmly fixed in their minds, is it any wonder that socialists hate private ownership of property and free market values? These fallacious socialist principles produce a society that is the antithesis of a liberty-based society and are the very source of the economic failure of all communistic communities and socialistic nations.

As shocking as it may sound to most Americans, it is nevertheless true that within fifty years of the adoption of the U.S. Constitution, there were numerous communistic and socialistic communities in the United States. The obvious question is, "Where did they come from?" With the failure of various European socialist revolutions in 1848, the United States became the place of asylum for an increasing number of radical socialists. However, most of these radicals did not leave their proclivity for revolutionary politics in Europe. These radical European socialists may have changed their abode but not their socialist political dogma. Their new beginning in America included many old European habits. Yet there is more shock in store! Shock number one—the growth of the Republican Party was enhanced by this growing number of European socialist and communist emigrants who made the United States their new home. Shock number two—as will be demonstrated in the

---

2 *Ibid.*, 42.

succeeding chapters, these radical socialists played prominent roles in Abraham Lincoln's nomination and election as president. Shock number three—when Lincoln's policies inaugurated war, these same radical socialists were eager to join the Union Army's attack upon the Southern states. For example, August Willich became a major general in the Union Army. Before coming to the United States, Willich had been a member of the London Communist League with Karl Marx and Fredrick Engels.[3] Robert Rosa and Louis Blenker are two more examples of communists in the Union Army; Maj. Robert Rosa of the Forty-fifth New York Infantry was a proud member of the New York Communist Club;[4] and, Brig. Gen. Louis Blenker of New York was said to be "a convinced Marxist."[5] These are but a few examples of communists, socialists, and other Red Republicans who gleefully waged war upon the South. In 1861, Germans, Frenchmen, Italians, and Hungarians rushed to assist the North in the struggle against the South. One historian, W. E. Dodd, pointed out, "The election of Lincoln and, as it turned out, the fate of the Union was thus determined not by native Americans but by voters who knew least of American history and institutions."[6] What a shocking revelation: The election of Lincoln and the destruction of thirteen sovereign states of these United States were accomplished with the assistance of European communists and socialists who "knew least of American history and institutions."

Think of it, one hundred years before Sen. Joseph McCarthy began looking for communists in every corner of American life (1950s), communists were working within the Republican Party, the Lincoln administration, and the Union Army. Before we

---

3 *Ibid.*, 154.

4 *Ibid.*

5 Arnold Whitridge, *Men in Crisis: The Revolutions of 1848* (Charles Scribner's Sons, New York: 1949) 316.

6 W. E. Dodd, as cited in, *American History Review*, XVI, p. 787.

proceed to exposing these Red Republicans, otherwise known as "Forty-Eighters," let us look at what was the driving influence that caused these radical socialists to set down roots in the United States.

Who were these European socialist revolutionaries and what political philosophy did they bring to America? Although these revolutionaries were from many European nations, the most influential and numerous were German revolutionaries. Depending upon the time frame in which their various revolutions failed, these men "blessed" our shores over a 25-year timespan from 1830 to 1855. Historians have labeled these socialist revolutionaries as "Forty-Eighters" because of the time frame for the bulk of European revolts. As many historians have noted, the Forty-Eighters came to the United States with a set of political, religious, and cultural values far removed from the average 19th century American. One historian noted that Forty-Eighters came to America with a "cultural mission" to remake America into their socialist's world view. This included their disdain for commonly held religious views because "They hated American Sabbatarianism, blue laws...and the more radical ridiculed what they called the *religious superstitions* of the American people"[7] [emphasis added]. Another historian noted that it was not love for the enslaved population nor love of the American Union as it existed at that time which incited Forty-Eighters to join in the War against Southern independence. According to this historian, Forty-Eighters were motivated by their socialist revolutionary zeal: "Their motive in the civil war and reconstruction sprang from the international mind of social democracy."[8] Carl Wittke, a respected observer of the times noted that the Forty-Eighters, "Actually dreamed of an intellectual conquest of the United States

---

7   Carl Wittke, 'The German Forty-Eighters in America: A Centennial Appraisal,' *The American Historical Review*, 53, No. 4, July, 1948, 714-15.

8   Heinrich H. Maurer, 'The Earlier German Nationalism in America,' *The American Journal of Sociology*, 22, No. 4, January 1917: 528.

which would become the fulcrum for world revolution." As can be seen, the Forty-Eighters had goals far removed from the intentions of America's Founding Fathers.

The years between 1830 and 1850 were an age of great unrest in Europe ultimately leading to many revolts against existing monarchs and the establishment of several republics. The socialist and communist movement of the day played a major role in the establishment of these new republics. Most if not all the new socialist governments fell due to a combination of inadequate leadership and outside military pressure. By 1850 many radical socialists found themselves on the run and looking for a place to make a new start in their lives. Many such men and women set their sights on the United States of America. Thus, European socialism and communism found its way across the Atlantic and put down roots in America. According to Theodore Draper in his book *The Roots of American Communism,* the first Marxist socialists in the United States were refugees of the 1848 German revolution.[9] As soon as these radical socialists established a home in the New World, they began practicing their Old-World political habits.[10] The newly arriving socialists were coming to a nation that was not devoid of socialist and communist societies. The philosophy of social reform already had a rather large following in the United States although for the most part it was in the North and not the South. For this and other reasons, the Northern states from Massachusetts to Wisconsin became the primary home of the newly arriving European socialists.

As the reader progresses through this work, he should be aware that there are several points that need clarification. The terms "communism" and "socialism" for the most part were interchangeable during the early part of the nineteenth century.[11] Although Karl Marx's *Communist Manifesto* was published in

---

9   Theodore Draper, *The Roots of American Communism* (The Viking Press, New York: 1957) 11.

10   *Ibid.*

11   Whitridge, 328.

1848, he did not coin the word "communist"; Marx did not play a major part in the socialist movement until after the failures of the 1848 revolutions. Before the time of Marx, anyone who believed in collective ownership of property and the ability of man to perfect his society was identified as either a communist or a socialist. Since the coming of the Bolshevik revolution in Russia in 1917, the term "communist" has been reserved for the followers of Marx. Nevertheless, the foundational principles of socialism/communism, whether in the nineteenth, twentieth, or twenty-first century, are the same.

The basic points of socialism/communism are as follows:

1. Collective ownership of the means of production and distribution, leaving little or no room for free market activity.

2. Centralized government. Since the means of production and distribution are to be controlled by the government (ostensibly for the benefit of all members of society), it is only natural that one large government is needed in order to discharge its manifold obligations. This leaves little or no room for local government—all local governments must be made subservient to the central government—the old dogma of States' Rights stood in their way.

3. Directly related to the second point is the view of absolute allegiance to the socialist government. Nothing is to come before the state. Being an authoritarian state, most socialist regimes will ensure loyalty to the state by propaganda (national education) or by the police power of the state with the use of organizations such as the KGB or the Gestapo. Political dissension is not allowed once the socialist state has been established. After all, only a "crazy" person would try to overthrow a utopian socialist paradise.

> The term "real" States' Rights is used to distinguish between States' Rights as announced by Thomas Jefferson and James Madison in the Kentucky and Virginia Resolves of '98, where States were sovereign and mere States' *Privileges* under a supreme all-powerful Federal government where the Federal government is supreme.

4. A near religious belief in the total equality of man. Advocates of socialism may vary in their socialistic philosophy from the humanism of a Robert Owen to advocates of socialist class warfare of a Karl Marx, yet their belief that circumstances or environment are key elements in the inequality of men remains intact. Man's sinful nature is never addressed because most socialists do not believe in God.

Keep these points about the nature of socialism and/or communism in mind as you read about early American socialists. The one great question that must be asked is, "Why did these radical socialists feel a kinship with Abraham Lincoln, his loathing of real States' Rights, and the desire for the destruction of an independent South?"

Even before slavery was made a war issue, these socialists were standing in line to join in the war effort. None other than Karl Marx voiced his support for a Union victory over the South. The embattled South should take pride in having such men as enemies; likewise, the Republican Party and the North should be embarrassed at having socialists and communists as friends and allies!

One last point needs to be made. While we are demonstrating the affinity that these radical socialists had for the Republican Party and Abraham Lincoln, we are not attempting to prove that either the

Republican Party or Lincoln was at heart socialist or communist. Lincoln was a member of the Republican Party and before that the Whig Party. Being the descendant of the Federalist Party, both political parties were advocates of a strong central government. As far as can be determined, Lincoln was never a member of any communistic society. Yet, socialists and communists did find something about Lincoln and the Republican Party that attracted them. We will endeavor to determine why these radicals found Lincoln and the Republican Party worthy of support, and also how this influence has had deleterious results for modern Americans.

Chapter 2

Red Invasion of America

Actually, the strictly political refugees who emigrated ...numbered only a few thousands, but the influence of these few thousand refugees was out of all proportion to their numbers.[12]

THE "POLITICAL REFUGEES" to whom Arnold Whitridge was referring in the above citation were the socialist radicals fleeing Europe after the failure of the 1848 revolutions. Whitridge was not alone in this assertion. Many historians of the American left have also noted that some of the first "Marxian Socialists" in the United States were immigrants from the ill-fated socialist revolutions of 1848.[13] In his book on the history of American communism, Theodore Draper noted that the 1848 radical socialist immigrants brought with them a "political consciousness then unknown in the United States" and that "they set about duplicating their old-world allegiances in their new homeland."[14]

---

12 Whitridge., 317.

13 Draper, 11.

14 *Ibid.*

Karl Marx

Marx was virtually Lincoln's unofficial European propaganda minister during the War for Southern Independence. Marx and Engels were strong advocates of a strong and indivisible government. The current politically correct view of the War for Southern Independence runs parallel to that of Marx and Engels. Today, both national political parties parrot Marx and Engels' views of the South's struggle for independence. (Photograph courtesy WiKi Media Commons.)

While acknowledging the profound influence of the socialist/ communist immigration to the United States in the post-1848 revolution, one must not forget that communism has a history in the United States that predates these "Red" European immigrants. Any society that holds all property in common and rejects the concept of private ownership of property is a communistic society. This does not mean that such societies are typical of the twentieth-century communist model. The first Europeans to settle in what would become the United States in Virginia and Massachusetts established communistic societies. This was true of the English who settled Virginia as well as the Pilgrims who settled Massachusetts. For the first year all property and profits were held in common by the Virginians in 1607 and by the Massachusetts Pilgrims in 1622, much as was done by early Christians in the first century. To the credit of both groups, our founding fathers soon realized that this "communal" concept looked good on paper but was a dismal failure in practice. After having to face down starvation, the concept of communal ownership and common reward for unequal work was abandoned and replaced with a free market society. It was after the establishment of free market principles of private ownership and rewards for personal efforts that the colonies began to prosper. In reality the first Thanksgiving by the Pilgrims took place after the abandonment of the communal system. The Pilgrim Fathers, like all those who embrace a collectivist society, discovered that socialism promises but cannot produce. Indeed, collectivism, socialism, and communism are idealistic social economic theories often driven by altruistic desires but ultimately tending only to make the *rich poor and the poor poorer.*

Most "communist" communities in the United States before and after the influx of the 1848 radicals were established and maintained by the free actions of their members, very unlike twentieth-century communist societies. These free associations of individuals were denoted "communist" or "socialist" because of their rejection of private property and free market commerce and their advocacy of communal ownership of profits and property. Individuals or groups of individuals were free to leave (secede) from the commune at their volition. Unlike twentieth-century communist societies, these communes never grew into nation-states; therefore, one can only speculate about the nature of freedom within these societies. These neophyte communist groups in America and Europe were breaking ground for the latter-day communistic and socialistic movements that haunted the twentieth century; they were in fact the grandparents of modern-day communism. Of these early groups of socialists and communists, socialist-historian Morris Hillquit noted, "The socialisms described by [John H.] Noyes [author of *The History of American Socialism* written in 1870] are merely the social experiments of early schools of communism."[15] Hillquit, who was writing a history of American socialism forty years after Noyes, pointed out how the early communist groups had grown and matured to become the "modern" socialism of his day, 1910: "The numerous isolated communities, with their multiform socialisms of various hues and shades, have given way to one organized and uniform socialist movement of national scope."[16]

Once again it must be pointed out that the terms "socialism" and "communism" as used by early socialists are synonyms. It should also be noted that one factor that the socialist-historian Hillquit was extolling was that the socialist movement was now a "movement of *national* scope" [emphasis added]. Many communists who gleefully joined in the suppression of Southern secession expressed the love affair that communists and socialists have for big government. Regardless of what "flavor" of socialism one considers, national socialist as in Nazism and Fascism, or Marxist communist governments, all tend to destroy local government and centralize power in the national government. Socialists and communists seem to have a natural affinity for national movements and national governments. General Louis Blenker, a radical socialist from Germany, wrote to the United States War Department that he could raise German troops who had "seen service and actual war abroad" and that he was seeking the *national*

---

15 Hillquit, 7.

16 *Ibid.*

government's approval to enlist "thousands of Germans ready to fight for the preservation of the Union."[17] What was missing from General Blenker's request was a declaration of his support of the Constitution of the United States with its checks and limits on the growth of big (national) government. Nor do we find in his letter to the War Department any expression of affinity for the defense of American liberty—only a defense of American Union. Here we must contrast the philosophy of Louis Blenker to that of Patrick Henry who stated, "The first thing I have at heart is American *liberty*, the second thing is American *union*."[18] Obviously Patrick Henry, the American patriot from Virginia, and Louis Blenker, the socialist Union general from Germany, had two different views on how free men should order their society. For Patrick Henry liberty was the *sine qua non* (something indispensable or essential) of American government. Without the *essential* element of liberty, union or government is worst than useless, it is tyrannical. This difference in opinion on the nature of the Federal government was the core issue driving secession and the War for Southern Independence. It must be pointed out once again that it was the South, i.e., the Confederate States of America, that was fighting for limited government, while Lincoln and the North were fighting to extend the power of the national government. Is it any wonder that European communists, including Karl Marx, and socialists, like Louis Blenker, would find Lincoln's view of government more to their liking?

When dealing with a political/economic philosophy that is more than two hundred years old, it must be remembered that words and expressions may have different connotations today than when they were used then. Every English word has both a denotation and a connotation. The definition of the word "communism" has remained relatively constant—common ownership of all

---

17 Louis Blenker, as cited in, The Official Records War of the Rebellion (ORWR), Sr. III, Vol. I, p. 459.

18 William Wirt Henry, Patrick Henry: Life, Correspondence and Speeches (1891, Sprinkle Publications, Harrisonburg, VA: 1993) III, 449.

means of production and profit. Yet, the connotation of the word "communism" has radically changed in the past one hundred years. Having succeeded in establishing a communist government in Russia, the Bolsheviks established a ruthless authoritarian and aggressive communist government. Therefore, today most Americans think of communism in relationship to an aggressive, ruthless, tyrannical government and the resultant subjugation and even murder of millions of people. Also, it must be recognized that in the post-Bolshevik revolution area, there has been a major division between communism and socialism. Whereas in the nineteenth century the words were essentially synonymous, in the twenty-first century they represent two different manifestations of the collectivist system. Whereas in the nineteenth century they were identical twins, today they are at best brothers. In this work these words will for the most part be used in the nineteenth-century connotation.

Another word that is often used by communists and socialists that has also been the source of much misunderstanding is the word "equality." As used by communists and socialists it reflects their belief in the absolute "sameness" of all humans. According to Marx and other socialists, all men are absolutely equal. Any observable inequality is the result of environmental modifiers. Thus, Marx is often quoted as saying, "Man is what he eats." It is a major tenet of socialism and communism that by equalizing the environment all men will become completely equal. With absolute equality mankind will be liberated from selfish desires, and therefore a utopian society will emerge, or so the theory goes. The foregoing concept of equality may represent the sense of the word as expressed by socialists and by communists, but in no wise represents what the founding fathers of these United States believed when they proclaimed in the Declaration of Independence that "all men are created equal." The author of, or at least the major contributor to, the Declaration of Independence was Thomas Jefferson, a slaveholder. Every delegate who signed the Declaration of Independence represented a slaveholding colony.

Those colonies that had the fewest number of slaves within their borders were the very colonies that were the leading agents of the African slave trade.

Although the term "all men are created equal" is part of the Declaration of Independence, our founding fathers were not Marxists or socialists. Remember, no one even suggested at the time of the signing of the Declaration of Independence that the slave trade had to end immediately; no one suggested at the signing of the Declaration of Independence that all slaves had to be freed; no one suggested at the signing of the Declaration of Independence that all class distinction had to cease. Obviously if our founding fathers had been socialist ideologues, they would have demanded the above-mentioned actions. What then did the founding fathers mean when they adopted a declaration proclaiming that "all men are created equal"?

At the time of the signing of the Declaration of Independence an aristocratic elite ruled most governments. In various ways this hereditary aristocratic class chose a monarch who was said to rule by "divine right." Two aspects of this system of government stand out. First, the aristocratic class was a hereditary class. Upper-class status was unobtainable for the rest of non-aristocratic society; the lower classes were not the equals of the upper class and could never obtain "noble" status. Second, holding special status within society that no one else could acquire and ruling by "divine right," monarchs (kings or queens) could never be equal to their subjects nor their subjects equal to them. In this system of government inequality was an established fact of life. Believing that no man was born "booted and spurred" to ride upon the backs of other citizens, our founding fathers expressed the republican view of government in which no class or individual has a superior right to rule the government. This then is the republican virtue of free men in free government that our forefathers were speaking of when they stated that "all men are created equal." Within this type of society, no man has a divine right to rule while others are denied this right; and no hereditary class is allowed to dominate the affairs of government to the exclusion of the "unequal" citizens. Vast forms of inequality exist within this society, but this inequality is based upon personal ability and not heredity or divine right. Within this free republic all citizens are allowed to compete for any social or economic prize. Not all will succeed, but all are equally free to attempt to do that which they set their mind to do.

The equality of the founding fathers is an equality of opportunity, not a governmental guarantee of equality of outcome. Social and economic inequality within a free-market society is a natural outcome of ability and effort. Furthermore, it is inequality that is a driving force of all free-market systems. A man with more money is unequal to a man with less money. When the man with more money desires to have a new roof put on his home, he will use this inequality of resources to hire a man to put a new roof on his home. A man who does not have gravel is unequal to the man with a lot of gravel. When gravel is needed, the one without gravel will seek out and hire the man with lots of gravel, and both men will prosper from this inequality. Multiply this little exchange a thousand times, and you will begin to see how a free-market system works, and why it works well. This type of activity is not possible within a socialist or communist system, and therefore *collectivist systems can only make the rich poor and the poor poorer.*

For the founding fathers "all men are created equal" was simply a statement recognizing the *political* equality of all free citizens of a society. Free men in a free society will by their own ability create an unequal citizenry. Socialist equality is and always has been the death knell for freedom. Thus, the socialist demand for abject human equality should be viewed with a jaundiced eye. Socialist and communist equality is obtainable only at the point of a bloody bayonet. Nowhere in the writings of the founding fathers is there to be found anything close to the Marxist concept of mandatory equality.

Another word that has "evolved" over the past two hundred years is "democracy." For most people today the term "democracy" or "democratic" has only a positive meaning. Yet for our founding fathers, democracy was a fearful form of government. The authors of the *Federalists Papers* warned of the corrosive effects of a democracy.[19] Because majority rule, unopposed by a strong constitutional guarantee of minority rights, leads ultimately to the dictatorship of the majority, the founding fathers established a constitutional republic of republics. Within a republic of republics numerous safeguards are in place to prevent the majority of citizens from plundering the property and liberty of the minority. These United States were established as a republic of republics. Even strong federalists such as Alexander Hamilton recognized the "compound" republican nature of the Federal government. When anti-federalists warned of the possibility of the Federal government usurping the rights of the states, Hamilton, replying to such criticism, assured the anti-federalists, "It may safely be received as an axiom in our political system, that the *state governments* will in all possible contingencies afford complete security against invasions of the public liberty by the national authority[20] [emphasis added]. The power exercised by the central government is a grant from the states, and this grant is clear and easy to discern. Furthermore, every power that is not delegated to the central government nor prohibited to the states is left intact to be exercised by the people at the local level; that is, the people of each state. Even within the central government the power granted to the central government is divided into three equally independent departments. The power to make laws for these United States is granted to a congress of elected representatives and does not reside in the body of citizens as a whole. All these measures are very anti-democratic. Whereas in a pure democracy the majority of the people can make and unmake laws at their volition, in a constitutionally limited republic of republics the majority must exist within several communities (states) and must elect a majority of representatives to the national government before its will is enforceable. Even then, constitutional barriers

---

19   James Madison, as cited in, The Federalists Number 10, George W. Carey and James McClellan, ed. (Kendall Hunt Publishing Company, Dubuque, IA: 1990) 46-48.

20   Alexander Hamilton, as cited in, The Federalists Number 28, Carey and McClellan, 141.

limit the will of the majority. All in all, this tends to attenuate the manifold evils of democracy and helps secure the rights and property of the minority.

As originally established, the government of these United States could be described as a representative democracy. The founding fathers were fearful of mass democracy; therefore, they opted for a representative republic instead of a pure democracy. This government was "democratic" only in the sense that any free adult male could qualify to be a voter. These voters then elected representatives who were responsible for making the laws of the Federal government. Speaking for the founding fathers, James Madison in *The Federalist* gave us the following warning about democracies:

> [A] pure Democracy, by which I mean, a Society, consisting of a small number of citizens, who assemble and administer the Government in person, can admit of no cure for the mischief of faction. A common passion or interest will, in almost every case, be felt by a majority of the whole; a communication and concert results from the form of Government itself; and there is nothing to check the inducements to sacrifice the weaker party, or an obnoxious individual. Hence it is, that such Democracies have ever been spectacles of turbulence and contention; have ever been found incompatible with personal security, or the *rights of property*; and have in general been as short in their lives, as they have been violent in their deaths[21] [emphasis added].

Madison also warned against believing that such governments would produce perfect equality. Thus, we see Madison warning against the prime tenet of modern socialism and/or liberalism, the belief in absolute human equality.

---

21 James Madison, as cited in, *The Federalists* Number 10, Carey and McClellan, 46.

Theoretic politicians, who have patronized this species of Government [democracy], have *erroneously* supposed, that by reducing mankind to a perfect equality in their political rights, they would, at the same time, be perfectly equalized and assimilated in their possessions, their opinions, and their passions[22] [emphasis added].

In one small paragraph James Madison destroyed the socialists'/liberals' philosophical keystone, i.e., their faith in equality and democracy. As Madison demonstrated, the American idea of equality is not the same idea that is held by socialists and communists. Nevertheless, it was the socialists' concept of democracy and equality that the European radicals of 1848 brought to the United States, to the Republican Party, and ultimately to Abraham Lincoln.

---

22 *Ibid.*

The Genesis of American Socialism

The theories of utopian socialism frequently led to experiments in communistic settlements.[23]

Long before Karl Marx became known as a leader in the socialist movement, numerous Americans had already joined in the effort to usher in a perfect or utopian society. As has already been explained, the very first European settlers in both Virginia and Massachusetts established communistic settlements. It soon became obvious that the theory of a collectivist society and the reality of a collectivist society are not one and the same. Despite the failure and repudiation of the collectivist attempts in early America, the socialists' dream persisted. The lingering dream of establishing a utopian society in which man would create a perfect world "where there will be no war, no crimes, no administration of justice...no government"[24] continued to be resurrected by socialist idealogues. Socialist idealogues assured the world that with their form of socialism, "there will be neither disease, anguish, melancholy, nor resentment. Every man will seek, with ineffable ardor, the good of all."[25] The eighteenth-century socialist philosophers taught that man's intelligence and reason could be applied to every problem and thereby create a harmonious society or a virtual heaven on earth. This socialist thesis should sound familiar to modern Americans because it is the theme used to promote every liberal, big government scheme in America. Unlike orthodox Christianity, which seeks to bring heaven to man by means of God's grace, this socialist "heaven on earth" was to be wrought by the hand of man.

---

23   Hillquit, 23.

24   W. Godwin, as cited in S. Hook, *Marx and the Marxists: The Ambiguous Legacy* (D. Van Nostrand Co. Inc., New York: 1955) 28.

25   *Ibid.*

One cannot avoid noticing the sharp contrast between orthodox Christianity and the philosophy of socialism. Christianity has always taught that man is sinful and therefore a fallen creature. The fallen nature of man was reinforced by the Nicene Church Council and other Church councils. Therefore, by his own efforts, Man cannot usher in a perfect society because he is not nor can he become perfect in and of himself. According to the Church, the only way man can be made perfect is by the grace of God. If God does not perfect man, then man is hopelessly doomed in any effort at establishing a "perfect" society. Yet, this is exactly what eighteenth, nineteenth, twentieth, and twenty-first-century socialist, communist, and liberal mankind has attempted to do. As has been noted, this dichotomy of worldviews is not something unique to modern man. During the fourth century one of the great theological debates was between a British monk, Pelagius, and Aurelius Augustine, Bishop of Hippo. Pelagius taught that man, although sinful, retained enough of the divine to essentially correct any wrongs or imperfections within himself, including working out his own salvation. Augustine, and eventually the Church in general council, repudiated the theology of Pelagius as heretical. The teaching of the Church from that time to now has been that man is a sinful creature and unable, apart from the grace of God, to work out his own salvation.

Although Pelagius was repudiated, his philosophy of man's ability to "save himself" has remained the cornerstone of humanistic ideology. All socialists, communists, free thinkers, and secular humanists firmly hold to the view that man can create nirvana, utopia, a workers' paradise, or some form of heaven on earth. Many early-American socialist communities were organized around this near religious philosophy. Nor has this nineteen century "near religious" view of socialism passed into oblivion. In 2015, David Priestland, in an article 'Anarchism could help to save the World,' noted that the Russian anarcho-communist, Peter A. Kropotkin, had been blessed by Oscar Wilde as the "beautiful white Christ."[26] At first glance this sounds strange, yet it must be remembered that there is a difference between religion and theology. Many theologians maintain that the subject matter of religion is man, whereas the subject matter of theology is God.[27] This is clearly displayed in the many communistic "religious" communities founded in early nineteenth-century America. In varying degrees these communities were attempting to plant a heaven on earth by their own intelligence and power. Here, once again, we see the specter of Pelagius attempting to challenge orthodox Christianity. The total failure of each of these communistic societies attests to the wisdom of St. Augustine.

This fundamental difference in worldviews has deep and abiding relevance to American history. The founding fathers of these United States were men who firmly held to a biblical worldview. This is not to suggest that all founding fathers were, in the vernacular of the twenty-first century, "born-again Christians." The founders of this republic were influenced by the commonly held view of that age, i.e., man was a fallen creature enslaved by sin; therefore, man, unlike angels, could not be trusted with power over other men. According to the biblical worldview, man's nature would push even the best of men into doing evil to his fellow citizens. The only way anyone could be trusted with the power to govern was if a *counter* power was retained by those governed to check any abuse of sinful man. Thus, we see in most state constitutions up and through the admission of Tennessee to the Union a firm statement in the belief in God, eternal punishment and rewards, and the right of the people to defend themselves against "arbitrary power" that

---

26 Oscar Wide, as cited in David Priestland, "Anarchism could help to save the world," *The Guardian*, July 3, 2015, 'Anarchism could help to save the world' | Politics books | *The Guardian* accessed January 5, 2022.

27 R. C. Sproul, *Grace Unknown: The Heart of Reformed Theology* (Baker Books, Grand Rapids, MI: 1997) 11.

was "destructive to the good and happiness of mankind."[28] People with a biblical worldview are more likely to produce a society with checks and balances on governmental power; whereas, people who see mankind as capable of ultimate perfection are more likely to create an all-powerful central government to do the will of "ultimately good" mankind. As stated, this dichotomy of worldviews has as much to do with how people are governed as it does with how they worship. Early in the history of these United States several groups of communistic communities were established with the aim of perfecting man and society. These communistic societies fall into two categories, sectarian socialists, aka, Christian socialists, and secular socialists.

The first and most prominent of the sectarian (Christian) socialists were the **Shakers**. Ann Lee, referred to as "Mother" Ann Lee by her followers, immigrated to America in 1774. Shakers rejected all privately owned property, living in a communal (communistic) community with perfect equality between men and women. Shakers prohibited marriage and any sexual activity among members. This group grew to around 5,000 members before beginning a decline. Around 1910 there were only 500 members, today they no longer exist. In their religious meetings Shakers would dance over long periods of time until they began a shaking and wild contorting of their bodies in which time, they were said to commune with the spirit world—thus obtaining their name, "Shakers."

Another group of Christian socialists were members of the **Oneida Community**, founded in 1811 by John H. Noyes of Vermont. Socialist historian Morris Hillquit, referring to Noyes, stated "The first historian of communism in the United States was himself the founder of one of the most noteworthy of communistic societies."[29] The bulk of members of this communistic society were from New England. The Oneida Society was started as a "Christian"

---

28   Constitution of Tennessee, as cited in, *The American's Guide to the Constitutions of the United States of America* (Moore and Lake, Trenton, NJ: 1813) 314.

29   Hillquit, 31.

community. They rejected the divinity of Jesus, believing him to be a good man. They did believe that the teaching of Jesus as a man could help them perfect society. After being influenced by other socialist groups, by 1848 Noyes' group had become an openly communistic society.[30] More information about these "Christian socialists" will be found in Addendum I.

Another group of early American communists were the secular socialists. Unlike their fellow socialists know as Christian socialists, the secular socialists rejected religion as the foundation for their attachment to socialist ideas. They held firm to the idea that man had within himself the means of securing the formation of a perfect society. They advanced the notion that the evils of society were due to the environment of man and not man's innate nature—bad people were bad because of the situation they found themselves in and not because of some inward moral defect. One of the leading men in this secular socialist movement was Robert Owen, the founder of the **Owenite Communities**.

According to Robert Owen, "Man becomes a wild, ferocious savage, according to the circumstances in which he may be placed from his birth."[31] Hillquit praised Robert Owen's work, especially Owen's "personal propaganda for the theories of communism, [which] has been too often overlooked. That propaganda has, however, had a powerful influence on many of his contemporaries."[32] Equally as important in promoting radical socialism in the United States was Robert Owen's son, Robert Dale Owen. Robert Dale Owen immigrated to the United States with his father and was "steeped in his father's socialist philosophy."[33] Robert Dale Owen assisted his father in establishing the New Harmony communistic community in Indiana and served three

---

30 *Ibid*, 43.

31 Robert Owen, as cited in Hillquit, 49.

32 *Ibid.*

33 Robert Dale Owen, *Encyclopaedia Britannica*, November 5, 2021, http://www.britannica.com/biography/Robert-Dale-Owen Access January 5, 2022.

terms as a Representative in the Indiana legislature as well as two terms in the United States House of Representatives from Indiana.[34] Long before AOC and the Squad were promoting their socialist views in the U. S. House of Representatives, Robert Dale Owens, a free thinker (secular humanist) who opposed evangelical religion, who advocated for liberal divorce laws, and who promoted the equal distribution of wealth, was pushing these ideas onto the American scene.

Another secular socialist group, although not as well-known as the Owenite community, is the **Fourierist** society. This group was established as a communal community in France by Charles Fourier. Albert Brisbane of New York brought Fourierism to the United States after an extended stay in Europe. Brisbane wrote and published *Social Destiny of Man* in 1840. Brisbane's book became a best-selling book on how to build a utopian society. It was Brisbane's book which was responsible for recruiting Horace Greeley to the communistic Fourier movement. Greeley, the editor of the *Tribune,* soon invited Karl Marx to be a contributing editor of his paper. The ardent "social reformers" from Massachusetts known as the "Transcendentalists" from Brook Farm fame were also soon avid supporters of the Fourier movement.

The influence of these sectarian and secular socialists and communists cannot be over emphasized. More than anything else, they laid the groundwork for the Forty-Eighters when they came to America and began propagandizing for their radical socialist worldview. For a more thorough look at who these early socialists and communists were and their influence upon the political stage in the United States, see Addendum I herein.

---

34 *Ibid.*

SUMMARY

As stated earlier, one notable 1848 European communist who was a member of the Union Army was Maj. Robert Rosa. Rosa was an early member of the New York Communist Club. The following preamble of the Communist Club's constitution gives insight into the worldview of these early American communists:

> The members of the Communist Club reject every religious belief, no matter in what guise it may appear, as well as all views not based upon the direct testimony of the senses. They recognize the perfect equality of all men, regardless of color and sex, and therefore they strive above all to abolish private property, inherited or accumulated, to inaugurate in its place the participation of all in the material and intellectual enjoyments of the earth. They pledge themselves with their signatures to carry out their aims in the present state of society as far as possible, and to support each other morally and materially.[35]

As stated in the constitution of the New York Communist Club, members were pledged to reject all religion. These early American socialists/communists did indeed reject accepted orthodox religion, but they maintained a near "religious" faith in their utopian dreams. Even today in the face of one socialist failure after another, the utopian mind-set is not predisposed to accepting socialism/communism as a failed system. In his book *How Capitalism Saved America*, Thomas DiLorenzo noted how left-wing intellectual Theodore Draper (author of *The Roots of American Communism*) expressed this "religious faith" in Cuba's communism: "The American writer Theodore Draper admitted that Cuban economic policy was 'murderous, mendacious...brutal and arbitrary,' but it should still be admired because, after all, 'it

---

35 Constitution of the Communist Club of New York, 1857, as cited in, Hillquit, 153.

is still socialist.'"[36] This "religious" faith in utopian socialism is the main characteristic that has flowed through the centuries from the Shakers, Owenites, Brook Farm participants, European socialists, members of the Communist Club of New York, and all other such utopian societies to America's modern-day neo-Marxists.

The near religious utopian philosophy has, unfortunately, been embraced by too many Americans. Regardless of the problem facing Americans today, the first question that is too often asked is, "When is the government going to save us?" At the most fundamental level, this question is a socialist response to private concerns. Free men in a free society do not look to government for solutions to private matters. Why? Because government is not God; it cannot "give" to one unless it first *takes* away from another. The "taking" mechanism of big government is that characteristic which tramples upon the liberty of its citizens. We do not live in a free society when the government can take our property in the form of taxes and give it to others. An individual's property is an extension of that person—an attack upon property is an attack upon an individual. This is the very reason that the founding fathers gave us a constitution that limited the power of the central government—to promote and secure the rights and liberty of "we the people."

The very foundation for modern-day liberalism/socialism was laid by the many and various utopian ideologues of the nineteenth century. The fact that these utopian socialists/communists found Abraham Lincoln and the Republican Party to be objects worthy of their zeal and efforts speaks volumes as to why post-Appomattox America has adopted most if not all of the early American socialist/communist goals. Universal suffrage was a dream of every socialist/communist movement in Europe and America; even Karl Marx spoke in favor of universal suffrage;[37] the same can be said to be true about a progressive income tax, abolition of the rights of inheritance, a system of national education, centralized banking,

---

36   DiLorenzo, *How Capitalism Saved America*, 38.

37   Robertson, 102.

and many other such socialist/communist measures. Indeed, it appears that even the most disheartened utopian ideologue of the nineteenth century would find much to celebrate in modern America.[38] Socialism and communism did not come to these United States from Communist Russia; these concepts were already well known by many Northern intellectuals of the nineteenth century.

In 1861, the South found itself in the unique position of fighting for the concept of small government while Lincoln and his supporters were fighting to expand the powers of the Federal government. By and large, most of the utopian dreamers were citizens of Northern states; few if any utopian dreamers fought in defense of the Southern point of view during the war. The preponderance of communistic societies in the United States were located in Northern states before the war. For example, of the ten states where the Shakers had communal societies, only two were in the South; the Oneida Community was organized by a man from Vermont and established its community in New York; Fourierist societies were formed in the states of New York, New Jersey, Pennsylvania, Massachusetts, Ohio, Illinois, Indiana, Wisconsin, and Michigan; the famous Brook Farm was in Massachusetts; the Icarians did have one community started in Texas but not from local Texans, this group later removed to Illinois. The point here is that it appears that the South never offered as pleasant an environment for utopian dreamers as did the North. This seems to have held true up and into the twentieth century. According to Theodore Draper by 1923 most communists in America could be found in cities such as New York, Chicago, Boston, Minneapolis, Cleveland, and Detroit.[39] Note that we do not see Charleston, New Orleans, or any Southern city mentioned in the above listed cities. Socialist-historian Morris Hillquit stated that by 1910, the electoral victories by American socialists were in the states

---

38 For a more comprehensive study of the failures of modern American "conservatism" in the face of socialism, see, James R. Kennedy, *Reclaiming Liberty* (Pelican Publishing Company, Gretna, LA: 2005) Chapter I.

39 Draper, 391.

of Wisconsin, Massachusetts, Montana, Ohio, Illinois, Colorado, and Pennsylvania.[40] Once again we see that it is the North and not the South where we find electoral victories for the Socialist Party in America.

The history of socialism and communism in America is a long and curious story extending from pious religious orders, New England Transcendentalists, European radical socialists, the Republican Party, Abraham Lincoln, a defrocked Baptist minister, and the author of a utopian novel that sold more than three million copies in America. Ultimately, all Americans have felt the influence of these socialist utopian dreamers. The thought of Lincoln as the first American president to have had a communist sympathizer working in a key part of his administration is and should be shocking to all Americans. Charles Dana, who visited Karl Marx in 1848, was an associate of Horace Greeley and an early convert to the communistic Fourierist movement. Dana served as assistant secretary of war under Edwin Stanton during the Lincoln administration, thus becoming the first communist, or at least the first communist sympathizer, to serve in a high position within the government of the United States.[41] Be that as it may, the result of Lincoln's victory over the South was to give the utopian dreamers a victory for big government. Lincoln and the Republican Party's victory assured that the first demand of the Communist Party for a "one nation indivisible" was not only made possible, it was made unavoidable. As a result, all Americans today are living in a nation far removed from that envisioned by America's Founding Fathers. At this juncture there is one question that stands begging to be asked: "Can the adverse effects of the socialists' victory at Appomattox be removed from this nation?" In a nutshell, will we Americans one day be as free as the founding fathers intended for us to be?

---

40 Hillquit, 352.

41 *Ibid.*, 91.

Fredrick Engels

Engels, co-founder with Marx of modern-day communism, was an associate of several radical socialists and communists who escaped Europe after the 1848 revolutions. In a letter to General Weydemeyer, Engels praised the efforts of building a strong, "indivisible," central government in Europe as laying the foundations for communist expansion. He foresaw the same results in the defeat of the South.

Chapter 3

Marx, Engels, and Lincoln

> The war of the Southern Confederacy is, therefore, not a war of defense, but a war of conquest, a war of conquest for the extension and perpetuation of slavery.[42]

KARL MARX'S COMMENT about the co-called American Civil War could just have easily been drawn from the proceedings of the NAACP or any politically correct liberal society of this age. Even more shocking is the fact that most conservatives hold very similar views of the cause of the War for Southern Independence, as do their liberal nemeses and Karl Marx. It is not uncommon to hear neo-conservative talk-radio show hosts promoting the idea that "the Civil War was fought to free the slaves," or that "the South fought to promote the cause of slavery in America." Having liberals and conservatives agreeing with Karl Marx and Fredrick Engels on the causes of the so-called Civil War should raise the proverbial "red flag" in the minds of rational Americans.

---

42   Karl Marx, "*The Civil War in the United States,*" Die Presse, November 7, 1861, as cited in, Karl Marx and Fredrick Engels, *The Civil War in the United States* (International Publishers Co., Inc., New York: 1971) 73.

The events surrounding the War Between the States were closely watched and commented on by both Karl Marx and Fredrick Engels. There were no less than sixty-one letters between Marx and Engels touching upon the war; at least two memorials by Marx, one to President Abraham Lincoln, and one to his successor President Andrew Johnson; and a host of letters from Marx to his socialist allies in the United States including several to an officer in the Union Army. In many ways Marx and Engels participated in the "Civil War" by serving as propaganda agents for the Northern cause in Europe. Not only did Karl Marx serve as a contributor to the American newspaper, the *New York Tribune,* but also, he and Fredrick Engels were contributors to several European newspapers. In November 1861, Marx wrote an article for *Die Presse* in Vienna titled, "The Civil War in the United States." In his introductory note to Marx's article the editor of *Die Presse* stated: "We have received from our London correspondent a fresh communication on the events in North America, in which the motives by which the secessionist South is guided are represented in an entirely new light. We will let our informant speak for himself."[43] In his article Marx condemned elements within the British government and press that were in sympathy with the right of the Southern states to withdraw from the Union. Marx proceeded to attack the idea that Southerners were fighting for independence just as their forefathers had done in 1776. He then attempted to place upon the South the entire burden of slavery in America. By doing so, Marx was attempting to fan the antislavery views of most Europeans. In this manner, Marx hoped the masses would oppose recognition of the Confederate States of America. Attempting to ignite the flames of European abolitionist passion against the South, Marx even claimed, "What the slaveholders, therefore, call the South, embraces more than *three-quarters* of the territory hitherto comprised by the Union"[44] [emphasis added]. It is obvious from

---

43 Marx and Engels, *The Civil War in the United States,* 71.

44 *Ibid.,* 72.

this citation that not only did Marx not understand the history of events leading to the War for Southern Independence, he also did not have a good grasp of American geography.

In today's politically correct environment it is not uncommon to hear the South slandered with the very same falsehoods enunciated by Marx and Engels. How many times has a Confederate flag, monument, holiday, or hero been condemned because "the South fought for slavery"? Often representatives of the political right and left in America use the very words of Marx to slander the South. From the left the NAACP demands the removal of all public display of Confederate flags; while, from the right we see Mr. Republican, George Bush, as governor of Texas, removing memorials to Confederate soldiers from the Texas Supreme Court Building. One wonders whether Karl Marx has become the social conscious moderator of the United States. If so, one is left with the question, "Who won the Cold War?"

Let us compare the words of Marx and Lincoln: From Marx: "The war of the Southern Confederacy is...a war for the extension and perpetuation of slavery."[45] From Lincoln: "One section of our country believes slavery is right, and ought to be extended, while the other believes it is wrong, and ought not to be extended."[46] Both Marx and Lincoln proclaimed that the South was attempting to defend and promote slavery. Yet, apart from the radical abolitionist scheme, the history of slavery in the United States demonstrates that the South was the leader in every effort of ending slavery and the slave trade. Let us examine the record of slavery in America to determine whether Marx and Lincoln were correct in their suggestion that the South was fighting for the "extension and perpetuation of slavery."

Before the War for American Independence, it was the Southern colonies that were petitioning the king of England to stop the importation of more slaves into their colonies. During this time

---

45   *Ibid.*, 73.

46   Abraham Lincoln, First Inaugural Address, March 4, 1861.

merchants from many nations as well as New England merchants were engaged in this nefarious commerce in slaves. While Southern colonial legislative bodies were petitioning the king to end the African slave trade, New England and English merchants were lobbying the English government to keep the slave trade open. Thomas Jefferson attempted to place into the Declaration of Independence a complaint against the king's government, criticizing that government for not allowing the colonies to end the African slave trade. Unfortunately, criticism of the African slave trade was deleted so as not to upset New England, which was profiting from it.[47]

When the War for American Independence was won, Virginia ceded control of the Northwest Territory to the Union. Virginia did so with the stipulation that slavery would not be allowed in the said Northwest Territory. When the Federal Congress voted to accept this large territory with the proviso of the elimination of slavery, every Southern representative voted in favor of that resolution. Now let us ask, with the Southern colonies demanding an end to the slave trade (while New England sought the continuance of the slave trade) and Virginia ceding a large area of land to the Union with the proviso that slavery be prohibited in that territory and every Southern representative voting *for* that resolution, how can anyone believe that the South was fighting for the "extension and perpetuation of slavery"? Let us continue. When the U.S. Constitution was adopted, the African slave trade was given a twenty-year grace period before Congress was allowed to outlaw the trade. In 1808 when Congress was authorized to legislate against the African slave trade, that nefarious trade was outlawed in the United States. When the vote was taken, 95 percent of all representatives both North and South voted to eliminate the African slave trade. Representatives from four states voted to maintain the African slave trade, two from the South and two from the North. Surely if the South was seeking the "extension" of slavery it would not have voted to end the African slave trade.

---

47 Robert L. Dabney, *A Defense of Virginia and the South* (1867, Sprinkle Publications, Harrisonburg, VA: 1977), 44.

Some of the most noted Southerners in American history were slaveholders and advocates for ending the "peculiar institution." America's first president was himself a slaveholder as well as Thomas Jefferson, Patrick Henry, and most of the signers of the Declaration of Independence who were from the South. Were these men engaged in a Southern conspiracy to extend and perpetuate slavery? The answer is seen in their actions. Most of these men voiced strong opinions against the institution of slavery, and many, at their own personal expense, manumitted (liberated) their slaves.[48] Even one of the most notable Southern nationalists, John Randolph of Roanoke, expressed his disdain for slavery by manumitting more than four hundred slaves. Not only did Randolph free his slaves, but he also provided homes and land for each family he liberated; all of this was done at great personal expense to the slave master.[49] When the freed slaves went to Ohio to claim their land, however, they were driven out of town by German immigrants. Many did settle in nearby counties, but were not compensated for the lost land. By the time of the War for Southern Independence more slaves had been freed and established in their own homes by the South than anyplace where slavery had existed. Yet, Marx and Lincoln stated that the South sought the "extension" of slavery.

The true history of the issue of slavery in America is much too complex to completely review in this chapter. Nevertheless, the aforementioned items should demonstrate that Marx and Lincoln were not expressing an irrefutable argument when they stated that the South was attempting the "perpetuation and extension of slavery." The very fact that a super-majority of Confederate soldiers were not slaveholders is proof enough to make an open-minded person question the notion that the South was fighting to promote slavery. As many observers of this war have noted, if Southern slaveholders wanted security for their slave property all they had to do was to remain in the Union. Abraham Lincoln himself

---

48   For more information on this subject, see, Walter D. Kennedy, *Myths of American Slavery*, 23-40.

49   Francis B. Simkins, *A History of the South* (Alfred A. Knopf, New York: 1959), 117.

made it clear that he had no desire to take away slave property then owned by a citizen of a state within the Union: "I have no purpose, directly or indirectly, to interfere with the institution of slavery in the States where it exists. I believe I have no lawful right to do so, and I have no inclination to do so."[50] Lincoln continued his argument that he was not an enemy of slavery in any state where it already existed: "Those who nominated and elected me did so with full knowledge that I had made this, and many similar declarations, and had never recanted them."[51] Lincoln reminded his audience that not only had he made these statements, but that his party platform clearly reinforced these views: "*Resolved,* That the maintenance inviolate of the rights of the States, and especially the right of each State to order and control its own domestic institutions according to its own judgment exclusively, is essential to that balance of power on which the perfection and endurance of our political fabric depends."[52]

From the previous citations it is clear that Abraham Lincoln and the Republican Party were offering the "slave oligarchy" security for its slave property. Why would any large slaveholder trade this security for a war to extend the domain of slavery, a war that if lost would lose him all of his property? Once more it must be pointed out that the secession of the Southern states was not predicated upon the promotion and extension of the slave system, regardless of what Marx and Lincoln would later state. Nevertheless, Marx and Engels would insist, and the politically correct and neo-conservatives of today would agree, that the South seceded from the Union to protect and promote slavery in America. Yes, slavery did have a great influence in the relationship between the North and the South in the last twenty years before the war. Just as slavery existed and was a point of contention between the colonies and Great Britain before and during the War for American Independence, the legacy of slavery, including the

---

50   Abraham Lincoln, First Inaugural Address, March 4, 1861.

51   *Ibid.*

52   Platform of Republican Party 1860, as cited in, *ibid.*

African slave trade, is a prominent fact of American history. Yet, no one ever demands the removal of American flags because each of the thirteen Original Colonies was a slaveholding colony. No one demands the elimination of monuments to the commander of the United States Army, George Washington, because he was a slaveholder. Apart from the fact that the commander of the Confederate Armies, Robert E. Lee, was a practicing abolitionist (having freed slaves left to his family by 1862), every argument used against the South, *vis-à-vis* slavery, by Karl Marx could be used against the United States in 1776.

PRELIMINARIES OF THE PROLETARIAN REVOLUTION

A natural question is, "Why did Marx and other radical socialists desire to paint the War for Southern Independence as a Southern war to promote slavery?" Perhaps a better question is, "Why did radical socialists and communists desire to fight for freedom for the slaves?" Most liberals and neo-conservatives will proclaim that it was the natural enthusiasm for freedom and hatred for human bondage that was the driving impulse behind the socialist and communist enthusiasm for freeing the slaves. Likewise, it will be said that this same love for humanity was the reason these socialists and communists flocked to Lincoln's cause. Thankfully, the advantage of more than eighty years of objective history of communist nations and regimes allows us to safely and vigorously assert that communists are not overly concerned with ending human bondage. Lenin and Stalin collectively were responsible for the deaths of more than twenty millions of their own people, the confiscation of all private property including that owned by peasants, and destruction of most houses of worship. Add to these twenty million the millions who after the death of Stalin were thrown into various gulags, most of whom never made it out alive. It is then that one begins to understand how much "communists hate human bondage." Add to these atrocities the murder, torture, and enslavement of countless millions from China to Cuba, and again one begins to understand that communists are not really concerned about human bondage and suffering.

In a letter to Joseph Weydemeyer (a future brigadier general of the Union Army), Marx's partner and co-author, Fredrick Engels, provided an insight into an essential element in the advancement of the communist cause: "The preliminaries of the proletarian revolution, the measures that prepare the battleground and clear the way for us, such as a single and indivisible republic, etc., things that *we* had to champion *against* the people whose natural, normal job it should have been to achieve or, at least, to demand them—all that is now *convenu* [taken for granted]."[53] Here (one communist talking to another communist) Engels confided in Weydemeyer that one of the preliminaries for the advancement of the communist revolution was the establishment of a "single and indivisible republic." This letter was written to Weydemeyer to explain how much "revolutionary" progress was being made in Germany in 1853. When in 1861 the South seceded from the Union, American and European communists saw that the United States was no longer going to be a single and indivisible republic. Recognizing the establishment of a single *indivisible* republic as setting the groundwork for communist revolution, it is not hard to understand why these radicals felt bound to fight for what Lincoln described as the "perpetual" Union. Remember the words of Col. Louis Blenker, a radical German socialist as he petitioned the "National government" to allow him to raise a regiment of German troops to fight "for the preservation of the Union."[54] It should be clearer now why he and his cohorts were so willing to fight for an indivisible government—after all, a perpetual Union would, according to Engels, "prepare the battleground and clear the way of us [communists]."

While most Americans think of the abolition of slavery as an end in itself, communists had a completely different view of abolition. As noted by the editor of Marx and Engels' collected letters on

---

53 Fredrick Engels, as cited in, Karl Marx and Fredrick Engels, *Letters to Americans: 1848-1895* (International Publishers Co., Inc., New York: 1953), 57.

54 Louis Blenker, as cited in, *Official Records War of the Rebellion, Series III*, Vol. I, p. 459.

the American Civil War, *The Civil War in the United States,* Marx understood that the proletarian revolution in America could not take place until after the emancipation of the slaves. Marx stated, "Labor cannot emancipate itself in the white skin where in the black it is branded."[55] In an article titled, "Address of the International Workingmen's Association to the National Labor Union," written by Marx, he set forth his view of the consequence of the American Civil War: "And the successful close of the war against slavery has indeed inaugurated a new era in the annals of the working class.... Still the Civil War offered a compensation in the liberation of the slaves and the impulse which it thereby gave to your own class movement."[56] Engels in a letter to General Weydemeyer stated his belief that the war would "doubtless determine the future of America for hundreds of years to come."[57] Note that the noble objective of ending slavery, an end viewed with equal admiration by most Southerners[58] from Thomas Jefferson to Robert E. Lee, was viewed by communists as a means of advancing the communist revolution, the ultimate objective of all communists.

As can be seen by these citations, Marx and Engels viewed the abolition of slavery in the United States in a totally different light from most Americans. First, Marx and Engels saw in Lincoln's war against the South the establishment of a "single and *indivisible*" nation. As has been pointed out in previous chapters, socialists love big (*indivisible* and perpetual) government. Engels unequivocally announced this fact to a fellow communist who would soon become one of Lincoln's generals waging war upon the South. Second, Marx and Engels viewed the liberation of the slaves as a means to advance the proletarian revolution. For Marx and Engels, the positive aspect of ending slavery was a mere side effect of the "preliminaries of the proletarian revolution."[59]

---

55   Karl Marx, as cited in, Marx and Engels, *The Civil War in the United States,* XIV.

56   Karl Marx, as cited in Marx and Engels, *Letters to Americans,* 76.

57   Fredrick Engels, as cited in, Marx and Engels, *Letters to Americans,* 63.

58   Walter D. Kennedy, *Myths of American Slavery,* 66-67.

59   Fredrick Engels, as cited in, Marx and Engels, *Letters to Americans,* 57.

As has been stated, the history of communism during the past eighty years demonstrates that communists do not highly regard human freedom. These men (Marx and Engels, communists and socialists) should not be viewed as great "freedom fighters"; rather, they should be viewed as evil proponents of big government who would willingly sacrifice human liberty and freedom to advance their concept of a "just" society.

MARX AND GENERAL WEYDEMEYER

Propagandizing for the cause of the North was not the only contact that Marx and Engels had with America's "Civil War." A longtime friend and fellow communist of Marx and Engels, Joseph Weydemeyer,[60] joined the Union Army early in the war and rose to the rank of brigadier general by the end of the conflict. During this time both Marx and Engels maintained personal correspondence with General Weydemeyer.

Weydemeyer had immigrated to the United States after the failure of the socialist revolution in his native land. Even in defeat, Weydemeyer was still dedicated to the communist cause. His friend Karl Marx wrote to him as he was departing Europe for America in 1851. Marx wrote: "I have just received your letter from Engels and hasten to reply. I should, of course, have very much liked to see you and talk with you before your departure— since it was impossible to keep you here. But once you are going to America, you can't be doing so at a more opportune moment, both to find a means of existence over there as well as to be useful to

---

60   Joseph Weydemeyer (1818-66) was born in Germany. He was active in the European socialist revolution of 1848; as a result, he had to flee to the United States in 1851. He maintained a close relationship with both Karl Marx and Fredrick Engels after he moved to the United States. He served as a literary agent for Marx in New York as well as publishing several newspapers in New York and Chicago, Die Revolution (1852), was on the staff of Die Reform, in 1860 founded the German-language newspaper Stimme des Volkes in Chicago. He retired from the Union Army with the rank of brigadier general and moved to St. Louis and edited Die Neue Zeit. For more information on Weydemeyer, see, Marx and Engels, *Letters to Americans*, 304.

our party."[61] Note that Marx viewed the dispersal of his followers not as a negative event but as one fraught with revolutionary possibilities. Marx then gave Weydemeyer the following advice: "When you are in New York, go to A. Dana [Marx was referring to Charles A. Dana, with whom he had a friendly relationship; this is the same Charles A. Dana who later served as assistant secretary of war in the Lincoln administration.] of the *New York Tribune* and give him my regards and regards from Freiligrath. Perhaps he may be of some use to you."[62] Marx felt close enough to Dana that he wrote a personal letter to him and recommended Weydemeyer to Dana. In his letter to Weydemeyer, Marx stated: "I wrote to A. Charles Dana [Charles A. Dana], one of the editors of the *New York Tribune*, and also enclosed a letter from Freiligrath, in which he recommends you. Hence, all you have to do is to go to him and mention our names."[63] The man Marx was referring to here as "Freiligrath" was Ferdinand Freiligrath, a German revolutionary poet and editor of *Neue Rheinische Zeitung*. He was a member of the Communist League and a friend of Marx and Engels.[64] From the tone and substance of Marx's letter it appears that this communist poet was also an acquaintance of Charles A. Dana.

In 1851, Marx commissioned Weydemeyer to publish one of the first editions of the *Communist Manifesto* in the United States. In his October 16, 1851, letter Marx directed Weydemeyer to "see whether it [the *Communist Manifesto*] cannot be issued as a pamphlet—in other words, printed, distributed, and sold. It stands to reason that the profits, if any, belong to you; all I want is 20-50 copies for my own use. I trust you have taken the ocean voyage well and your affairs in the United States will prosper."[65] Two points jump out at the astute reader of these lines: (1) A future general of Lincoln's Union Army was an agent of Karl Marx as they attempted

---

61 Karl Marx, as cited in, Marx and Engels, *Letters to Americans*, 23.

62 *Ibid.*, 24, 25.

63 *Ibid.*, 27.

64 Marx and Engels, *Letters to Americans*, 297.

65 Karl Marx, as cited in, *Ibid.*, 28.

to have published and distributed in America the first copies of the *Communist Manifesto*; (2) "It stands to reason that the *profits*... belong to you." It is somewhat ironic to read the words of the father of modern communism admitting that anyone deserved to receive the *profits* of his labor. Discovering that Adolf Hitler was Jewish or that Abraham Lincoln owned slaves could not be any less shocking than to read the pronouncement from the father of communism that a man deserves to keep his well-earned profits.

Not only did Marx and Engels have close contact with a Union Army general, but also Marx wrote congratulatory letters, published in England and America, congratulating Lincoln on his election victory. In November of 1864, Marx sent Weydemeyer a letter with a copy of a resolution he had written for the International Workingmen's Association congratulating Lincoln on his second electoral victory. In his letter to Weydemeyer, Marx stated:

> I am sending you simultaneously by mail copies of a printed address drafted by me. The newly established International Workingmen's Committee, in whose name it is issued, is not without importance. Its English members consist mostly of the chiefs of the local trade unions, the actual labor kings of London, the same fellow who prepared the gigantic reception for Garibaldi and prevented Palmerston from declaring *war* upon the *United States,* as he was on the point of doing, through the monster meeting in St. James Hall (under Bright's chairmanship) .... Although for years I rejected working with this group, I accepted *this time*, because it involved a matter where it is possible to do some important work.[66]

---

66   Karl Marx, "Address of the International Workingmen's Association to Abraham Lincoln," as cited in, Marx and Engels, *Letters to Americans*, 65-66.

The following is an address written by Marx for the International Workingmen's Association congratulating Lincoln on his second presidential victory.

To Abraham Lincoln,

President of the United States of America.

Sir: We congratulate the American people upon your re-election by a large majority. If resistance to the Slave Power was the reserved watchword of your first election, the triumphant war-cry of your re-election is, Death to Slavery.

From the commencement of the titanic American strife the workingmen of Europe felt instinctively that the star-spangled banner carried the destiny of their class. The contest for the territories which opened the dire epopee, was it not to decide whether the virgin soil of immense tracts should be wedded to the labor of the emigrant or prostituted by the tramp of the slave driver?

When an oligarchy of 300,000 slaveholders dared to inscribe, for the first time in the annals of the world, "slavery" on the banner of armed revolt; when on the very spots where hardly a century ago the idea of one great democratic republic had first sprung up, whence the first declaration of the Rights of Man was issued, with systematic thoroughness, gloried in rescinding "the ideas entertained at the time of the formation of the Old Constitution," and maintained "slavery to be a beneficent institution, indeed the only solution of the great problem of the relation of labor to capital," and cynically proclaimed property in man "the cornerstone of the new edifice"; then the working classes of Europe understood at once, even before the fanatic partisanship of the upper classes for the Confederate gentry had given its dismal warning, that the slaveholders' rebellion was to sound the tocsin [wakeup call or alarm bell] for a general holy crusade of property against labor, and that for the men of labor, with their hopes for the future, even their past conquests were at stake in that tremendous conflict on the other side of the Atlantic. Everywhere they bore therefore patiently the hardships imposed upon them by the cotton crisis, opposed enthusiastically the pro-slavery intervention, importunities of their "betters," and from most parts of Europe contributed their quota of blood to the good cause.

While the workingmen, the true political power of the North, allowed slavery to defile their own republic; while before the Negro, mastered and sold without his concurrence, they boasted it the highest prerogative of the white-skinned laborer to sell himself and choose his own master; they were unable to attain the true freedom of labor or to support their European brethren in their struggle for emancipation, but this barrier to progress has been swept off by the red sea of civil war. [From the time of the socialist revolts of 1848, the color red has been inevitably linked with left-wing, socialist, or communist causes.]

The workingmen of Europe feel sure that as the American War of Independence initiated a new era of ascendancy for the middle class, so the American anti-slavery War will do for the working classes. They consider it an earnest of the epoch to come, that it fell to the lot of Abraham Lincoln, the single-minded son of the working class, to lead his country through the matchless struggle for the rescue of an enchained race and the reconstruction of a social world.[67]

---

67 *Ibid.*

Note that in the third paragraph Marx referred to the formation of the United States as the "idea of one great democratic republic." These are virtually the same words as those spoken by Lincoln himself. After all, it was Lincoln who was proclaiming that the United States was one indivisible and perpetual republic—Marx was just echoing Lincoln's ideas. In the same paragraph Marx proclaimed that the "slaveholders' rebellion" (Marxist euphemism for the War for Southern Independence) was to sound a warning bell for a crusade of property against labor. In other words, the South, i.e., property, was fighting against everything that communism, i.e., labor, held dear. In the fourth paragraph Marx informed his readers that the barrier of progress for the communist revolution had been "swept off by the red sea of civil war." In conclusion Marx reminded the world that it had fallen to the lot of Abraham Lincoln to do those things necessary to insure the "reconstruction of a social world." After eighty years of communism, it is not necessary to speculate too hard to discover what type of world Marx and his friends sought to establish. In the closing lines of his work, the *Communist Manifesto*, Marx proclaimed, "Workers of the world, unite; you have nothing to lose but your chains." After eighty years of communism that line should be rewritten to state, "Workers of the world, beware; you have everything to lose—your property, your freedom, your life."

Upon the death of Abraham Lincoln, Marx addressed a letter to President Andrew Johnson in which he railed against the defeated South and encouraged Johnson to punish and reconstruct the South. Marx's vitriolic hatred for the South was clearly displayed in the first paragraph: "The demon of the 'peculiar institution,' for the supremacy of which the South rose in arms, would not allow his worshipers to honorably succumb on the open field. What he had begun in treason, he must end in infamy. [Here Marx was referring to the assassination of Abraham Lincoln by John Wilkes Booth, which he viewed as just one more plot by evil Southern slaveholders.] As Philip II's war for the Inquisition bred a Gerard, thus Jefferson Davis's pro-slavery war a Booth."[68] Marx continued

---

68 Karl Marx, "Address of the International Workingmen's Association to President Johnson," as cited in, Marx and Engels, *Letters to Americans*, 71.

in his address to President Johnson pleading with the president to use his newfound powers to "uproot by the law what has been felled by the sword, to preside over the arduous work of political reconstruction and social regeneration.... [T]o initiate the new era of the emancipation of labor, the American people devolved the responsibilities of leadership upon two men of labor—the one Abraham Lincoln, the other Andrew Johnson."[69] Notice how Marx addressed the Southern people and President Davis. The words of Marx are almost identical to the words of the modern-day politically correct woke establishment when they speak of the Southern cause. Marx insisted that the South fought for *slavery,* that the act of secession was *treason,* and that the South had to be *reconstructed.* Whether it is Marx, Lincoln, the politically correct left, or the neo-conservative right, all seem to agree that the South is the epitome of evil in America. If that is so, one can only wonder why it is that so many great Americans came from the South.

MARX'S FALSE IMPRESSIONS OF THE SOUTH

While reading the correspondences of Marx and Engels as it pertains to the War for Southern Independence, one becomes acutely aware of many misconceptions these communists held about the South and the many outright inaccuracies they stated about it. Some of the more ludicrous, such as the South occupying *three-quarters* of the territory of the Union, can stand or fall on their own merit. Neither time nor space allow for a complete correcting of the record, but the following four Marxist falsehoods will be addressed:

> 1.The South prepared years ahead of time for the War. "The South had prepared in secret for years, but particularly since the treason of Buchanan's ministers it had obtained money and arms *en masse* at the last moment."[70]

---

69   *Ibid.*, 72.

70   Fredrick Engels, as cited in, Marx and Engels, *The Civil War in the United States*, 223.

2. Jefferson Davis was a Southern dictator. "Mississippi, which has given the Southern Confederacy its dictator, Jefferson Davis..."[71]

3. The Confederate Constitution, unlike the United States Constitution, recognized slavery as a "good thing." "The Confederate Congress boasted that its new-fangled Constitution, as distinguished from the Constitution of the Washingtons, Jeffersons, and Adams, had recognized for the first-time slavery as a thing good in itself, a bulwark of civilization, and a divine institution."[72]

4. The United States Supreme Court was a willing agent of the slaveholding South. "This Supreme Court, which numbers nine judges, five of whom belong to the South, had been long the most willing tool of the slaveholders. It decided in 1857, in the notorious Dred Scott case, that every American citizen possesses the right to take with him into any Territory any property recognized by the Constitution."[73]

ANSWERING MARX AND ENGELS

I. *The South prepared years ahead of time for eventual secession.* From the beginning of the war to the end, one thing is for sure, the South was never well prepared for war. As has been borne out by history, the South had only the advantage of a large group of very good officers who were willing to follow their respective states in secession, and nothing else. There is no proof of large movements of military supplies into the South other than that which was necessary to provide for arming and maintenance of the state militia. As each state seceded from the Union, the military forces of that state took control of any military supplies within

---

71   Karl Marx, as cited in, Marx and Engels, *The Civil War in the United States*, 76.

72   Karl Marx, "The American Question in England," *New York Daily Tribune*, October 11, 1861, as cited in, Marx and Engels, *The Civil War in the United States*, 4.

73   *Ibid.*, 63.

the limits of that state. Each state in the Union, North or South, had the right to request supplies from the Federal government; Mississippi was no different from New York in this respect.

With the election of Lincoln, for the first time in American history a political party controlled the White House with both the President and the Vice President from only one section of the country. Lincoln from Illinois and Hamblin from Maine were both from the North, leaving the South completely closed off from the Executive Branch of government. Having become a minority in the House of Representatives, having lost any influence in the Executive Branch, and seeing itself becoming a minority in the Senate, the South which had rejected the idea of secession many times, now sought safety in the act of secession.[74] Just ten years before the secession crisis, a convention of Southerners was held in Nashville, Tennessee. Many people thought this meeting would lead to disunion at that time, but as it turned out, "the convention showed the loyalty of the South to the Union and the willingness of southerners to compromise to preserve national unity."[75] Most Southerners viewed secession as a last-ditch measure, not something one would plan for years ahead—unfortunately, this attitude may have cost the South its independence.

2. *Jefferson Davis was a dictator.* One has to think that Marx was exercising his right as an author to use hyperbole to get his point across because nothing in recorded history indicates that President Davis had any such dictatorial powers as described by Marx. As any good socialist knows, and surely Marx was a good socialist, a federal republic composed of several sovereign states cannot be ruled by a dictator. If the Confederate States of America was anything, it was a federal republic of sovereign states. From one end of the Confederate Constitution to the other it dripped with States' Rights language. Jefferson Davis's authority ranged

---

74 For more information on the lack of willingness of the South to rush into secession, see, Thelma Jennings, *The Nashville Convention: Southern Movement for Unity, 1848-1850* (Memphis State University Press, Memphis, TN: 1980).

75 *Ibid*, v.

somewhere between that of the president of the United States under the Articles of Confederation and that of George Washington under the new Federal government after the adoption of the U.S. Constitution. In no way could this power be logically called dictatorial. One thing Marx completely overlooked when accusing President Davis of being a "dictator," is that any state within the Confederate States of America that did not like the way it was being treated could secede from that union and exist as a sovereign republic or join a union that treated it fairly. Not a bad idea—that is if one loves liberty more than government.

3. *The Confederate Constitution unlike the United States Constitution recognized slavery as a "good thing."* Many politically correct liberals and neo-conservatives condemn the Confederacy because as they assert, "The Confederate Constitution defended slavery and demanded that every state recognize slavery." Nowhere in the Confederate Constitution was there a prohibition against ending slavery within a state. What the Confederate Constitution did stipulate was that the central government of the Confederacy did not have the right to interfere in the ownership of slaves; these matters were left in the hands of "we the people of the sovereign states." Even Abraham Lincoln affirmed that the United States Constitution recognized the right of ownership of slaves and the return of runaway slaves—he even went so far as to state his willingness and desire to enforce such laws.[76]

Once again it must be pointed out that if by some folly of judgment, the government of the Confederate States trampled upon the right of the people of a sovereign state to abolish slavery, that state had the right to secede from the Confederate Union. Both the people at the state level and the politicians in the Confederate government understood this principle and acted accordingly. In other words, the people at the local level and not the central government had the final word in how they were to be governed— what a novel idea! Furthermore, the United States Constitution did indeed recognize slavery in three important ways: (1) In Article

---

76   Abraham Lincoln, First Inaugural Address, March 4, 1861.

IV, Section 2, the United States Constitution recognized a master's right in his slave property by establishing a means for the return of any runaway slave from one state to another. This portion of the Constitution is a near perfect copy of America's first fugitive slave law, passed by the United Colonies of New England more than one hundred years before the adoption of the U.S. Constitution. In his history of slavery in Massachusetts, George H. Moore stated: "The original of the Fugitive Slave Law provision in the Federal [U.S.] Constitution is to be traced to this Confederacy [United Colonies of New England], in which Massachusetts was the ruling colony."[77] In other words, this was not an exclusively Southern element in the Constitution. (2) In Article I, Section 2, we read slaves would be counted as three-fifths of a person for establishing congressional districts. Misunderstanding this section has caused many detractors of the South to accuse the South of viewing a slave as only three-fifths human. When this portion of the Constitution was being debated, Northerners did not want to count slaves as human at all, while Southerners desired to count slaves as any other human. A compromise was reached in which slaves were counted as three-fifths of a person when establishing congressional districts. (3) In Article I, Section 9, the United States Constitution gave the African slave trade a twenty-year grace period in which Congress was not allowed to legislate against the nefarious trade. In three important areas the Constitution dealt with slavery. In the entire document not one negative word was placed in the Constitution about the subject of slavery. Every state that adopted this Constitution understood full well the meaning of each article, section, and paragraph of the document. There was no Southern conspiracy to use the United States Constitution to promote slavery.

The Confederate Constitution followed the United States Constitution on the issue of slavery with one major exception. Whereas the United States Constitution protected the African slave trade for twenty years after its adoption, the Confederate Constitution unequivocally prohibited further importation of

77 George H. Moore, *Notes on the History of Slavery in Massachusetts* (D. Appleton and Company, New York: 1866), 27.

slaves into the Confederate States of America. No new slaves were allowed into the Confederacy *via* the African slave trade. Only slaves from slaveholding states of the United States would be allowed into the Confederacy, and the Confederate Congress was authorized to close that trade at any time. The very first veto by President Jefferson Davis was issued when the Confederate Congress passed a law that President Davis stated violated the "spirit" if not the letter of this constitutional prohibition; the Confederate Congress upheld President Davis's veto. This does not sound like the action of a "slaveholding conspiracy" seeking to promote the cause of slavery.

4. *The United States Supreme Court was a willing tool of the slaveholding South.* As Marx understood the issue, "This Supreme Court, which numbers nine judges, five of whom belong to the South, had been long the willing tool of the South." Enraged by the Dred Scott decision, Marxist and radical abolitionist propagandists pulled no punches in their attacks on what they viewed as the slaveholders' control of the U.S. Supreme Court. The chief object of their criticism was Chief Justice Roger Brooke Taney.

Justice Taney was the second chief justice of the United States Supreme Court. A native of Maryland, a very Southern state at that time, Justice Taney was a very well-respected member of the Maryland bar. The foremost point of irritation between the chief justice and the radical abolitionists was his insistence that the Constitution had to be interpreted as it was currently written and not according to the mode of thinking of a particular section of the country. Judge Taney would not agree with the concept of what in the twentieth century became known as "judicial activism." According to Taney's view, the court was to interpret the law, not create law. This judicial philosophy is common for those holding a strict construction view of the Constitution, something very common for Southerners but also a view held by many Northerners. Even Federal judges from the North who did not always agree with the strict construction philosophy of interpretation of the Constitution felt bound by the Constitution when dealing with the issue of slavery. For example, when Supreme Court justice Joseph

Story of Massachusetts upheld the Fugitive Slave Law in *Prigg v. Pennsylvania,* he was relentlessly attacked in the abolition press because, as the issue was stated, he "voted for slavery." In reply to these attacks, Story, a constant foe of slavery, stated: "You know full well that I have ever been opposed to slavery. But I take my standard of duty as a judge from the Constitution."[78] Again, in *Jones v. Van Zandt,* the issue of upholding the fugitive slave section of the Constitution came before the court. Justice Levi Woodbury of New Hampshire, a longtime foe of slavery, wrote the majority decision for the court upholding the fugitive slave section of the Constitution. Responding to this decision, the abolition press excoriated this antislavery judge because he ruled according to the Constitution and not according to what was perceived as a higher moral authority, i.e., "higher law." Arguing in favor of overruling the fugitive slave section of the Constitution were: Salmon P. Chase, future chief justice of the Supreme Court, nominated by Lincoln; and William H. Seward, future secretary of state in Lincoln's administration.

Both Chase and Seward insisted that slavery was so iniquitous that no court should recognize it as worthy of constitutional protection. In his response to this "higher law" assertion, Justice Woodbury stated: "That is a political question, settled by each State for itself; and the Federal power over it is limited and regulated by the people of the States in the Constitution itself, as one of its sacred compromises, and which we possess no authority as a judicial body to modify or overrule. Whatever may be the theoretical opinions of any as to the expediency of some of those compromises, or of the right of property in persons which they recognize, this Court has no alternative while they exist, but to stand by the Constitution and the laws with fidelity to their duties and their oaths."[79] Justice Woodbury, an opponent of slavery, made it clear that interpretation of the Constitution is the legitimate

---

78   Judge Joseph Story, as cited in, Walker Lewis, Without Fear or Favor (Houghton Mifflin Company, Boston: 1965) 355.

79   Justice Levi Woodbury, as cited in, Lewis, 366.

function of the Supreme Court and not to legislate on "political questions." The Constitution itself provides a means for the people of the United States to change any section of the Constitution by the amendment process. The amending process, and not judicial activism, is the appropriate means for changing the Constitution. Understanding the Constitution, as Justice Joseph Story of Massachusetts and Justice Levi Woodbury of New Hampshire understood it, is something that Marx, radical abolitionists, and modern-day liberals are unwilling to do.

Because Taney was a Marylander, he was denoted by Marx as part of the Southern slaveholder power structure on the Supreme Court. Yet, Taney, like so many other men of the Old South, was a practicing abolitionist. Taney's brother-in-law, Francis Scott Key (of "Star-spangled Banner" fame), was a leading member of the American Colonization Society, organized to establish a home in Africa for freed slaves. Taney was an officer in the local chapter of this society. In 1818 at great expense to himself Taney freed seven of his slaves and an eighth slave in 1821. Each slave was not only given freedom, but was also established in a profession and housing before being freed. Taney and his brother freed two slaves they had inherited from their father at his death. The only slaves owned by Taney that he did not free were two elderly slaves too old to support themselves; Taney supported them until their death. While radical abolitionists were fanning the flames of hatred for Southerners, men such as Justice Taney were busy, quietly and at their own expense, liberating enslaved people. It is somewhat ironic that with money jingling in their pockets that was made from the selling of slaves, both their own and those sold as a result of the African slave trade, Northerners condemned Southerners who were in the process of freeing at their own expense slaves bought from Northerners or freeing slaves inherited from their families who had been bought from Northerners.

Marx and the radical abolitionists unreservedly condemned Taney and the Supreme Court for the Dred Scott decision. This decision was the focal point of Marx's charge that the Federal Supreme Court was a "willing tool of the South." Yet, as has been pointed out, even staunch antislavery judges from the North felt compelled to rule as the Constitution was written and not as they would have liked to rule *vis-à-vis* slavery. Marx was correct when he stated that five of the nine judges of the Supreme Court were from the South, which left four from the North. If as Marx contended the Supreme Court was the "willing tool of the South," why was the vote on the Dred Scott decision not along sectional lines, i.e., five to four? The final vote by the justices was seven to two, not five to four. Moreover, at least two of the five Southern justices voting for the Dred Scott decision were practicing abolitionists, having freed their slaves many years earlier: Taney of Maryland and Campbell of Alabama.

Responding to the Supreme Court's Dred Scott decision, Horace Greeley's (remember that Greeley and Dana were both on very friendly terms with Karl Marx) abolition newspaper, the *New York Tribune,* opined: "*You* may 'cheerfully submit,' of course you will, to whatever the five slaveholders and two or three doughfaces on the bench of the Supreme Court may be ready to utter on this subject. But not one man who really desires the triumph of Freedom over Slavery in the Territories will do so."[80] Note how wrong the *Tribune* was when asserting that there were *five* slaveholders on the Supreme Court. As has been stated, four members of the court were from the North, and two of the five Southern justices were non-slaveholding Southerners, having at great personal expense freed their own slaves—something that few if any Marxists or radical abolitionists ever did.

Closely related to the Dred Scott decision, as seen in the remark in the *Tribune,* is the relationship of slavery in the United States territories. This issue became so emotional that it resulted in the breakup of the Democratic Party in 1860. The South held to the concept that the Constitution recognized slavery as an institution regulated by the states; therefore, only states could eliminate slavery. Nowhere in the Constitution was the right to regulate slavery, other than the importation of slaves, delegated to the

---

80 Horace Greeley, writing in the *New York Tribune*, as cited in, Lewis, 395.

Federal government nor was it denied to the states. That being the case, only states had the right and the power to abolish slavery. From the beginning of the republic under the Constitution, slavery was dealt with in this manner. Any commonly held territory of the United States was acquired by the common treasury of the country; and therefore, any citizen had the right to immigrate into said territory with his property. Only when the territory became a state could the people of that state determine the fate of slavery. Two factors were militating against the formation of new slave states within the "territory of the Union." First, the soil and climate of the territories were not conducive to the formation of Southern-style plantations. Without the need of a large labor force, as in cotton or sugar cultivation, slavery would not survive. Second, the growth of population both through natural birth and through immigration from Europe gave the North a large population advantage in settling the territories. In other words, the tumult being raised by the radical abolitionists was unfounded—but unfounded or not, the ruckus being raised would lead to a bloody war.

SUMMARY

LIKE OUR ANCESTORS—WE WILL BE FREE.

No, these words were not the words of Abraham Lincoln, Karl Marx, or the radical abolitionists. These words were taken from the Confederate battle flag of the Fifth South Carolina Volunteer Infantry, C. S. A., of King's Mountain, South Carolina. It was during the War for American Independence that a group of Southern militias defeated the British at the Battle of King's Mountain. This defeat was a major factor in the eventual British retreat to Yorktown, Virginia, where the War for American Independence was won. Seventy-five years later, the sons and grandsons of these patriots reminded the world what the War for Southern Independence was all about. Regardless of what Lincoln, Marx, radical abolitionists, or modern politically correct liberals and neo-conservatives declare, the South was fighting for freedom, not slavery.

The close connection between the views of Lincoln and the views of Marx, Engels, and other socialists and communists within the Union Army has been demonstrated in this chapter. Just as stated in the chapter on Lincoln and Hitler, the question must be asked once again, "Why did communists and socialists feel such a strong connection with the Republican Party and Abraham Lincoln?" As has been stated, it is obvious from recent history that communists do not have a high regard for human liberty and well-being. Therefore, it can be safely assumed that human freedom was not the prime purpose behind the efforts of these communists and socialists in their war against the South. Engels wrote to his communist associate and Union general Joseph Weydemeyer stating that the "Civil War" constituted "[t]he preliminaries of the proletarian revolution, the measures that prepare the battle ground and clear the way for us." Preparing the way for "us," i.e., communism was the central reason for Marx, Engels and their communist friends pursuing the war against the South. The last question that must be asked is: "Has this 'preparing the way' had deleterious results for modern Americans?"

Chapter 4

ADOLF HITLER AND ABRAHAM LINCOLN

[Hitler] The states that make up the American Union are mostly in the nature of territories... formed for technical administrative purposes. These states did not and could not possess sovereign rights of their own. Because it was the Union that created most of these so-called states. [81]

[Lincoln] The Union is older than the States and, in fact created them as States. The Union, and not themselves separately, procured their independence and their liberty. [T]he Union threw off their old dependence for them and made them States, such as they are. [82]

THE NOTION THAT the Union preceded the states is more than a lie; it is a "spectacular lie." This "spectacular lie," like Hitler's "big lie," would become the driving force behind the North's war against the right of secession and Southern Independence.[83] Early in the

---

81   Adolf Hitler, *Mein Kampf* (Hurst and Blackett, LTD., New York: 1942), 312.

82   Abraham Lincoln, July 4th Message to Congress, July 4, 1861.

83   Thomas J. DiLorenzo, *The Real Lincoln* (Prima Publishing Company, Roseville, CA: 2002), 113.

Adolf Hitler

"It is absurd to speak of the 'Statal sovereignty' for the constituent states of the Reich." In his autobiographical book Mein Kampf, Hitler expresses admiration and approval of what Lincoln did during the War for Southern Independence. Hitler's views of States' Rights, of perpetual government, and of "Higher Law," when breaking traditional moral and constitutional law, run parallel to Lincoln's views. (Photograph courtesy Library of Congress.)

history of the republic under the Constitution, a small but potent group of High Federalists maintained that the Federal government was superior in every aspect to the government of the states. Men such as John Marshall, Joseph Story, Daniel Webster, and of course Abraham Lincoln promoted this view of big government. These men held that the people of the United States as delegates of their various states adopted the Constitution. This being the case, so they argued, no "state" can undo that which the people of the United States had done.

A little review of history demonstrates the weakness and actual fault with this High Federalist argument. The United States Constitution in Article VII stated that the Constitution would become the law of the land when the delegates of nine states had ratified the same and that the Constitution would become the law only in those states so ratifying the same. In other words, "we the people" of each state, acting for our own benefit, acceded to the Union. No state was compelled by a majority vote of "the people" of the United States to join this Union. Furthermore, most states so ratifying the Constitution did so with the provision that the people of each state had the right to judge for themselves how they were to be governed. In other words, it was the will of "we the people" of each state who had to determine how they would be governed. Note for example what the people of the state of New York said about how they were to be governed: "That the power of government may be resumed by the people whensoever it shall become necessary to their happiness; that every power, jurisdiction, and right, which is not by the said constitution clearly delegated to the Congress of the United States, or the departments of the Government thereof, remains to the people of the several States, or to their respective State governments, to whom they may have granted the same." In its ratification of the Constitution, Massachusetts asserted its right as a sovereign state thusly: "That it be explicitly declared, that all powers not expressly delegated by the aforesaid constitution, are reserved to the several States, to be by them exercised."

These are just two of many examples of "States' Rights" language seen in the official documents of the states as they acceded to the new Union. These actions demonstrated that early Americans did indeed believe that they were members of sovereign states and that those states were forming a new government. By establishing the new government under the Constitution, the people of the various sovereign states created a new Union. Regardless of what Lincoln and Hitler believed, "we the people" of the sovereign states created the Union—the Union did not create the states. By ratifying the Constitution on the condition that certain amendments would be added to it, the Bill of Rights with its guarantee of American liberty became a reality. The Tenth Amendment of the Bill of Rights states, "The powers not delegated to the United States by the constitution, nor prohibited by it to the States, are reserved to the States respectively, or to the people." Note that in this amendment it is the "States" who are addressed as the primary recipient of this protection—one more proof that the states were central in the formation of the United States of America and therefore, the Union.

A comparison of the beliefs of Hitler and Lincoln demonstrates that these two men held very similar views on how a government should be organized and function. First, let us compare Hitler's views on perpetual government. Most observers of National Socialism remember Hitler's proclamation that he was building a "thousand-year Reich." Although not "perpetual," any state that lasts for one thousand years must be as close to perpetual as most humans would ever see. In Mein Kampf, Hitler addressed his love for strong national government:

> We, National Socialists...would adopt the following axiom: A strong national Reich.... Every State in the world has to face the question of unification in its internal organization.... In the sphere of commerce as well as that of administration the importance of the individual states has been steadily decreasing. Modern means of communication and mechanical

progress have been increasingly restricting distance
and space. What was once a State is to-day only a
province[84] [emphasis added].

By the end of World War I in 1918, the Federal Republic of
Germany was composed of twenty-five German states. Each of
these states was at one time a free, independent, and sovereign
state. One of the first things done by Hitler and the Nazis after their
ascension to power was to deny any claim of state sovereignty by
these states and to consolidate all power into one big government.
For Hitler the "national" state was the embodiment of the German,
Aryan, people, and was the center of all political life. This state
had to live longer, have more rights, more power, and ultimately
control the fate of all citizens within the Reich. Hitler's Reich was
one very big authoritarian national government. Nothing would
be allowed to stand in the way of the achievement of the desires
of this big government—certainly not the liberty and freedom of
the people composing the little German states that made up the
Federal Republic. Hitler made his view of States' Rights and/
or state sovereignty very clear: "[I]t is absurd to speak of 'statal
sovereignty' for the constituent states of the Reich."[85] It cannot
be clearer that Hitler was following Lincoln's philosophy of
government by asserting that the states were to be subservient
to the will of the central government. One begins to wonder: Was
Hitler following Lincoln, or was Lincoln reincarnated in Germany?

Let us now look at Lincoln's view of "perpetual" government.
"But if destruction of the Union, by one, or by part only, of the
States, be lawfully possible, the Union is less perfect than before the
Constitution, having lost the vital element of perpetuity. It follows
from these views that no State, upon its own mere motion, can
lawfully get out of the Union"[86] (emphasis added). There are three
points that Lincoln made in these sentences: (1) Perpetuity is a vital

---

84   Hitler, 315.

85   *Ibid.*

86   Abraham Lincoln, First Inaugural Address, March 4, 1861.

element in the government of the United States; (2) the Union is less perfect than before the adoption of the Constitution if secession is permissible; and, (3) no state can upon its "mere motion" get out of the Union. Let us consider Lincoln's three points.

1. PERPETUITY IS A VITAL ELEMENT OF GOVERNMENT

Adolf Hitler believed his Reich would last at least one thousand years, whereas Abraham Lincoln went much further; he believed government should have everlasting life! According to Lincoln, this everlasting and therefore perpetual nature of American government was so essential he referred to it as "vital." Surely, any political principle this important would show itself in one of the major documents of American history—say, the Declaration of Independence or the United States Constitution. The Declaration of Independence states that a free people have the unalienable right to "alter or abolish" any government that does not conform to the desires of the people. Surely, any government organized along such principles cannot be said to be "perpetual." It should be noted here that when asserting the right of the people to alter or abolish a government, the Declaration of Independence is not suggesting a "revolutionary" right but rather, an intrinsic right of free men. Lincoln often stated his belief that a people could exercise a revolutionary right of abolishing any government, but he never believed in an intrinsic and unalienable right of men to abolish a government. While a member of the House of Representatives in 1845, Lincoln stated: "Any people anywhere, being inclined, and having the power, have the right to rise up and shake off the existing government, and form a new one that suits them better. This is a most valuable, a sacred right."[87] In Lincoln's first inaugural address he stated: "This country...belongs to the people who inhabit it. Whenever they shall grow weary of the existing government, they can exercise their constitutional right of amending it, or their revolutionary right to dismember, or overthrow it." In Lincoln's

---

87   Abraham Lincoln, as cited in, Edgar Lee Masters, Lincoln: The Man (1931, The Foundation for American Education, Columbia, SC: 1997) 319.

view, secession was an act of revolution, something everyone had a right to try but did not have a right to do! The question is simply this: "How can one man have a right to do something if another man has the right to negate that act?"

The exercise of one's innate right is not an act of revolution; rather, trampling upon a free man's right to exercise his unalienable right is revolutionary vis-à-vis the American Republic. It was Lincoln who was rebelling against the teaching of the Declaration of Independence—not the Southern states. But if one views government as did Lincoln and Hitler, it is only natural to believe that there is no inherent right to abolish any government because, after all, governments (Reichs) are perpetual or at least should last one thousand years.

Lincoln's claim of perpetuity for government is not found in either the Declaration of Independence or the U.S. Constitution. The only place where the term "perpetual" is found in relation to government is in the Articles of Confederation. It is these same Articles of Confederation that formed the first weak government of the United States. Without the permission and in total disregard for the instructions given by the government under the Articles of Confederation, the states wrote and adopted a new Constitution, thereby seceding from the government under the Articles of Confederation—so much for perpetual government in America.

We shall now look at how Hitler and Lincoln viewed the Constitution as a grantor of political power. Here is how Hitler viewed States' Rights and the U.S. Constitution: "[I]n speaking of the United States of America one must not consider them [the several states] as sovereign states but as enjoying rights or, better perhaps, autarchic powers, granted to them and guaranteed by the Constitution. Originally these states did not and could not possess sovereign rights of their own. Because it was the Union that created most of the so-called states."[88] Hitler maintained that the states of the United States were never "sovereign"; therefore,

---

88 Hitler, 312.

they possessed not "rights" but only "powers." These powers were held by the states at the discretion of the national government from whom, by way of the Constitution, these powers have been granted to the states.

Now let us hear from Lincoln: "Having never been States, either in substance, or in name, outside of the Union, whence this magical omnipotence of 'State rights,' asserting a claim of power to lawfully destroy the Union itself? Much is said about the 'sovereignty' of the States; but the word, even, is not in the national Constitution; nor, as is believed, in any of the State constitutions."[89]

Let us now dissect Lincoln's and Hitler's argument against the sovereign rights of "we the people" of the states of the United States of America: (1) Both Lincoln and Hitler agreed that the states were never "sovereign." Lincoln stated that the word "sovereignty" does not even appear in the Constitution; therefore, according to Lincoln's logic, no state can be sovereign. Let us apply Lincoln's logic to the Federal government. If states cannot be sovereign because the word "sovereign" does not appear in the Federal Constitution then, what does that say about the United States? Is then the Federal government the agent of a non-sovereign power because this word "sovereign" cannot be found in the Federal Constitution? The word "marriage" is not found in the Constitution. Does this mean that there is no such thing as a legal marriage in the United States? Lincoln and Hitler's argument is not just illogical—it is ridiculous!

Equally impotent is Lincoln's statement that the term "sovereignty" does not appear in any state constitution. Petitioning Congress for admission into the Union as a state, Louisiana sent Congress a copy of its state constitution that in part proclaimed that Louisiana would be: "a free and independent state."[90] Most states in the Union on seeking admission into the Union at that time

---

89 Abraham Lincoln, July 4th Message to Congress, July 4, 1861.

90 Constitution of the State of Louisiana, as cited in, *The American's Guide to the Constitution of the United States of America* (Moore and Lake, Trenton, NJ: 1813) 341.

had similar language; Louisiana was not unique in proclaiming itself to be "free and independent"—something Lincoln must have overlooked. Having the attributes of a "free and independent state" is emblematic of "sovereignty." Sovereign states are free and independent states, and vice versa. Lincoln and Hitler overlooked this matter, resulting in the loss of many lives.

When considering the rights of Americans, one should remember that the U.S. Constitution is not a cookbook of American rights. The Constitution is a document that explains the grant of power from "we the people of the sovereign states" to the Federal government and the self-imposed limits on the rights of the states. As we read in the Tenth Amendment, "The powers not delegated to the United States by the constitution, nor prohibited by it to the States, are reserved to the States respectively, or to the people." Now, we ask this question: "Mr. Lincoln, Herr Hitler, what powers do the states of the American Union hold according to the Tenth Amendment?" Let us answer—y'all have already proven you don't understand the Constitution—any powers not delegated from the states to the Federal government, or any rights not prohibited to the states by the Constitution belong to the states. We don't have to try and name every right we possess; after all, we might overlook one. Simply put, unless "we the people of the sovereign states" have delegated a right to the Federal government or prohibited the states from exercising a power or right, those rights belong to "we the people of the states," otherwise known as States' Rights. The right to exist as a sovereign state or the right of secession has not been prohibited to the states nor have those rights been delegated to the Federal government—therefore, they exist with "we the people of the sovereign states" as one of our many States' Rights.[91]

---

91   For a more complete answer to the question of the nature of the sovereign states of America, please refer to: James R. Kennedy and Walter D. Kennedy, *The South Was Right!* and *Jefferson Davis: High Road to Emancipation and Constitutional Government.*

Lincoln stated, and Hitler agreed, that the states never had an existence outside of the Union, and therefore depended upon the Union for their very existence. Let us analyze that assertion by considering the following historical facts. Before the Declaration of Independence was signed, the people of each colony took up the functions of a sovereign state. Each colony expelled the royal governor, assumed all legislative functions, raised its own military force, and sent delegates to Philadelphia and empowered those delegates to vote for independence. Please note that the power and authority to vote for independence did not originate from some mystical Union but from the legislature of each state. The people of each state did all of this with no state compelling any other state to act against its own will.

Not only did the states authorize the vote for independence, but they also fought the first battles in the war for independence. In one example of many such instances North Carolina soldiers and not Union soldiers fought the Battle of Moore's Creek Bridge in North Carolina in 1775—one year before the signing of the Declaration of Independence. It is true that thirteen states were united in their war against their common foe, Great Britain. Nevertheless, being united against a common enemy does not make a "perpetual" Union; otherwise, the Allies of World War II would be in a "perpetual" Union to this day! Without question, during the War for American Independence, the only political entity with sufficient power to raise taxes, provide for defense, and enforce both local and international law[92] resided in the several states, not in some ill-defined mythical Union.

2. SECESSION CREATES A LESS PERFECT UNION

The second point Lincoln made in his first inaugural address was that secession makes a "less perfect" Union and not a "more perfect" Union: "But if destruction of the Union...be lawfully

---

92 International law, as cited in, James R. Kennedy and Walter D. Kennedy, *The South Was Right!* (Shotwell Publishing Co., Columbia, SC: 2020) 284.

possible, the Union is less perfect than before the Constitution." Here Lincoln was referring to the phrase in the preamble of the Constitution that states, "in Order to form a more perfect Union." For Lincoln, a more perfect Union was obviously a "perpetual" Union. If one accepts Lincoln's premise of perpetuity as the earmark of a more perfect Union, then of course secession makes for a less perfect Union. At this point the question must be asked, "What is the earmark of a more perfect Union of free men?" Study the words of that great defender of American liberty, Patrick Henry: "The first thing I have at heart is American liberty, the second thing is American union."[93] According to Patrick Henry, it is liberty and not Union that is of prime importance to Americans. In other words, the Union is of great benefit as long as it is subservient to the cause of liberty—liberty never takes a back seat to Union. James Madison, who is often referred to as the "Father of the Constitution," stated thus: "[T]he safety and happiness of society are the objects at which all political institutions must be sacrificed."[94] Madison made it clear that the safety and happiness of society are to take precedence over any institution of government, such as Union, or even government itself. The impression given from reading this statement of Madison is that a "more perfect" Union is that Union which guarantees the safety and happiness of the people. In his *Commentaries on American Laws*, Chancellor James Kent of New York noted under what condition the Union would be preserved: "...for on the concurrence and good will of the parts, the stability of the whole depends."[95] What will hold the Union together? According to Chancellor Kent, concurrence and good will, not bloody bayonets, will hold the Union together. For free men living in a free government, a more perfect Union is that Union which more perfectly defends and protects liberty—a point Lincoln missed.

---

93   Patrick Henry, as cited in, Herbert J. Strong, *What the Anti-Federalists Were For* (The University of Chicago Press, Chicago: 1981) 24.

94   James Madison, *The Federalist* No. 43.

95   James Kent, *Commentaries on American Law* (1826: Da Capo Press, New York: 1971) I, 195-6.

Only if one accepts Lincoln's High Federalist view of the government of the United States under its Constitution can one justify Lincoln's statement on a "more perfect" Union. But early American history demonstrates that this view was rejected in favor of Jeffersonian republicanism. The rejection of the High Federalist view was so complete that it caused the demise of the first American political party, the Federalist Party. Although the ideas of the High Federalists never completely vanished, as demonstrated by the ascension of Lincoln, they never had the backing of the American people in general. Remember, Lincoln was elected by only 39 percent of the American voters; 61 percent of American voters cast votes for other candidates for president rather than voting for Lincoln. Lincoln was a minority president espousing a minority view on the formation of the Union. This minority view of the Constitution stands the Constitution on its head and makes it a document that defends government and not liberty. Most constitutional scholars would agree with the statement that the people of the states would have never ratified the Constitution if those delegates had thought that this Constitution would serve the interests of government over the liberties of the people.

3. SECESSION IS UNLAWFUL

Lincoln's third point was the unlawfulness of a state seceding from the Union. "It follows from these views that no State, upon its own mere motion, can lawfully get out of the Union."[96] Lincoln here explained why he felt that a state cannot "get out of the Union," when he stated, "It follows from these views..." As already pointed out, only if one unquestionably imbibes in the High Federalist philosophy of the Union creating the states, as did Hitler and Lincoln, will the third point "follow from these views." By pointing out that a minority of the American people held these views and that a woeful minority (39 percent) of voters elected Lincoln, there is no reason to grant him this point. Why did the people of the Southern states feel that they could upon their "own

---

96 Abraham Lincoln, First Inaugural Address, March 4, 1861.

mere motion" secede from the Union? The first question is, "How did the people of South Carolina, the first state to secede, get into the Union?" Was there a great American plebiscite or general election to vote for acceding to the new Union? The answer is no. No general vote by the American people was ever held to "vote in" the U.S. Constitution. By the action of each state legislature, a convention of the people of that state was called to accept or reject the proposed Constitution. In other words, the state of South Carolina got into the Union by its "own mere motion"! South Carolina was not unique in this action but rather symbolic of the action taken by all the states as they separately and individually ratified the Constitution. According to Samuel Rutherford in *Lex Rex*, "Those who have power to make have power to unmake a king."[97] Rutherford here was using the term "king" as a metaphor for "government." This principle of making and unmaking a king was the justification for the removal of a tyrannical king and replacing him with one more in keeping with the desires of the people during the English "Glorious Revolution." Likewise, each seceding state would "get out of the Union" in the same manner it got into the Union, by its "own mere motion."

It is of some interest to note that Lincoln described the act of secession in the same manner as did King George's government. Both the government in London in 1776 and the government in Washington in 1861 referred to the action of free men in a free society altering or abolishing (using the words of the Declaration of Independence) their government as "insurrectionary or revolutionary." Within eighty-five years so much had changed in America. In 1776 Americans both North and South were demanding their unalienable right to live under a government by the "consent of the governed." Patriots from Massachusetts to South Carolina were standing firm in the belief that these rights were more sacred than "King and Country"! Yet, with the election of this minority

---

97 Samuel Rutherford, *Lex Rex* (1644: Sprinkle Publications, Harrisonburg, VA: 1982) 126.

president, the United States now looked and sounded more like the government of King George in 1776 than the noble army of patriots who with their blood secured our freedom.

As just demonstrated, in Lincoln's view, States' Rights and state sovereignty had to yield to the necessities of the Federal government. Hitler noted that those parties who, "placed the interests of their own states...before the Reich had now to look on passively while the pressure of events forced the Reich, in its own interests, to abolish the existence of the individual states. It was an unparalleled example of hypocrisy to raise the cry of lamentation over the loss which the federal states suffered in being deprived of their sovereign rights."[98]

Both Lincoln and Hitler would seem to agree that the central government is of much more importance than the rights of sovereignty of a few small states. In Hitler's view, forging a super-state whose authority could not be questioned was a patriotic venture. According to Hitler, "This principle of combining absolute authority with absolute responsibility will gradually cause a selected group of leaders to emerge."[99] The world should have known what the results of this hideous combination of "authority and responsibility" had in store. Unfortunately, the world did not heed the warnings about Hitler, and as a result big government proved just how ugly and tyrannical it could be. After the end of the War for Southern Independence in a letter to Lord Acton, General Lee stated that he believed that the maintenance of the reserved rights (States' Rights) under the Original Constitution was essential "to the continuance of a free government."[100] Lee went on to emphasize what would happen if those reserved rights were concentrated into a central government; he believed this action would result in a nation that would be "aggressive abroad

---

98 Hitler, 314.

99 *Ibid*, 252.

100 Robert E. Lee, in letter to Lord Acton, original on file, Washington-Lee University, Lexington, VA.

and despotic at home."[101] Without real States' Rights to counter the abuse of power by the Federal government, the warnings of Lee are becoming a reality.

This spirit of "authority and responsibility" was not missing from the actions of the followers of Lincoln during the war. Congressman Zachariah Chandler had this to say about the rights of Southerners: "A rebel has sacrificed all his rights. He has no right to life, liberty, property, or the pursuit of happiness. Everything you give him, even life itself, is a boon which he has forfeited."[102] Lincoln's men moved from suppression of rebellion to nothing less than Nazi-like acts of genocide. Even men such as Union general William Sherman were caught up in this Nazi-like practice of "authority and responsibility" as demonstrated by Sherman's formal dispatches: "The Government of the United States has...any and all rights which they choose to enforce in war—to take their lives, their homes, their lands, their everything.... [W]ar is simply power unrestrained by constitution.... To the persistent secessionist, why, death is mercy, and the quicker he or she is disposed of the better."[103] Hitler and Sherman both understood that "disposing" of men and women who stood in the way of big government was a "responsibility" of one who was in "authority." Sherman continued in this vein, even enlarging his target for "disposing" to include children: "There is a class of people [Southerners] men, women, and children, who must be killed or banished before you can hope for peace and order."[104] Does this sound like a peace-loving, Constitution-respecting, defender of liberty, or does it sound more like something Adolf Hitler set loose?

---

101   *Ibid.*

102   Zachariah Chandler, Congressional Globe, 37th Congress, 1st sess., 45, 75, 91, pt. 3:1338.

103   William Sherman, as cited in, Official Records War of the Rebellion, Vol. XXXII, pt. II, pp. 280-81.

104   William Sherman, as cited in, *ibid*, Vol. XXXIX, pt. II, p. 132.

Another historical coincidence is the faith that both Lincoln and Hitler held in what is called "Higher Law." It is not uncommon for Christians to believe that God's law is of higher value and importance than the laws of men and nations, but this is not the definition embraced by the advocates of "Higher Law." Orthodox Christians hold firm to their faith in God's Word as supreme, but they do not advocate using that faith to negate existing law. God's Word is used by Christians to shape their view of how to make and construe laws for their government. Advocates of Higher Law believe that no law that is made by a government can be enforced if it runs contrary to their belief in some unwritten spiritual wisdom. Therefore, radical abolitionists did not believe that the constitutional guarantee of returning runaway slaves had to be enforced. Instead of amending the Constitution and removing the fugitive slave section, Higher Law advocates believed that they had the right (a power given to them from a "Higher" source) to ignore that part of the Constitution.

Lincoln disagreed with the radical abolitionists on the point of ignoring the fugitive slave section of the Constitution, but he did hold to the view of a higher power than written law. His view of government having a fundamental right to life is an example of the Higher Law mentality. Even though the foundation of these United States was set upon the principle of a free people having the unalienable right to "alter or abolish" their government, Lincoln still demanded the right of government to exist forever. The rather mystical view Lincoln held of the Union as the creator of the states demonstrates this Higher Law idealism. The Union was seen as a near god-like creature capable of working the wonders of creation itself! Lincoln's Union was so divine that setting aside the Constitution became acceptable, as in denying the rights of habeas corpus; ignoring the Supreme Court, as was done in the Merryman Case; jailing legislators of states loyal to the Union, as was done in Maryland; shutting down dissenting newspapers, as was done in New York, Ohio, and Illinois; arresting unfriendly political opponents and trying them in military courts and banishing them from the United States, as was done to Representative Clement Vallandigham of Ohio; and, creating a new state out of a portion of another state in flagrant violation of Article 4, Section 3, of the U.S. Constitution as was done by the creation of the state of West Virginia. These represent a very small sample of some actions taken by Lincoln which unbiased historians admit were unconstitutional; but as Lincoln and his defenders insisted it was being done for a "higher" purpose—saving the Union. They all believed that "history" would judge them as men who were willing to do "tough things" in order to save the Union.

Let us now hear from another advocate of Higher Law, Adolf Hitler: "The judges of this State may tranquilly condemn us for our conduct at that time, but History, the goddess of a higher truth and a better legal code, will smile as she tears up this verdict and will acquit us of the crime for which this verdict demands punishment.[105]" According to Hitler, it was not the written law of the German Republic that had to be obeyed but some mystical "higher truth" and a "better legal code." This is the same rationale that refuses to look at the history of the American Republic and its founding documents for guidance in dealing with the issues of state sovereignty, States' Rights, and secession. Rather than looking to established facts, Lincoln and his sycophants looked to a "higher law" that demanded preserving the Union regardless of the loss of life and liberty for all Americans.

At this point we must ask, "What was the general opinion and history of the act of secession in early America?" Was secession a new political fantasy dreamed up by a few radical members of the "slaveocracy?" Did "evil slaveholders" concoct the idea of secession to protect their slave property? As shocking as it may sound to the average American today, there is a strong tradition and history about secession in these United States that can teach us much about Lincoln's ill-advised philosophy and real American liberty.

In their attempt to paint the Federal government with near divine attributes, High Federalists often distorted the historical record about state sovereignty and secession. Therefore, let us depart from

---

105   Hitler, 377.

the historical record about secession in America and look at the very words of some noted American patriots. It is after all much easier to distort the nature of a historical event or philosophy than it is to distort the very words spoken about that event or philosophy. Let us call upon a noted American patriot, St. George Tucker of Virginia. Tucker took a leading part in the defense of his home state during the War for American Independence, serving throughout the war and being wounded at Yorktown. Also, Tucker was well known as a leading legal scholar, having edited and published one of the first American editions of Blackstone's *Commentaries on the Laws of England*. As a colonel in the Continental Army, Tucker not only fought for American Independence but also took an active part in forming the new government under the Articles of Confederation and the Constitution. Surely his thoughts on such issues as States' Rights, state sovereignty, and secession would be more in keeping with the founders of this nation than those of Abraham Lincoln, who was not even alive at that time. The following is St. George Tucker's views on:

1. State sovereignty: "From the moment of the revolution they became severely independent and sovereign states, possessing all the rights jurisdiction, and authority, that other sovereign states."[106] "The Constitution of the United States, then being that instrument by which the federal government hath been created; its powers defined, and limited; and the duties, and functions of its several departments prescribed; the government, thus established, may be pronounced to be a confederal republic, composed of several independent, and sovereign democratic states, united for their common defense, and security against foreign nations, and for the purposes of harmony, and mutual intercourse between each other; each state

---

106 St. George Tucker, *A View of the Constitution of the United States*, as cited in, A View of the Constitution of the United States: With Selected Writings, Clyde N. Wilson, ed. (Liberty Fund, Inc., Indianapolis, IN: 1999) 100.

retaining an entire liberty of exercising, as it thinks proper, all those parts of its sovereignty, which are not mentioned in the constitution, or act of union, as parts that ought to be exercised in common. It is the supreme law of the land, and as such binding upon the federal government; the several states; and finally upon all the citizens of the United States."[107] [Note that here Tucker made two statements that totally destroy Lincoln's view of the Federal government and state sovereignty: (1) The Federal government, i.e., the Union, was created by the adoption of the Constitution; it did not create the states; and, (2) the Constitution was binding upon the Federal government first, then upon the states and citizens. Lincoln's view had the Constitution binding the states to the will of the Federal government first, with no constitutional limits that could be overstepped by the Federal government if it was acting to "save the Union."]

2. States' Rights: "[T]he state governments will clearly retain all the rights of sovereignty, which they had before, and which are not by that act exclusively delegated to the United States.... The right of sovereignty, therefore, in all cases not expressly ceded to the United States by the constitution, or prohibited by it to the several states, remains inviolably, with the states, respectively."[108] [A more clear and definite assertion of States' Rights cannot be found outside of the writings of Thomas Jefferson and James Madison in the Kentucky and Virginia Resolves of 1798. The right of the people of the

---

107 *Ibid*,121.

108 *Ibid*, 126.

sovereign states to judge for themselves how long they will remain in a Union with other sovereign states is not prohibited by the Constitution nor has that right been delegated to the Federal government—it is the vital right that protects the citizens of these United States from Federal abuse and tyranny.]

3. Secession: [In the following citation Tucker demonstrated the right that the states had to secede from the first Federal government under the Articles of Confederation. He summed up the matter by explaining that the right of secession had not been lost by the adoption of the Constitution.] But the seceding states were certainly justified upon that principle; and from the duty which every state is acknowledged to owe to itself, and its own citizens by doing whatsoever may best contribute to advance its own happiness and prosperity; and much more, what may be necessary to the preservation of its existence as a state. Nor must we forget that solemn declaration to which every one of the confederate states assented...that whenever any form of government is destructive of the ends of its institution, it is the right of the people to alter or abolish it, and to institute new government. Consequently whenever the people of any state, or number of states, discovered the inadequacy of the first form of federal government to promote or preserve their independence, happiness, and union, they only exerted that natural right in rejecting it, and adopting another, which all had unanimously assented to, and of which no force or compact can deprive the people of any state, whenever they see the necessity, and possess the

> power to do it....We may infer that that right has
> not been diminished by any new compact which
> they may since have entered into.[109]

Note that these words were written circa 1803. The United States had been independent for less than thirty years, and the Constitution was only fifteen years old when Tucker was writing these words. Even still, we see this American patriot who had a living memory of the events surrounding the signing of the Declaration of Independence, the bloody struggle for independence, and the adoption of the Constitution stating facts that fifty-eight years later Lincoln would claim were untrue. St. George Tucker wrote about the sovereign nature of the states and the right of secession, fifty-seven years before South Carolina seceded from the Union.

In 1825, William Rawle of Philadelphia, Pennsylvania, wrote and had published one of the first textbooks on the United States Constitution, *A View of the Constitution of the United States of America*. Rawle was a contemporary of the founding fathers of this nation, being a young man at the time of the War for American Independence. Rawle was a friend of both Benjamin Franklin and George Washington. His textbook was used for several years as a textbook and a reference book for the study of the Constitution at the United States Military Academy at West Point, New York. Not only did Rawle advocate the philosophy that the states were sovereign, but also that the states created the Union. But the greatest shock for modern Americans is that in one complete chapter of his book, Rawle defended the right of secession. Once again, let us look at the following subjects, this time from Rawle's viewpoint:

1. State sovereignty: Each state was naturally tenacious of its own sovereignty and independence, which has been expressly reserved in their antecedent associations, and of which it was still meant to retain all that it did not become

---

109   *Ibid*, 85.

unavoidably necessary to surrender.... [T]he people, formed into one mass, as citizens of the union, yet still remaining distinct, as citizens of different states, created a new government, without destroying those which existed before.[110]

2. States' Rights: [Rawle explained that, in all cases, the will of the people of the state was supreme, and he explained why this was the case.] To deny this right would be inconsistent with the principle on which all our political systems are founded, which is, that the people have in all cases, a right to determine how they will be governed.[111]

3. Secession: The secession of a state from the Union depends on the will of the people of such state. The people alone as we have already seen, hold the power to alter their constitutions.... Still, however, the secession must in such case be distinctly and peremptorily declared to take place on that event.... But in either case the people is the only moving power.[112]

It must once again be stressed that Rawle was a contemporary of Franklin and Washington and was also their friend. Yet we see here in Rawle's textbook the very ideas and language that Lincoln some thirty-six years later would scorn and deny that they ever existed! Not only was Rawle's textbook used at West Point Military Academy, but one year after the publication, Rawle's book was

---

110 William Rawle, *A View of the Constitution of the United States of America*. This book was originally published in 1825 and has been edited, annotated, and republished by Walter D. Kennedy and James R. Kennedy under the title, *A View of the Constitution: Secession as Taught at West Point* (Scuppernong Press, Wake Forest, NC: 2020) xiii-xiv.

111 *Ibid.*, 252.

112 *Ibid.*, 256.

reviewed by the eminent journal of American political orthodoxy, The North American Review of Boston, Massachusetts. Surely if no state was ever sovereign (as Lincoln and Hitler contended) and secession is nothing less than revolution (as Lincoln and Hitler contended), the good people in Boston, Massachusetts, would have exposed this secession heresy in their review of Rawle's book. But once again, Lincoln and Hitler would find no such allies for their opinions. In a well-written and thorough review of Rawle's book by The North American Review we find only mild criticism of Rawle's view of how the electoral college should be organized, but not one word about his error (according to Lincoln and Hitler) on the right of secession! In a concluding remark the editors of The North American Review stated that Rawle's book was "a safe and intelligent guide to understanding the Constitution."[113] Unfortunately for America and the world, Lincoln and Hitler did not follow this "safe and intelligent guide" to the Constitution. This review by The North American Review was written only thirty-four years before South Carolina seceded from the Union.

Even foreign observers of these United States took note of the rights of the people of the various states within the Union. Here is how the French observer, Alexis de Tocqueville in his famous book, *Democracy in America*, described the Federal Union in 1833: "The Union was formed by the voluntary agreement of the states; and these, in uniting together, have not forfeited their nationality, nor have they been reduced to the condition of one and the same people. If one of the states chose to withdraw its name from the compact, it would be difficult to disprove its right to do so, and the Federal Government would have no means of maintaining its claims directly, either by force or by right."[114] This view of States' Rights and secession by De Tocqueville was made twenty-seven years before South Carolina seceded from the Union.

---

113 The North American Review (1826: AMS Press, Inc., New York: , 1965) Vol. XXII, pp. 446-51.

114 Alexis DeTocqueville, *Democracy in America* (1838, The Classics of Liberty Library, New York: 1992) 368.

Even presidents and former presidents spoke of the Federal government as originating from a compact among states, with the states having the right to secede from the Union. Here are the words of President John Q. Adams as spoken to the Historical Society of New York in 1839:

> With these qualifications we may admit the same right in the people of every state in the Union, with reference to the general government, which was exercised by the people of the colonies with reference to the supreme head of the British Empire, of which they formed a part; and under these limitations have the people of each state of the Union a right to secede from the Confederated Union itself. Here stands the right. But the indissoluble Union between the several states of this confederated nation is, after all, not in the right, but in the heart. If the day should ever come (may heaven avert it), when the affections of the people of these states shall be alienated from each other; when the fraternal spirit shall give way to cold indifference, or collision of interest shall fester into hatred, the bands of political asseveration will not long hold together parties no longer attached by the magnetism of conciliated interests and kindly sympathies; and far better will it be for the people of the dis-United States, to part in friendship from each other, than to be held together by constraint.[115]

These words of a former president of the United States from Massachusetts were spoken only twenty-one years before South Carolina seceded from the Union.

---

115   John Q. Adams, as cited in, Masters, 336.

Add to these noted Americans the works of President Thomas Jefferson and President James Madison, authors of the Kentucky and Virginia Resolves. From the Kentucky Resolves:

> Resolved, That the several states composing the United States of America, are not united on the principle of unlimited submission to their general government; but that by compact...they constituted a general government for special purposes, delegated to that government certain definite powers, reserving, each state to itself, the residuary mass of right to their own self-government; and whensoever the general government assumes undelegated powers, its acts are un-authoritative, void, and of no force.... [A]s in all other cases of compact among parties having no common judge, each party has an equal right to judge for itself, as well of infractions, as of the mode and measure of redress.[116]

What could fly in the face of Lincoln and Hitler's philosophy more than the notion that the states are not subject to unlimited submission to the Federal government? Not only did Thomas Jefferson state that the states are so constituted as not to be subject to an unlimited submission to the Federal government, but he also stated that the people of the states are the proper judge of "infraction" and "mode and measures of redress."

Let us look at what James Madison had to say in the Virginia Resolves:

> The powers of the Federal government as resulting from the compact to which the States are parties, as limited by the plain sense and intention of the instrument constituting that compact; as no further valid than they are authorized by the grants enumerated in that compact; and that in

---

116   Thomas Jefferson, as cited in, Kennedy and Kennedy, *Was Jefferson Davis Right?* 282.

cases of a deliberate, palpable, and dangerous exercise of other powers not granted by the said compact, the States, who are the parties thereto, have the right, and are in duty bound, to interpose for arresting the progress of the evil, and liberties appertaining to them.

Note that Madison asserted that the states are the parties of the "compact," i.e., the Constitution and the Union so formed, and not "we the people in general" as Lincoln believed. Also, Madison as well as Jefferson pointed out that it is within the power and rights of the states to "judge of infraction," determine "mode and measures of redress," and to "interpose" the power of the state to thwart the abuse of power by the Federal government. Every point that Jefferson and Madison were making in the Kentucky and Virginia Resolves vis-à-vis States' Rights, state sovereignty, and secession were rejected and excoriated by both Lincoln and Hitler.

SUMMARY

This chapter was commenced by looking at the shocking similarities between Abraham Lincoln's views of state sovereignty, States' Rights, and the life expectancy of government and those of Adolf Hitler. In chapter one we noted the close ties between radical European socialists/communists and Lincoln. In that chapter we pointed out that we are not suggesting that Lincoln was a communist, only that for some reason, these early American socialists/ communists found the new Republican Party and Abraham Lincoln very attractive. Likewise, in this chapter we are not suggesting that Lincoln was an early Nazi or that Hitler based his total philosophy on Lincoln's ideas. Yet, there is a shocking similarity between the views of these two men on these key points: Endurance of government, supremacy of the central government over the "so called states," and, the belief in some form of mystical justification of what was being done, regardless of what the law stated.

What a shame that upwards of one million Americans died directly or indirectly as a result of the war Lincoln was willing to wage. His willingness to wage this war was based as he said in the fact that secession was rebellion against the lawful authority of the United States. Lincoln even insinuated that secession was something new in American political history and that only evil slaveholders could hold such a view. As has been pointed out, the issue of secession, and state sovereignty from whence the right of secession springs, has real American antecedents:

1. St. George Tucker wrote in defense of both, fifty-seven years before South Carolina seceded from the Union.

2. William Rawle wrote one of the first textbooks on the United States Constitution in which he defended the right of the people of a state to secede from the Union, thirty-five years before South Carolina seceded from the Union.

3. One year after Rawle's textbook on the U.S. Constitution was published, The North American Review of Boston, Massachusetts, reviewed Rawle's book and had nothing negative to say about one whole chapter of his book that advocated the right of secession, thirty-four years before South Carolina seceded from the Union.

4. John Quincy Adams spoke in New York and acknowledged the rights of the sovereign states and the right of secession, twenty-one years before South Carolina seceded from the Union.

In 1798 only ten years after the adoption of the Constitution, Thomas Jefferson and James Madison wrote the Kentucky and Virginia Resolves that unequivocally stated that the states created the Federal government. Jefferson and Madison did not stop at making an empty assertion but went on to point out that the people of the sovereign states have the right and duty to oppose any Federal measure they find incongruent with their rights even to the point of nullifying said act or any other measure the people of the state find necessary. The words of these two great American presidents were written in defense of real States' Rights, rights that belong to the people of sovereign states.

Here is what is being demonstrated in this chapter: States' Rights, state sovereignty, and secession were not new ideas in America when Abraham Lincoln was elected president. Lincoln's views of these issues are the views held by those who love big government more than local government, be they socialists, communists, or Nazis. All such men will naturally follow Lincoln's view of government because they believe in the righteousness of their cause. In their mind's eye they see a better world if only the little people at the local level will get out of their way and allow the "experts" to do their job and run big government—of course for the good of all!

Advocates of big government always clothe their grab for power in high and praiseworthy rhetoric: Socialists are struggling to uplift the workers; Communists are bringing economic freedom to the masses; Nazis are trying to free the workers from the parasitic influence of an alien culture; and Lincoln was saving the Union and freeing the slaves. As was pointed out in chapter one, socialism cannot economically uplift anyone because socialism (and therefore communism and Nazism) only makes the rich poor and the poor poorer. Likewise, Lincoln did not save the Union if that term is used to refer to the Union as described by Thomas Jefferson and James Madison among many others. Lincoln completely destroyed that Union and replaced it with something more akin to an empire. Julius Caesar took the Roman Republic and in the process of creating the Roman Empire destroyed the Republic; likewise, Hitler destroyed the Federal Republic of Germany and created the Nazi Empire. In both cases liberty and freedom were exchanged for the exercise of power and trappings of glory. Lincoln's effort at "saving the Union" had the same deleterious result. The Union of free men in free states federated with like-minded free men in free states was destroyed, and in its place now stands an all-powerful Federal empire, an empire that is the sole judge of its powers. Just as shocking as the fact that Lincoln did not save the Union is the fact that Lincoln did not free the slaves; rather, he enslaved free men.[117]

Recurring to St. George Tucker once again, we will note that Tucker described three classes of slavery—all which Tucker openly opposed:

> (1) Domestic slavery. "That condition in which one man is subject to be directed by another in all his actions; and this constitutes a state of domestic slavery; to which state all the incapacities and disabilities of civil slavery are incident, with the weight of other numerous calamities superadded thereto."[118] It should be noted that Tucker wrote and published an early tract opposing both domestic slavery and laws that discriminate against free people of color, making this defender of States' Rights and secession one of America's first total civil rights advocates.

> (2) Civil slavery. "Civil liberty being no other than natural liberty, so far restrained by human laws, and no further restrained than is necessary and expedient for the general advantages, a state of civil slavery commences immediately."[119] Anytime a government passes laws that infringe upon its citizens' unalienable rights or gives special

---

117 For a more complete account of Lincoln and slavery, please review *Myths of American Slavery* by Walter D. Kennedy. For a more complete account of Lincoln's enslaving free men, please see *Emancipating Slaves, Enslaving Freemen*, by Jeffery Hummel.

118 Tucker, 409-10.

119 *Ibid.*, 407.

advantages to one class of persons over another class of persons, this action results in reducing otherwise free men into a condition of civil slavery.

(3) Political slavery. "When a nation is, from any external cause, deprived of the right of being governed by its own laws, only, such a nation may be considered as in a state of political slavery. Such is the state of conquered countries, and generally, of colonies, and other dependent governments. Such was the state of united America before the revolution. In this case, the personal rights of the subject may be so far secured by wholesome laws, as that the individual may be esteemed free, whilst the state is subject to a higher power: this subjection of one nation or people, to the will of another, constitutes the...species of slavery, which, in order to distinguish it from the other two, I have called political; inasmuch as it exists only in respect to the governments, and not to the individuals of the two countries."[120]

As Tucker explained it, when one nation conquers another nation and forces the conquered to live in a government when the people do not wish to do so, political slavery exists. Note that even if the people of the conquered nation have all the freedoms of the citizens of the conquerors, without the right to live in a government by the "consent of the governed," the people are not free—in reality they are slaves! This is an apt description of the people of the former Confederate States of America.

---

120   *Ibid.*

Chapter 5

A FREETHINKER LOOKS AT LINCOLN

Hundreds of people are now engaged in smoothing out the lines of Lincoln's face—forcing all features to the common mold so that he may be known, not as he really was, but, according to their poor standards, as he should have been.[121]

A FORMER CHAPLAIN in Robert E. Lee's army once had the occasion to shed a little light on how the "lines of Lincoln's face" had been smoothed out by Lincoln's admirers. While discussing the Christian character of Lee and his many Christian acts, the chaplain was interrupted by a lady who was amazed to find out that Lee was indeed a Christian. Her shock on learning about Lee's Christian character was confirmed by her comment; "I knew that President Lincoln was a Christian, but I never knew that Lee was one also." Whereupon the chaplain explained that yes indeed Lee was a Christian, but there was a major difference between the Christianity of Lee and that of Lincoln. According to the chaplain,

---

121   Robert G. Ingersoll, "Abraham Lincoln, a Lecture," speech given by Ingersoll, New York City, 1894, as cited in http://www.archive.org/stream/abrahamlincolnle00inge/ abrahamlincolnle00inge_djvu.txt, accessed March 16, 2009.

Col. Robert G. Ingersoll

Col. Ingersoll was a nineteenth century freethinker. Freethinkers rejected any authority outside of man's reasoning. Thus, freethinkers viewed Biblical theology and ideas as unauthoritative. In addition to being one of the most prominent freethinkers of his day, Ingersoll was a colonel in the eleventh Illinois Cavalry during the War; a Republican, a radical abolitionist, and an admirer of Lincoln. Ingersoll, as did other freethinkers, led the charge in defending Lincoln of being a Christian, while insisting that Lincoln was a freethinker. (Photo courtesy of WiKi Media Commons.)

the difference between Lee's Christianity and Lincoln's Christianity was that Lee had been a Christian all his adult life, whereas Lincoln did not become a Christian until *after* his death!

Martyrdom or at least the appearance of martyrdom has a unique way of metamorphosing the reputation of a slain individual. Surely this has been the case with the sixteenth president of the United States, Abraham Lincoln. Even though Lincoln received only 39 percent of the popular vote in 1860, and in 1864 had to fight hard to win reelection—and this is without any anti-Lincoln votes being cast from the South—today Lincoln is acknowledged as the most beloved president of the United States, and most evangelical Christians view Lincoln as a fellow Christian.

Which Lincoln are Americans talking about when they routinely stand in awe and reverence of this man? Is it the man of equality and love whom the politically correct society worships, or is it the man who defended white supremacy? Is it the man of liberty and freedom whom liberal commentators froth and swoon over, or is it the man whom Marx adored and Hitler admired? Is it the man who believed in the Constitution as Mark Levin and Sean Hannity would have us believe, or is it the man who invaded sovereign states, pillaged private property, jailed political opponents, and visited starvation and death upon innocent women and children? Which Lincoln is the real Lincoln? Perhaps we shall never completely understand the sixteenth president of the United States because, as Robert Ingersoll stated, "Hundreds of people are now engaged in smoothing out the lines of Lincoln's face." What was true in Ingersoll's day is true also today.

There seems to be spiritual tug-of-war between evangelical Christians and freethinkers for the possession of bragging rights to the moral character of Abraham Lincoln. This conflict commenced shortly after Lincoln's death and continues to this day. In an effort to prove that Lincoln was indeed a freethinker and not a Christian, Joseph Lewis published an article in 1924 titled "Lincoln, the Freethinker." Before we scrutinize the evidence about Lincoln's religious beliefs, let us first offer a definition of the term "freethinker." The following definition of a freethinker comes to us from the Freedom From Religion Foundation, Inc., a freethinking advocacy group: "A person who forms opinions about religion on the basis of reason, independently of tradition, authority, or established belief. Freethinkers include atheists, agnostics, and rationalists."[122] From the other extreme let us look at how the Roman Catholic Church defines freethinkers: "Freethinkers, those who, abandoning the religious truths and moral dictates of the Christian Religion, and accepting no dogmatic teaching on the ground of authority, base their beliefs on the unfettered findings of reason alone."[123] Taken together we can now simply say that a freethinker is one who does not believe in religious or mystical knowledge. According to this teaching, one can only know that which his senses can verify. As just stated, a freethinker believes only in those things substantiated "on the unfettered findings of reason alone."

Both Robert Ingersoll and Joseph Lewis give strong evidence of the fact that Lincoln was not a typical believer in orthodox Christianity. Yet even biographers who are somewhat critical of Lincoln point out that, regardless of Ingersoll and Lewis's comments, "Lincoln is not that easy to classify."[124] Strange, is it not? It was never hard to "classify" John F. Kennedy or Jimmy Carter as to their religious beliefs. Yet even contemporaries of Lincoln found it hard to identify his religious or lack of religious beliefs. Nevertheless, dogmatic freethinkers have found in Lincoln a man whom they believe was a fellow freethinker. What is the evidence that these freethinkers give to support their assertion that Lincoln was a freethinker?

---

122 Freedom From Religion Foundation, Inc., "What is a Freethinker," www.ffrf. org/nontracts/freethinker.php, accessed March 18, 2009.

123 The Original Catholic Encyclopedia, "Free Thinkers," http://oce.catholic.com/index. php?title=Free_Thinkers, accessed March 18, 2009.

124 Masters, 149.

By examining the speeches of Robert Ingersoll and Joseph Lewis one can recognize no less than four major points these men use to support their contention that Lincoln was a fellow freethinker: (1) In his early life, before he became a major player in politics, Lincoln expressed his lack of faith in the Bible and accepted religion; (2) Lincoln held a view of life more akin to pagan fatalism than to Christianity; (3) Lincoln was not then nor was he ever a member or frequent visitor of any church; (4) Lincoln held to his negative view of orthodox Christianity until his death.

In his biography of Lincoln, William H. Herndon, Lincoln's close friend and law partner, noted that Lincoln was greatly influenced by the writings of rationalist authors such as Constantin François Chasseboeuf Volney, *Les Ruines*; Thomas Paine, *The Age of Reason*; and various works of Arouet de Voltaire.[125] Lincoln's youthful exuberance for his newfound philosophy had to be throttled by his friends after he had written an essay exposing the Bible as a book of falsehoods and Jesus as a common man, not the Son of God. After reading his essay to several people, a friend of Lincoln, Samuel Hill, took the essay and threw it into a nearby stove and, according to Herndon, "The book went up in flames, and Lincoln's political future was secure. But his infidelity and his skeptical views were not diminished."[126] If not orthodox Christianity, then what was the religious faith of Lincoln? John T. Stuart, Lincoln's first law partner, explained Lincoln's religious faith thusly: "He was an avowed and open infidel and sometimes bordered on atheism. Lincoln always denied that Jesus was the Christ of God—denied that Jesus was the son of God as understood and maintained by the Christian Church."[127] As Herndon points

---

125   William H. Herndon and Jesse W. Weik, *Herndon's Lincoln* (1889, University of Illinois Press, Chicago: 2006) 266. Also see, Joseph Lewis, "Lincoln, the Freethinker," www.positiveatheism.org/hist/lewis/lewis07.htm, accessed March 15, 2009.

126   Herndon and Weik, 266.

127   *Ibid.*

out, these testimonies are about Lincoln the young man, but as shall be demonstrated, there are witnesses who attest to Lincoln's lifelong rejection of the basic principles of the Christian Church.

If he was not a Christian in the orthodox meaning of the word, what were Lincoln's religious beliefs? Again, we have the testimony of his close friend and law partner, William H. Herndon, who testified that Lincoln "held most firmly to the doctrine of fatalism all his life. His wife, after his death, told me [Herndon] what I already knew, that 'his only philosophy was, what is to be will be, and no prayers of ours can reverse the decree.'"[128] According to Herndon, Lincoln was enslaved to a superstitious mind. Herndon stated, "This superstitious view of life ran through his being like the thin blue vein through the whitest marble."[129] Note that Lincoln's view of "what will be will be" is nothing less than pagan fatalism— that there is no higher purpose to events; they just happen, and nothing can be done about it. Christians believe that every act of the natural world is either directed by God (Calvinism) or known to and overseen by God (Arminianism) and the prayers of the faithful "availeth much." As described by his wife, Lincoln's view was that man is subject to the whims of fortune with no one of higher power to call upon for assistance. Where Christians believe in Divine Providence, pagans trust in luck. For example, Ward Hill Lamon in his *Life of Abraham Lincoln* stated that Lincoln believed in "providence," but this providence was the outworking of *natural law and order*, which is firmly in place in the world.[130] Herndon, Lincoln's longtime friend, attested to the fact that Lincoln held many views in common with Christians, but he did not embrace what is known as "orthodox or evangelical views of Christianity."[131] Lamon states that Lincoln's religious views were limited to "practical and rationalistic order."[132] According to

---

128 *Ibid.*, 264.

129 *Ibid.*

130 Ward Hill Lamon, as cited in, *ibid.*, 268.

131 Herndon and Weik, 268.

132 Lamon, as cited in, *ibid.*, 269.

Lamon, the only religious author whose views were close to those of Lincoln was the Unitarian preacher Theodore Parker.[133]

Theodore Parker was a radical Unitarian, a member of Brook Farm, a Transcendentalist, and a radical abolitionist, having supported the bloody work of John Brown. After Brown's arrest, Parker intervened on his behalf by writing letters and articles in defense of Brown.[134] Parker's theology was so radical that he was shunned and eventually denied access to other Boston Unitarian churches. Yet this radical Unitarian preacher may have been responsible for one of Lincoln's most famous quotes. In 1850 Parker gave a speech at an abolitionist convention in Boston in which he spoke in part of "[a] democracy—that is a government *of all the people, by all the people, for all the people*"[135] [emphasis added]. Is this line not rather like Lincoln's famous "of the people, by the people, and for the people" declaration in the Gettysburg Address? This being the case, it appears that Lamon's assertion that Parker was a man whom Lincoln could agree with is a valid statement.

Even though Lincoln has been proclaimed by many to be a Christian, there is no evidence that he was ever baptized or otherwise became a member of a Christian church. In an interview with Herndon after Lincoln's death, Mary Todd Lincoln noted, "Mr. Lincoln had no faith and no hope in the usual acceptation of those words. He never joined a Church...and he was never a technical Christian."[136] The fact that Lincoln believed in some form of god, or some form of providence does not qualify him as a Christian, regardless of how often he intoned those words. It is not unusual in today's political arena to hear politicians speak in language that would endear them to voters of strong religious

---

133 *Ibid.*

134 Dictionary of Unitarian and Universalist Biography, "Theodore Parker," http://www25.uua.org/uuhs/duub/articles/theodoreparker.html, accessed March 18, 2009.

135 Bartlett's Quotations, Theodore Parker, "The American Idea: Speech at N.E. Anti Slavery Convention, Boston, May 29, 1850," http://www.bartleby.com/100/459.html, accessed March 18, 2009.

136 Mary Todd Lincoln, as cited in, Herndon and Weik, 269.

faith. Likewise in the mid-nineteenth century when orthodox Christianity was strong and vigorous, anyone seeking office would pepper his speeches with words and phrases that would endear said candidate to the masses of voters. To assume that because an individual is "religious" or believes in God therefore he is *ipso facto* a Christian is to strain the definition of Christianity. Only biblical standards are adequate when defining who is and who is not a Christian. Any member of a satanic cult can be said to have religion; any pagan can be said to believe in God, but this does not qualify them for the title of Christian. Holding principles common to the Christian faith is equally insufficient to make one a Christian. As Herndon points out, "Whilst he [Lincoln] held many opinions in common with the great mass of Christian believers, he did not believe in what are regarded as the orthodox or evangelical views of Christianity."[137] Lincoln did not belong to a church, did not attend worship services, did not tithe to a church, and "did not believe in...orthodox or evangelical...Christianity." Whenever I hear an evangelical minister praising and lauding Lincoln, I often wonder how that minister would react if all his church members adopted Lincoln's style of Christianity.

While many sycophants of Lincoln will admit that indeed Mr. Lincoln did at one time question the Bible and orthodox Christianity, these views dramatically changed after witnessing the horror of the Civil War. It is somewhat strange that this very same "oh yes, but he changed" argument is used by liberal and neo-conservative Lincoln devotees when dealing with his blatantly racist statements and attitude. John G. Nicolay, a German-born friend and personal secretary to Lincoln, made the following statement to Herndon about Lincoln's religious beliefs: "Mr. Lincoln did not to my knowledge in any way change his religious ideas, opinions, or beliefs from the time he left Springfield to the day of his death. I do not know just what they were, never having heard him explain them in detail; but I am very sure he gave no outward indication of his mind having undergone any change

---

137 *Ibid.*, 268.

in that regard while here."[138] In closing his review of Lincoln's religious life, Herndon made the following observation: "My own testimony, however, in regard to Mr. Lincoln's religious views may perhaps invite discussion. The world has always insisted on making an orthodox Christian of him, and to analyze his sayings or sound his beliefs is but to break the idol....The benevolence of his impulses, the seriousness of his convictions, and the nobility of his character are evidences unimpeachable that his soul was ever filled with the exalted purity and sublime faith of natural religion."[139] So now we have the startling testimony of a friend and associate of Lincoln that Lincoln's soul was filled not with the amazing grace of God, or covered with the Holy Blood of Christ, or baptized in the Holy Spirit, but that his soul was "filled with the exalted purity and sublime faith of *natural religion*" [emphasis added]. No wonder that Colonel Ingersoll, a contemporary of Lincoln and fellow Republican, and Mr. Lewis felt sure that Lincoln was a freethinker. Who can fault them for drawing such a conclusion? After all, *natural religion* is nothing less than code words for the rejection of orthodox Christianity and the embracing of humanistic theology.

But what about Herndon's allegation that Lincoln was a man characterized by "benevolence of...impulses...nobility of character... [and] exalted purity"? Just how noble is someone who institutes a war against his fellow citizens upon the most spurious of grounds? How benevolent is it to wage war upon innocent women and children? Where is that exalted purity of soul when men such as Karl Marx laud and praise a man's every action and when men such as Adolf Hitler admire and replicate that man's exploits? Not since the dreaded terrors of Attila the Hun have a Christian people been put to such horrors as those visited upon the civilian population of the South during Lincoln's war on the South. Lincoln's commanders left a trail across the South of mass starvation, murder, rape, pillaging of private homes and churches, looting of cemeteries, destruction of colleges, libraries, hospitals, and any means of

---

138   John G. Nicolay, as cited in, Herndon and Weik, 267.

139   Herndon and Weik, 269.

production of medicines and medical supplies. How do these acts compare with the laudatory statements of Herndon about Lincoln? Nothing in the annals of Western civilization other than the attacks of pagan infidels can compare to that which Lincoln loosed upon the South. Surely there will be those who will say that this was war and therefore justifiable. How can a Christian justify such acts? In 1864 Sherman, upon being informed about continued attacks on his army by Southern partisans, issued this order: "Cannot you send over about Fairmount and Adairsville, burn ten or twelve houses of known secessionists, kill a few at random, and let them know that it will be repeated...?"[140] This is the same Sherman who stated, "There is a class of people [Southerners] men, *women, and children,* who must be *killed or banished* before you can hope for peace and order"[141] [emphasis added]. Notice that these were non-combatant civilians whom Sherman was talking about killing or banishing. Sherman was not alone in committing these atrocities. Grant stated, "It is our duty to weaken the enemy, by destroying their means of subsistence, withdrawing their means of cultivating their fields, and every other way possible."[142] From the highest level of the military in Washington, Gen. Henry Halleck, army chief of staff, wrote to General Grant the following order: "...make all the valley south of the Baltimore and Ohio road a desert."[143] How do old men, the sick and infirmed, or the women and the children live in a "Federal" desert?

One is left wondering that if indeed Lincoln was fighting the war to "save the Union," for whom was he saving it? If a person exterminates the population of the South, if he lays waste the productive capacity of the South, and if he pulls down all structures of government in the South, the Union is left with nothing

---

140   William T. Sherman, as cited in, John Bennett Walters, *Merchant of Terror: General Sherman and Total War* (Bobbs-Merrill, New York: 1973) 137.

141   William T. Sherman, as cited in, Official Records of the Rebellion, Vol. XXXIX, pt. II, p. 132.

142   U. S. Grant, as cited in, *ibid.*, Vol. XXIV, pt. III, pp. 186-87.

143   General Halleck, as cited in, *ibid.*, XXXVII, pt. II, p. 366.

saved. As has been pointed out in other works, Lincoln was not unknowledgeable about what was going on in the prosecution of his war against the South.[144] Nevertheless, evangelicals and freethinkers both adore and swoon before the icon of Lincoln. Ironic, is it not, that the crowd kowtowing before the icon of Lincoln is populated by Marx, Hitler, freethinkers, and evangelical Christian ministers?

Robert Lewis Dabney was quick to answer Colonel Ingersoll's attack upon those holding a biblical worldview. Dabney, a Presbyterian theologian and friend of Gen. Stonewall Jackson, wrote a rebuke of Ingersoll's freethinking philosophy titled *The Latest Infidelity: A Reply to Ingersoll's Position*. Notice that Dabney linked freethinking to the philosophy of an infidel. Dabney stated: "The phase of infidelity most current among those who do not profess to accept the gospel is marked by two qualities: It is aggressive, and it is extreme. It refuses to stop short of that last result, blank atheism, or, at least blank agnosticism, from which even the skepticism of previous ages recoiled with abhorrence."[145] Dabney, who is criticizing Ingersoll, is the same Dabney who predicted, that as a result of the North's victory over the South, a loss of moral virtue would sweep away the proper relationship between men and women in America. According to Dabney, the North's victory over the South would also lead to the Bible and Christianity being purged from American society. All of this, and more, Dabney predicted just after the defeat of the South. It is rather eye-opening to note that all this, plus much more, has become reality in modern America—and yet many evangelical Christian ministers loathe Dabney and adore Lincoln. The work of "smoothing out the lines on Lincoln's face" appears to have been very successful.

---

144   Kennedy and Kennedy, *The South Was Right!* 387-89.

145   Robert Lewis Dabney, Discussions, "The Latest Infidelity: A Reply to Ingersoll's Positions" (1897, Sprinkle Publication, Harrisonburg, VA: 1979) VI, 506.

Chapter 6

THE BIG LIE COMES TO AMERICA

LINCOLN'S SUPERNATURAL AND MYSTICAL UNION

IN HIS FIRST INAUGURAL ADDRESS, March 1861, Abraham Lincoln stated, "The Union is much older than the Constitution.... It follows from these views that no state...can lawfully get out of the Union." To add insult to ignorance, in Lincoln's July 4, 1861, message to Congress, he informs Congress that, "The Union is older than the States and, in fact created them as States... The Union threw off their old dependence for them and made them States, such as they are." It seems as if Lincoln viewed the Declaration of Independence as a "Union document." Abraham Lincoln had a most unique and unusual view of the Union and the States. Historian and economist, Dr. Thomas DiLorenzo often referred to Lincoln's view of the Union as a "spectacular lie." Like their twenty-first century counterparts, nineteenth century socialists understood the force of what Adolf Hitler's henchman, Joseph Goebbels, called the "Big Lie." In his book *The Lincoln No One Knows* author Webb Garrison provided a view into Lincoln's rather convoluted concept of the Union. Lincoln's Big Lie advanced the fable that the Union existed before either the States or the Constitution. According to Lincoln's view, the mystical and supernatural Union hovered over the American Colonies and ushered them into independence, statehood, and pointed the way to writing and adopting the Constitution. Strange is it not, that no

John G. Nicolay, Abraham Lincoln, and John Hay

Lincoln's two secretaries, Nicolay to Lincoln's right and Hay to his left. Lincoln brought Nicolay with him from Illinois when he was elected president. It was Nicolay who stated that Lincoln was not an orthodox Christian before he was elected president and also that Lincoln's views on religion did not change while he was president. (Photograph courtesy of the Library of Congress.)

other United States president had ever seen this mystical Union before Lincoln? Like DiLorenzo, Garrison noted that Lincoln repeatedly insisted on the concept that the Union existed before the Constitution was written and adopted by the states. "The Union is much older than the Constitution," Lincoln stated. "It was formed, in fact, by the Articles of Association in 1774." As many historians have noted, the "government" or association of the colonies before the adoption of the Articles of Confederation was a body that could suggest anything but conclude or demand nothing. Until the adoption of the government under the Articles of Confederation, 1783, the only political body that could act with the force of law was the legislature of the various States. Any recommendation or suggestion that the Continental Congress passed, had to be submitted to the States for their official action. It must be noted that there was no mystical or supernatural Union commanding or directing these actions. Said commanding and directing had to be performed by the act of sovereign States.

Lincoln asserted that this mystical bond of union, "was further matured by the Articles of Confederation in 1778." Lincoln, who proclaims that no State in the Union is or was ever sovereign, completely overlooks the fact that the Articles of Confederation boldly states in Article II, "Each state retains its **sovereignty, freedom,** and **independence** and every Power, Jurisdiction and right, which is not by this confederation expressly delegated to the United States, in Congress assembled" [emphasis added]. Notice that each State is declared to be a sovereign, free and independent State. This is the same Lincoln that stated in his July 4, 1861, Message to Congress that no State had ever been sovereign.

According to Lincoln's reasoning, the Constitution was created by the supernatural agency of a mystical Union not by the action of sovereign States. Remember that Lincoln proclaimed that the Union preceded the Constitution and the States in time. Yet as demonstrated, this mystical Union did not direct the State delegates to vote for independence in 1776, the State directed their delegates on how to vote; the mystical Union is not seen in the adoption of the Articles of Confederation in 1783, the Articles boldly proclaim these States to be sovereign and as such each State, acting for itself, acceded to the Article of Confederation; likewise, as proven by Article VII of the Constitution, it was not a mystical Union that directed the adoption of the Constitution, thereby forming a new Union, but the act of each sovereign State in 1787-88. The Federal government and therefore Union of States came about when nine States ratified the Constitution (see Article VII of the Constitution). When nine out of thirteen States ratified the Constitution, at that time the Union then existed only among those States so ratifying the Constitution, see Article VII. It is as ridiculous to say the Union existed before the Constitution was ratified by the States as it is to say a marriage union existed before two people were married!

Lincoln's mystical view of the Union and the Constitution seemed to have governed how he responded to Constitutional issues which obstructed his presidential actions. Lincoln believed that his view of the Constitution allowed him, when necessary, to do "a little bending of it." One million Americans killed, political opponents in the North jailed, the total impoverishment of generations of Southerners is more than just "a little bending" of the Constitution! With such a high cost in lives, liberty, and property, one is left wondering, "What type of Union is being saved and for whom is this Union being saved?"

Garrison noted that Lincoln viewed the pre-constitutional Union as eternal or everlasting. Lincoln repeatedly stressed that states could not secede from this eternal Union and was therefore in a state of rebellion against lawful authority if secession was attempted. Lincoln warned that if secession destroyed the Union, the whole world would suffer from this dire catastrophe. One might be tempted to ask, "Are bloody bayonets the instrument that *free* governments use to hold a union of free men together?" What does one call a place in which one is not free to leave? Unless one believes a prison is a suitable place for free men, it must be admitted that free men cannot be held in a situation against their will without ceasing to be free. Looking at the world situation today, one can only wonder if Lincoln's forcing the Union to remain intact through the power of the bloody bayonet has, indeed, helped the world to be a better place. From the gulags of the Communist empires to the gas chambers of Nazism, many people would not agree with the use of bloody bayonets to preserve unity.

Some people, according to Garrison, argued that the states had come together in order to form the Union and not, as Lincoln stated, the Union formed the states. President Ronald Reagan said as much in his first inaugural address. He stated that the states had formed the Federal government and not the other way around. On January 20, 1981, President Reagan proclaimed, "It is my intention to curb the size and influence of the Federal establishment and to demand recognition of the distinction between the powers granted to the Federal Government and those reserved to the States or to the people. **All of us need to be reminded that the Federal Government did not create the States; the States created the Federal Government**" [emphasis added]. John C. Calhoun, Jefferson Davis, Robert E. Lee, could not have said it better! Apparently, Lincoln would have disagreed with Reagan's statement. Sadder yet is the fact that many so-called "conservative" leaders embrace Lincoln's fabrication rather than Reagan's truth.

Lincoln's view that to preserve the Union "a little bending" of the Constitution might be necessary was little more than the 1860s' version of "the end justifies the means," which is a concept firmly held by socialists from Lenin to Hitler.

Columnist Joseph Sobran agreed with Garrison's assessment of Lincoln's ideas about the Union. In a column published in August 2001 Sobran noted that Lincoln's mystical view of the Union being older than the States and the Constitution was completely false. Lincoln was completely wrong when he stated that the Union was older than the Constitution and the States. As Sobran observed, "How could a union of things be older than the very things it was a union of? Isn't that a bit like saying that a marriage is older than either spouse? Well, said Lincoln, the Union had been formed while the future states were still colonies—then they declared their independence of Britain—but not of each other, mind you—then the Union was 'further matured' in the Articles of Confederation—then it was matured still further in the Constitution; but at every stage, the states had had no existence outside the Union."[146]

In another article published later that same month, Sobran points out Lincoln's total lack of factual history when dealing with the adoption of the Declaration of Independence. Sobran notes that Lincoln said the States never existed independent of the Union and as dependents of the Union, they could not withdraw from the Union. According to Lincoln, even the Declaration of Independence was not the act of individual States but rather a group of colonies, being directed by a mystical union, and acting as a unit to break the union between the group of colonies and Great Britain. In other words, every act of the American people was being done by "one people indivisible" and not by the people of sovereign States. [147]

Lincoln's chief task as he saw it was to preserve that mystical Union which up until his administration had never existed. As has been pointed out in previous chapters, this view of the Union as eternal and supreme was a view held by High Federalists. This view had been so rejected by Americans that it caused the demise of the Federalist Party and the ascension of the Jeffersonian States' Rights Party in the United States. What should be obvious is that Lincoln was holding a view of the Union that had been rejected by Americans, and as a minority president, only being elected by 39 percent of the vote, his political philosophy did not represent the commonly held view.[148]

---

146   Joseph Sobran, "The Imaginary Abe," www.lewrockwell.com, August 4, 2001.

147   Joseph Sobran, "Who Killed the Iceman?" www.lewrockwell.com, August 10, 2001.

148   Garrison, 147.

Alexander Stephens, vice-president of the Confederate States of America, noted of Lincoln's view of the Union: "The Union with him in sentiment, rose to the sublimity of a religious mysticism; while his ideas of its structure and formation in logic, rested upon nothing but the subtleties of a sophism!"[149]

A modern psychobiographer, Dwight G. Anderson, stated that by 1864 Lincoln's mystical Union and his own personality were so closely identified that Lincoln and the Union had become one and the same.[150] One commonly heard slogan in Nazi Germany was, "Hitler is Germany, Germany is Hitler." This is what happens when a people place persons or government above liberty. Therefore, Patrick Henry insisted on placing American liberty first, and American Union second. Even if one rejects Anderson's view of Lincoln and the Union, it is difficult to comprehend how Lincoln formulated his view of the American Union and why he became so dedicated to that view.[151]

In his book *The Real Lincoln,* Professor Thomas DiLorenzo noted that Emory University professor Dr. Donald W. Livingston referred to Lincoln's assertion that the Union created the states was not just a lie but also a "spectacular lie." Although Lincoln declared that the South's claim to the right of secession was "an ingenious sophism," it was in reality Lincoln who was engaged in twisting both language and the Constitution into something heretofore unknown in American history.[152]

DiLorenzo pointed out that Lincoln's argument that secession would destroy the government of the United States was nothing less than "foolish." A little historical reflection clearly demonstrates just how incorrect was Lincoln's view. After the secession of thirteen Southern states and the formation of the government of the

---

149　Alexander H. Stephens, A Constitutional History of the late War Between the States (National Publishing Company, Philadelphia: 1868) II, 448.

150　Garrison, 147.

151　*Ibid.*

152　DiLorenzo, The Real Lincoln, 113.

Confederate States of America, the Federal government (the same one that Lincoln stated would be destroyed by secession) created and maintained one of the world's largest armies and navies. This same government that Lincoln said would be destroyed by secession waged near total war upon the Confederate States of America for four years and forced its will upon the South. How can a government that is "destroyed" by secession do such things? Equally ridiculous was Lincoln's contention that representative government would perish from the face of the earth if secession were successful. To refute Lincoln's assertion one only has to note that the United States, less the Confederacy, would still be a "representative" government; that the Confederate States of America was also a "representative" government; and that Great Britain, with its long history of "representative" government, would not cease to exist if secession was successful in America.[153] DiLorenzo pointed out that those who advocated the right of secession and nullification understood that these were powerful checks on the growth of Federal power. The right of secession and nullification was an effective means to compel the Federal government to live within the limits as established by the founding fathers in the Constitution. Absent these checks and balances on the Federal government, what is left is a government that knows and respects no limits on its power—an apt description of any Marxist or Nazi government.[154]

In his book *The Real Lincoln*, Charles L. C. Minor (this book should not be confused with DiLorenzo's book by the same title) has observed: "The logic of the Civil War was that the right to govern is paramount over the right to live, that man is made for government, rather than that government is made for man, and that for men to claim the right of self-government is to deserve and incur the death penalty. Lincoln's arguments against the right of the South to independence were drawn from baseless exaggerations, the fatalistic sequence of mechanistic logic, and imperial and

---

153   *Ibid.*, 114.

154   *Ibid.*

authoritarian interpretation of the Constitution which ignored its humanitarian purpose, a strange hodgepodge of the maxims of monarchical political science, and an instinctive metaphysical attitude toward government."[155] In other words, Lincoln had an almost supernatural view of government; not a view based upon the realities of his day but based on what he desired the nature of the Federal government to be. Unfortunately for American liberty, the mystical demon big, all powerful, one nation indivisible government had total sway of Lincoln and today of the United States of America.

---

155   Charles L. C. Minor, *The Real Lincoln* (1928, Sprinkle Publishing Co., Harrisonburg, VA: 1988) 259.

Having been expelled from Europe for his radical socialist revolutionary views, Blenker was more than eager to enlist "thousands of Germans ready to fight for the preservation of the union." The "Union" Blenker and his fellow radical socialists/ communists "saved" was not the same Union given to America by her Founding Fathers. Several non-Southern historians have described Blenker as "a convinced Marxists." (Photograph courtesy of the Library of Congress.)

Chapter 7

THE UNION, ITS TRUE NATURE AND CHARACTER

IN 1840, JUDGE ABLE UPSHUR wrote *The Federal Government: its True Nature and Character; Being a Review of Judge Story's Commentaries on the Constitution of The United States.*[156] His work is now referred to as *The Federal Government: Its True Nature and Character*. As his original title notes, Judge Upshur sought to counter Story's High Federalist view of the Federal government as the supreme power of government and the States as subservient to the Federal government. Story's view of the Federal government and therefore the Union runs counter to the Jeffersonian view of real States' Rights. As Jefferson and Madison point out in the Kentucky and Virginia Resolves, "we the people" of the sovereign States hold the ultimate right and power to determine how we shall be governed. The rejection of the High Federalist view of big government caused the demise of the Federalist Party early in the history of the United States. The political successors to the High Federalist view were represented by the Whig Party (Lincoln entered politics as a Whig) which was soon absorbed into the Republican Party. Judge Upshur's book destroys Story's view of

---

156   Able Upshur, *The Federal Government: Its True Nature and Character; Being A Review of Judge Story's Commentaries on the Constitution of the United States* (Van Evrie, Horton & Co., NY: 1840).

the United States being "one people" with the Federal government as the sovereign agent of all Americans. As noted, his work is in essence a study of the "true nature and character" of the Union.

To understand the true nature and character of the Union, we must ask several questions: (1) Was the Union, as given to us by America's Founding Fathers, an indivisible entity and did it exist before the States and Constitution as Lincoln proclaimed? (2) Is the United States one nation indivisible, thereby denying that States were ever sovereign? (3) Who authorized the Union under the Constitution and did that authorization make the new Union/government perpetual?

No better answer to the first question can be given than from the pen of Thomas Jefferson in the Kentucky Resolves of 1799. Is the Union indivisible and did it exist before the States and Constitution? Let Jefferson speak on those subjects: "RESOLVED, That this commonwealth [Kentucky] considers the federal union, upon the terms and for the purposes specified in the late **compact** [the Constitution], as conducive to the liberty and happiness of the several states: That it does now unequivocally declare its attachment to the Union, and to that compact, **agreeable to its obvious and real intention,** and will be among the last to seek its dissolution: That if those who administer the general government be permitted to transgress the limits fixed by that compact, by a total disregard to the special delegations of power therein contained, annihilation of the state governments, and the erection upon their ruins, of a general consolidated government, will be the inevitable consequence: That the principle and construction contended for... that the general government is the exclusive judge of the extent of the powers delegated to it, stop nothing short of despotism; since the discretion of those who administer the government, and not the constitution, would be the measure of their powers: That **the several states who formed that instrument, being sovereign and independent,** have the unquestionable right to judge of its infraction; and that a nullification, by those sovereignties, of all unauthorized acts done under colour of that instrument, is the rightful remedy"[157] [emphasis added]. Note that Jefferson states that the Constitution is a compact among the States. Lincoln's assertion that the Constitution preceded the States is proven false by Jefferson's words. Notice also that Jefferson proclaims the States to be "sovereign and independent," and he also points out the danger of allowing the Federal government to be the exclusive judge of what powers it possesses. According to Jefferson, allowing the Federal government to be the sole judge of its powers would lead to "annihilation of the state governments, and the erection upon their ruins, of a general consolidated government." In the Virginia Resolves of 1798, James Madison also notes the danger to American liberty if the Federal government rather than the States became *the* sovereign agent in the United States. Madison notes that if the Federal government is allowed to, "consolidate the states by degrees, into one sovereignty, the obvious tendency and inevitable consequence of which would be, to transform the present republican system of the United States, into an absolute, or at best a mixed monarchy."[158] Here we have the words of the "Father of the Constitution" warning Americans of the danger of transforming the republic of sovereign States into "one sovereignty," aka, "one nation indivisible." What Madison predicted would happen, an all-powerful Federal government that recognizes no limits on its power or as Madison warned, "an absolute or at best a mixed monarchy," is America's current reality.

It is apparent from reading the words of Jefferson and Madison, that their view of the Union and Lincoln's view of the Union are not simply a little different, they are polar opposites. The following is a list of the four most important and fundamental documents relating to the formation of these United States and therefore, the Union. These documents prove that Jefferson and Madison,

---

157   Thomas Jefferson, The Kentucky Resolutions of 1799, Kentucky Resolution 1799 < 1786-1800 < Documents < American History From Revolution To Reconstruction and beyond (rug.nl) http://www.let.rug.nl/usa/documents/1786-1800/kentucky-resolution-1799.php accessed December 29, 2021.

158   James Madison, The Virginia Resolves of 98, The Tenth Amendment Center, Virginia Resolutions of 1798 | Tenth Amendment Center Accessed December 30, 2021.

unlike Lincoln, viewed the Union correctly. These documents are: The Declaration of Independence, The 1783 Treaty of Paris, The Articles of Confederation and The Constitution. While many people praise the Union, yet there is no definition or description of the Union found in these four fundamental documents of this nation. Yet, Lincoln drove this nation into its most bloody and costly war to save *his* mystical Union.

Many historians have pointed out that the independence and sovereignty of each state was clearly recognized in Article II of the Articles of Confederation and plainly stated in the Treaty of Paris of 1783. In that treaty His Britannic Majesty, the King of Great Britain, "acknowledges that said United States, viz (herein is named each of the thirteen states) to be sovereign and independent States."[159] We see here that the very treaty that ended the War for American Independence acknowledged that each state was indeed a sovereign state. Lincoln's mystical Union was not even mentioned. Add to this the words of a founding father of these United States, Luther Martin: "At the separation from the British Empire, the people of America preferred the Establishment of themselves into thirteen separate sovereignties instead of incorporating themselves into one."[160]

Even that arch-nationalist, Alexander Hamilton, had to admit to preexisting state sovereignty. In No. 15 of the *Federalist Papers* Hamilton wrote: "In our case the concurrence of thirteen sovereign wills is requisite under the Confederation to the complete execution of every important measure that proceeds from the Union."[161]All of these men recognized that the United States was, in fact, not one unitary nation, but rather a republic of separate republics, or as William Rawle of Pennsylvania referred to it, a republic of republics. Each, in his own way, gives evidence supporting the fact that the States, as sovereign entities, existed before the Union was formed.

---

159   The Treaty of Paris, 1783, 'Virtual Library of Inter-American Peace Initiatives, Microsoft Word - Antigua&Barbuda.doc (oas.org) accessed December 30, 2021.

160   Luther Martin, as cited in, Berger, 30.

161   Alexander Hamilton, The Federalists Papers (Mentor Books, New York: 1961) 112.

Lincoln asserts that by some mystical maneuver, a benevolent, all-wise and unseen supernatural Union acted the part of a foster parent to the thirteen colonies from somewhere around 1774 through the writing and adoption of the Declaration of Independence and the adoption of the first government under the Articles of Confederation, and ultimately shepherded the states into the adoption of the government under the present Constitution in 1788. According to Lincoln, all of this was done by an unseen, all-powerful and everlasting Union. Lincoln's description of the actions of his mystical Union sounds more like the attributes of a god and not an agent of the people.[162]

Strange as it may sound, the Union of the states under the Articles of Confederation was denoted as a *perpetual* Union. What happened to that so-called perpetual Union? That Union ended in 1788 by the secession of its member states as they acceded to the new Union under the Constitution. It should be noted that the one thing that was missing in the *new* Union's Constitution, in contrast to the Union under the Articles of Confederation, was the statement that the new Union would be a *perpetual* Union!

It is also worth noting that the new Union under the Constitution would become a reality when adopted by nine states and the new Union would be enforceable only on *those states so ratifying the Constitution.* In other words, those states not ratifying the Constitution would not be in the Union—so much for Lincoln's statement that no state ever existed outside of the Union. Two states, North Carolina and Rhode Island, did not accede to the new Union for more than a year and a half after it was the "law of the land" in the other eleven states.

As clearly demonstrated by the act of acceding to the new Union under the Constitution, it was the act of the people of each *state* that was forming the new government and not the people of America in general (see Article VII, United States Constitution). As

---

162   James Ostrowski, Secession, State, and Liberty (Transaction Publishers, New Brunswick, NJ: 1998) 160-63.

has been pointed out, Lincoln believed that the term "more perfect Union" in the preamble of the Constitution meant "perpetual Union." Yet, there is nothing in the Constitution to indicate that this view is correct. We do know that Patrick Henry believed that a more perfect Union is that Union that more perfectly protects American liberty and not American government: Henry stated, "The first thing I have at heart is American *liberty*, the second thing is American *union*."[163] Nothing could be further from true American freedom than a state of perpetual force, which is what Lincoln was advocating in defense of his mystical union.

Obviously, the true nature and character of the Union as described by Judge Upshur in 1840, William Rawle in 1825, Thomas Jefferson and James Madison in 1798 is far removed from the mystical and unseen Union that Lincoln advocated. It's time to unequivocally answer the questions posed earlier in this chapter: (1) Is the Union indivisible? No, the Union is not indivisible, or the very words of the Declaration of Independence would be made of no effect. (2) Is the United States "one nation?" No, the Treaty of Paris, which acknowledges the independence of thirteen sovereign states points out that these United States (plural) are thirteen sovereign states. (3) Who authorized the formation of the new Union and was it denoted to be "perpetual"? As the Constitution in Article VII points out, we the people of sovereign states ratified the Constitution thus forming a new Union. Nowhere in the Constitution is there a claim of perpetuity. The only Constitution that did claim to be perpetual, the Articles of Confederation, died as a result of the secession of states from that Union as they acceded to a new Union under the Constitution.

Lincoln's view of the Union, Constitution, and state sovereignty was at odds with the Union as established by America's Founding Fathers. This fact is more than just a historical oddity because his view laid the foundation for an all-powerful, one nation indivisible, Federal government—*a government that recognizes no limits*

---

163   Patrick Henry, as cited in, Patrick Henry: Life, Correspondence, and Speeches (1891, Sprinkle Publications, Harrisonburg, VA: 1993) III, 449.

on its power. Washington DC's ability to close down churches, enforce vulgar sexual values, force medicate its subjects, impose laws and regulations that Deep State bureaucrats and politicians do not have to abide by, and provide unlimited amounts of money to special interests was made possible by Lincoln and his Red Republican socialist allies' victory in his war to *prevent* Southern Independence.

General Franz Sigel

Sigel served as the commander of socialist troops during the abortive 1849 revolution in Germany. At the outbreak of the War for Southern Independence, Sigel volunteered for service in the Union Army and rose to the rank of major general. (Photograph courtesy Library of Congress.)

Chapter 8

LINCOLN, BIG GOVERNMENT AND SOCIALISM

AS STATED IN CHAPTER I, it is not being asserted that Lincoln and the Republican Party are socialists. What is being demonstrated is that Lincoln was an advocate of big government, and the Republican Party was assisted in its formation and electoral victories by radical socialists, Marxists and communists (remember that all Marxists are communists but not all communists are Marxists). Big government is the *sine qua non,* the essential element, for the life of a socialist nation. Never in the history of man has a socialist or communist government existed without big government— herein resides the danger of Lincoln's victory over the Jeffersonian compound republic of limited government. Before the advent of the Republican Party, there were two political parties that can be identified as "big government parties," the Federalist Party and the Whig Party. Lincoln entered politics on March 9, 1832, by announcing his intention to run as a Whig candidate for the Illinois legislature. His platform was purely a Whig, big government platform. Lincoln announced "I am in favor of a national bank... and a high protective tariff. These are my sentiments and political principles."[164] As previously noted, the policies of the Whig Party, internal improvement, national banking, and high protective tariffs, were opposed by the advocates of limited and therefore

---

164   Lincoln, as cited in, Edgar L. Masters, *Lincoln: The Man* (1931, The Foundation for American Education, Columbia, SC: 1997) 32-32.

small, government. Men such as Jefferson, Madison, Jackson, and other leading Democrats held the line against those advocating the unlimited growth of government.

Lincoln's political idol at the time of his March 1832 announcement was Henry Clay. Clay was the leading figure in Whig politics and the author of the American System, an economic plan that supported a national bank, internal improvements, and high protective tariffs. The one firm and stable aspect of Lincoln's political philosophy from the time he entered politics to the time he entered Ford's Theater was his love for big government policies as advocated by Alexander Hamilton and Henry Clay. Lincoln's policies made big government not only possible, but they made it inevitable. Without Lincoln's policies, there would be no Deep State tyranny in the United States.

Looking at Lincoln's view of the Union and his preferred means for holding the Union together forces one to conclude that Lincoln had socialist tendencies; that is, he tended toward the concept of centralized power. The fact that he identified with first the Whig and then the Republican Party demonstrates his love for big government.

Lincoln's embracing of big government policies and his advocacy of eternal life for government places him alongside other political figures holding similar views. For example, Lenin also had a mystical view of government and believed in the rights of big government to order and perfect society. The specter of Lincoln holding views so similar to those of Lenin prompted author L. Neil Smith to suggest that when America comes to this "painful but illuminating truth, it will finally have begun to recover from the War Between the States."[165]

Award winning author and historian, James McPherson, observed that Lincoln often remarked favorably about the leadership and efforts of European revolutionaries, many of whom came to the United States and became known as Forty-Eighters.

---

165   Arthur L. Neil Smith, "The American Lenin," www.sierratimes.com, February 12, 2001.

As these communist and socialist revolutions were ongoing, Lincoln gave a speech in Congress on the 12ᵗʰ of January 1848, in which he stated: "Any people anywhere, being inclined and having the power, have the right to rise up and shake off the existing government, and form a new one that suits them better. This is a most valuable, a most sacred right—a right which we hope and believe is to liberate the world. Nor is this right confined to cases in which the whole people of an existing government may choose to exercise it. Any portion of such people, that can, may revolutionize, and make their own of so much of the territory as they inhabit."[166]

Lincoln's January 1848, speech sounds like he was defending the concept of secession, something he fought so strongly to suppress thirteen years later. Unfortunately, this is not what Lincoln is saying. Lincoln is simply stating that any people who can take up arms can *revolt* against an existing government. This is the very definition of revolution. America's Founding Fathers in 1776 were not revolting against the British government, they were fighting for their Constitutional Rights as Englishmen. Defending one's Rights is not an act of revolution, regardless of what King George said. Likewise, fighting to maintain Constitutional Rights as Americans against a usurper of those Rights, which our Confederate Forefathers were doing, is not an act of revolution. Thus, Lincoln, believing the South was in revolt, felt no shame in "putting down the insurrection."

As previously noted, Lincoln's actions laid the foundation for advancing the aims of socialism and communism. As the conservative commentator, the late Joseph Sobran proclaimed, "Lincoln's war changed this country." Sobran noted that what was once a limited federal Union had morphed into a "centralized monolith... since 1865" and that the once sovereign States had been reduced to a condition of being "powerless to defend their constitutional powers against federal usurpation."[167] This is consistent with the aims of socialism—the centralizing of power

166 Abraham Lincoln, as cited in, Minor, 66.

167 Joseph Sobran, "Crossfire on Lincoln," The Wanderer, St. Paul, MN, June 8, 2000.

in the hands of the state. In fact, columnist Vin Suprynowicz has gone so far as to tell us that Northern fanatics were nothing less than American Bolsheviks.[168]

Lincoln's socialist proclivities are reflected in the fact that he adopted many of the ideas promoted by Karl Marx in the *Communist Manifesto* and in *The Demands of the Communist Party of Germany*. Few Americans think of Lincoln or Marx when they get a letter from the IRS. Yet Marx advocated ideas later embraced by Lincoln. Marx advocated: "The introduction of severely progressive taxation"[169] and today we call this "progressive taxation" the income tax. The first progressive income tax and Federal income tax collectors were established during Lincoln's administration. Marx and Engels advocated, "One state bank shall replace all private banks and its notes shall be legal tender." [170] Marx and Engels also advocated "Universal and free education for the people."[171] Most important of all the Demands of Marx and Engels is the first demand, "The Whole of Germany shall be declared a single and indivisible republic."[172] Does this sound like a pledge all "patriotic" Americans are supposed to say, "one nation indivisible"? All these measures were, to one degree or another, made a part of Lincoln's program. By embracing Henry Clay's "American System," Lincoln became the foremost advocate of national banking, a similar system to that advocated by Marx. Lincoln went so far as to pronounce President Andrew Jackson's attack upon the High Federalist national banking scheme as unconstitutional.[173]

---

168 Vin Suprynowicz, "Celebrating America's First Bolsheviks," Mountain Media, Las Vegas, NV, February 27, 2000, www.infomagic.com.

169 Karl Marx and Fredrick Engels, 'The Demands of the Communist Party in Germany The Demands of the Communist Party in Germany' - Marx and Engels (libcom.org) accessed December 30, 2021.

170 *Ibid.*

171 *Ibid.*

172 *Ibid.*

173 DiLorenzo, *The Real Lincoln*, 67-68.

This being Lincoln's position (as well as that of Marx and Engels), when Lincoln was elected president, he signed the Legal Tender Act into law in February of 1862, as well as the National Currency Acts of 1863 and 1864. These acts resulted in the creation of a system of nationally charted banks, something both the High Federalists and Karl Marx desired. This act had the effect of creating a near monopoly on all bank notes in the United States. As part of the Republican Party's plan for creating a national banking monopoly, the Federal government obtained the assistance of financier Jay Cook to demonize state banking systems while making flattering statements about the national bank. This was not the first time that big government has had a working relationship with rich and powerful people—Hitler was a master at this method of increasing his power. One of the leading supporters of nationalized banking was Sen. John Sherman of Ohio. Senator Sherman did not hide the reasons why he sought to nationalize and centralize every center of power in Washington. Senator Sherman stated: "Nationalize as much as possible [and thereby] make men love their country before their states."[174]

Lincoln and the Republican Party soon enacted Marx's "Heavy, progressive or graduated income tax," when in 1862 Lincoln signed America's first income tax into law. This was one of the largest tax systems ever enacted in the history of the United States up until that time. The following is an overview of Lincoln's tax: (1) The bill consisted of seventeen pages, tripled columns; (2) With more than 119 sections it imposed taxes upon inheritance and gross receipts as well as a license tax for many occupations, stamp taxes, and a tax on many items in common commerce of that day; and, (3) It created the first embryonic IRS service. All of the above-mentioned items and more began the process of centralizing all power into the hands of the government in Washington. From that day to the present the Federal government has grown in power and influence—no one appears capable of controlling its lust for power and taxes.[175] Marx's idea of public education financed by

---

174   John Sherman, as cited in, *Ibid.*, 252-53.

175   DiLorenzo, *The Real Lincoln*, 255.

the government also became a central part of Lincoln's agenda. Writing in *Chronicles* magazine for March 1989, author and playwright John Chodes revealed that "Washington jumped squarely into education in 1862. The Civil War was raging. The Union Army had been suffering major reverses. Robert E. Lee maneuvered to bring the war to the North, and the Union was not sure it would win. In such an atmosphere the Morrill Act passes Congress. Its stated objective was to fund colleges that teach agriculture and mechanical arts, via money raised through federal land-grant sales. The true objective was to bring the Northern perspective to the re-conquered areas of the South, to teach the rebel's children 'respect for national authority'—to break their rebellious spirit forever. The three Rs had absolutely nothing to do with this landmark bill."[176] Karl Marx must have been deliriously happy with America adopting his ideas.

"Senator Justin Morrill, in explaining his authorship of the Morrill Act, said, 'The role of the national government is to mold the character of the American people.'... The land grants had hidden strings; Washington controlled curriculum. To insure a uniformly nationalized, anti-Southern slant, land and money could be taken from one state and given to another."[177]

Morrill's comment about the role of the national government portrays the socialist mind-set this man possessed in the 1860s. John Sherman's comment about "nationalizing" as much as possible also betrays his collectivist mentality. Willingly signing these measures into law clearly demonstrates that Lincoln was more than ready in 1860 to implement in the United States what Marx had given his blessing to in Europe in 1848; that is, centralism, collectivism, and socialism. This adoption of socialist schemes has had an impact on this country from the 1860s down to present-day America. As Americans, we need to begin to grapple with this fact or we will never understand how we lost so much freedom; and more important, how we can regain our lost liberty.

---

176 John Chodes, "Education for a Conquered Nation," *Chronicles*, March 1989, 20.

177 *Ibid.*, 21.

Chapter 9

THE FORTY-EIGHTER'S "ONE NATION INDIVISIBLE"

FOR THOSE LIVING THROUGH the Cold War era, the term "War of liberation" has a distinctly Marxist's ring to it. From Cuba to Vietnam and hundreds of other revolutions, these "wars of liberation," if successful, were followed by the imposition of communist and/ or socialist tyranny. One only must look at the once free and prosperous nation of Venezuela before and after the introduction of a socialist regime to understand what "socialist's freedom" looks like. As has been noted several times in the preceding chapters, the lexicon of communist revolution is full of terms that mean one thing to Americans who hold firm to the Jeffersonian view of liberty and quite another to those with a Marxist view of liberty. The term republic has a positive connotation for Americans but yet the Union of Soviet Socialist Republics was not a good republic. The German Democratic Republic (Communist East Germany) was denoted as both "Democratic" and a "Republic," but again these words do not mean what freedom-loving Americans understand them to mean.

It is not uncommon to hear modern historians and journalists characterizing the 1848 European socialist revolutions as "wars of liberation." Unfortunately, these so-called "wars of liberation," rather than liberating men from the confines of an all-powerful government, became the mid-wife for delivering big government tyranny. When these "1848" revolutions were defeated in Europe,

Charles A. Dana

*Dana, a friend of Karl Marx, Fredrick Engels, and Joseph Weydemeyer, rose to the
level of assistant secretary of war in Lincoln's administration. Prior to the Bolshevik
revolution in Russia, no other American did more to promote the cause of communism
in the United States than did Dana. (Photograph courtesy Library of Congress.)*

the radical revolutionaries sought a place of refuge and America offered them a "safe -space" from which to continue pushing their radical socialist's agenda. When in America, these revolutionaries pushed their concept of "liberation" and "freedom" which was radically different from that bequeathed to Americans by America's Founding Fathers. Nevertheless, these radical socialists, communists, and Marxists, aka, Forty-Eighters, were to become instrumental in the founding of the Republican Party, the election of Lincoln, and the War to *Prevent* Southern Independence. A quick evaluation of the worldview and history of the Forty-Eighters is useful in understanding how their efforts adversely impacted these United States. As noted in chapter 2 of this work, these deleterious consequences are with us to this day.

The group of Forty-Eighters who had the greatest influence in bringing Europe's socialist revolution to America was the German Forty-Eighters. The "nation" of Germany as is presently known did not exist in 1848. At that time the German Federation was composed of 39 free, independent, and sovereign States. Radical socialists loathed the loose confederation of German States and demanded the unification of Germany into one indivisible nation. In *The Demands of the Communist Party in Germany*, the very first "demand" of the German communists was that "The whole of Germany shall be declared a single and indivisible republic."[178] The reader's attention is again drawn to the fact that this was the very *first* demand of the German Communist Party. These demands were written by Karl Marx and Fredrick Engels for the Communist Party in Germany to assist in a revolt in one of the many German States. These Demands were an attack upon the German Constitutional government as it then existed and as author Walter Schmidt noted it was necessary for "upholding the revolutionary democratic principle of French Jacobinism of 'nation une et undivisible,' one nation indivisible." Marx and Engels wrote these Demands while in France and they were first published in Paris, France. Like their socialist cohorts in Germany,

---

178 Marx and Engels, 'Demands of the Communist Party in Germany,' Collected Works, Moscow 1977, VII, 3-7.

they too embraced the notion that France should be "one nation indivisible." In Germany, the concept of *eine nation unteildar* (one nation indivisible) was not completely realized until the advent of Adolf Hitler, see chapter 4. As is pointed out in chapter 17, it was an American socialist, Francis Bellamy, who boldly introduced this concept in the pledge of allegiance in 1892. As demonstrated in chapter 3, it was Fredrick Engels who stated that it was essential for promoting communism to replace republics of small sovereign states with "a single and indivisible republic." As noted, many times herein, big government is *essential* for the life of any socialist government. The irony of so many good Americans placing their hand over their heart and declaring the United States to be "one nation indivisible" should not be lost on thinking Americans.

Nineteenth century Germany was composed of many free, sovereign, and independent States closely resembling these United States before Lincoln's war upon the sovereign States of the South. Another interesting similarity between pre–Lincoln America and pre-revolution Germany is that neither nation was politically aggressive on the international scene. After the consolidation of the sovereign German States into "one nation indivisible," she became an aggressive international player, as two World Wars testify. Likewise, after Lincoln, the United States became, as General Lee warned, "aggressive abroad and despotic at home."[179]

In their supposed quest for liberation and freedom, Karl Marx and his disciples were trying to create a large, omnipotent, centrally controlled, communist government. With a strong central government under their control, they could control all property, means of production, and distribution of goods and services. This would of course entail the complete destruction of the small individual state governments, which as Engels noted was a prime objective of the socialists—exit the Jeffersonian concept of "that which governs less, governs best." The socialist concept of freedom freed people from a decentralized system of government

---

179   Robert E. Lee, as cited in, Kennedy and Kennedy, *Yankee Empire: Aggressive Abroad and Despotic at Home* (Shotwell Publishing, Columbia, SC: 2020) 51.

and replaced it with an all-powerful, indivisible, perpetual big government. Now admittedly, human nature being what it is, the various state governments in Germany and these United States were far from perfect, nor were those who administered them perfect. However, to replace these various locally controlled state governments with a centralized socialist or communist government was an even less perfect solution to Germany's or America's problems.

In his 1864 letter to Lincoln, Karl Marx referred to Lincoln as "the single-minded son of the working class [who] lead his country through the matchless struggle...and the reconstruction of a social world."[180] The "reconstruction of a social world" is the driving force behind every radical socialist scheme, regardless of whether that scheme is in France, Germany, Hungary, or the United States. America's "reconstruction" did not end with the withdrawal of Federal troops from the conquered Confederate States of America but continues to this day. In an article "Demands of the Communist Party," writer Walter Schmidt noted that the Forty-Eighters' revolutionary intention was for a total remake, "reconstruction," of society. Schmidt explained how the German revolutionaries desired to unite the "German proletariat, workers, peasant farmers, and lower middle-class Germans into a "democratic order."[181] A total dismantling of the old social order with its plethora of unequal stations of society and the remaking of society into a more social and economic society of equals was the ultimate design of the radicals. Not only was the social and economic fabric to be remade but the nation itself was to undergo a radical change so as "to overcome the partition of Germany into a number of states, and to create a unified German state of a decidedly democratic character."[182] If one stops and analyzes what Schmidt wrote, it is obvious that the purpose of the revolutionaries was to

---

180 Karl Marx, "Address of the International Workingmen's Association to Abraham Lincoln," as cited in, Marx and Engels, *Letters to Americans*, 66.

181 Walter Schmidt, "Demands of the Communist Party," www.ohiou.edu.

182 Walter Schmidt, *Ibid.*

bring about a "radical-democratic transformation" of Germany and to do away with a Germany in which the various states ran their own affairs. The term "decidedly democratic" should be read as "socialist"—this is demonstrated when one recalls the name of communist East Germany, the German Democratic Republic. Schmidt indicated that the revolutionaries were attempting to create the same amount of "democracy" that prevailed during the French Revolution. It should hardly be necessary to state that the bloody political excesses of the infamous French Revolution are something from which France, even in our day, has yet to fully recover. In dealing with the revolutionaries' agenda, Schmidt stated: "With its first claim, 'All Germany is declared to be a united indivisible republic,' the program was directed against liberal constitutionalism and against a moderately democratic federal system, thereby upholding the revolutionary democratic principle of French Jacobinism of the 'nation une et undivisible'" (one nation indivisible).[183] We also note here that Schmidt stated that the aim of the revolutionaries was opposed to "a moderately democratic federal system." A federal system is what the founders of this nation gave us, though, admittedly, that system has been turned upside down since 1865. A federal system in which the powers of government are separated between the states and the federal government, as in the case of our own republic before Lincoln, was not what the promoters of revolution desired. They sought to place all power in the hands of the central government, rather than having it diffused among the various states. As Engels and Marx keep pointing out, big government is necessary to advance the cause of communism.

Many scholars today are not at all bashful about stating that the 1848 revolts were socialist in origin and in agenda. On one Internet site that carries various historical documents it is reported that the 1848 revolts in Europe were a result of the abuse of power by established politicians and an ongoing economic recession. The site names no less than nine European nationalities

---

183   Ibid.

that took part in this revolt; chief among them were Germans and Hungarians. These revolutions, according to this site, ultimately failed but did manage to set the foundation for future socialist victories.[184] Although the writer doesn't identify which country he is referring to in his article, nonetheless, it seems to him to be quite an accomplishment that the revolutionaries could undermine a government and establish what the author refers to as "liberalism and socialism." The article also mentions Gieuseppe Mazzini and his attempts to unify Italy into one state. The author bemoans the fact that Mazzini's socialist plot to unify Italy was a failure. According to the author, the cause of Mazzini's failure was the desire of the local people in Italy to keep government local and not centralized in a big impersonal Roman government.[185] A revelatory statement if ever there was one! Socialism in Italy failed at that point in time because people sought to protect their independence. The desire by the Italians for maintaining their independence at the local level is reflected by Southerners who in 1861 did not wish to be governed by a big impersonal government in Washington. Eventually this desire for local independence by Italians was defeated, thus setting the stage for the socialist dictator Benito Mussolini and his Fascist government. Quite possibly there is a lesson here for the rest of the world.

At this point we may well be tempted to think that terms such as "democracy" or "liberalism" don't really sound too offensive. As was pointed out earlier, the word "democracy" was not a word or term fondly held to by the founding fathers. However, it is a documented fact that communists and socialists often employ what is called Aesopian language—the use of terminology that sounds harmless but which really means something entirely different to those who understand how to interpret it. In 1972 Professor Roy Colby wrote a book titled, *A Communese-English Dictionary.* Professor Colby's book describes how certain common terms in our language are used by totalitarians to mean something entirely different from

---

184   Jaffer Zaidi, "Essay—Revolutions of 1848," http://www.pvhs.chico.k12.ca.us.

185   *Ibid.*

what we think they mean. Thus, to the communists or socialists, the term "liberalism" means "advocacy of socialistic or collectivistic policies and practices to be enforced by the State; pseudo-liberalism."[186] The term "democratic" is defined as "of or pertaining to the Marxist-Leninist version of democracy."[187] Using the logic of a Marxist, any word, phrase, group or person that promotes the cause of communism or socialism is a "democrat" or someone that is promoting "democracy." This is how, with a straight face, neo-Marxists can promote the virulent anti-white Critical Race Theory as a non-racist program to "bring people together."

We would do well to note that the founding fathers gave us a republican form of government, not a democratic one. Due to their understanding of history, America's Founding Fathers understood the problems inherent in a democracy, and they sought to avoid those problems. That we today do not grasp truths that were quite apparent to them is a testimony to the wretched quality of what passes for education in the government schools of this country.

Many commentators on the failed socialist revolts of 1848 have contended that the revolts did, in fact, have major consequences for the future of Europe. Prior to 1848 workers did not hold an overly negative view of forming political associations with (using Marxist phraseology) the "bourgeoisie." Middle-class liberals, that is, advocates of constitutional government as opposed to monarchy, could be found side by side with workers and peasants during the early portion of the revolts. But as it became obvious that a general attack upon property rights was the ultimate goal of the socialists, these middle-class "bourgeoisie" property owners rejected the revolution. Thus, we see the final end of the first attempt by socialists to capture control of the governments of Europe.[188]

---

186   Roy Colby, *A Communese-English Dictionary* (Western Islands Publishers, Belmont, MA: 1972) 60.

187   *Ibid.*, 24.

188   "Permanent Results of 1848," http://www.unlv.edu/faculty/gbrown/westernciv.

In 1906, Peter A. Kropotkin, a Russian-born, self-proclaimed anarchist communist, noted that there was one feature common to all socialists, that is, a view of socialism as a religion. Kropotkin wrote that socialists viewed socialism as a "new revelation, and upon themselves as upon the founders of a new religion. Socialism had to be a religion, and they had to regulate its march, as the heads of a new church."[189]

One seldom hears socialism heralded as a religious entity. Most of its adherents prefer to refer to themselves as "scientific socialists," and they downplay any religious connotation whatever. Nonetheless, Kropotkin has given us a little insight into the "religious" mind-set of socialist man, despite their protestations to the contrary.

In an article titled "United States and the 1848 Revolutions," author James B. Chastain noted that many newspaper editors and politicians of the North believed that the time was right for a more aggressive "progressive" political agenda to be advanced in the United States to reflect what was happening in Europe in 1848. These "progressives" pushed for American assistance, both monetary and military, for the fledgling European socialist republics. Parades and banquets were held to raise public support for the European revolutionaries; yet, many Americans, remembering the warning of President Washington about getting involved in European conflicts, refused to become involved with the troubles in Europe. Alas, the most that these advocates for European interventionism could muster was mere symbolic American support.[190]

In his article Chastain pointed out that although the advocates of European interventionism were unsuccessful in their attempts to entice Americans into direct support of the socialist revolts in Europe, those revolutions did indeed have far-reaching consequences for America. As a result of the 1848 revolts, the

---

189   *Ibid.*

190   James B. Chastain, "United States and the 1848 Revolutions," http://cscwww.cats.ohiou.edu.

"reform" element of the United States received a major boost. From that time onward every reform from abolition to prison reform became the *cause célèbre* of Northern society. Chastain also pointed out that many of the European revolutionaries sought and received asylum in America after the failure of their revolts. These men and women did not leave their socialist and revolutionary proclivity in Europe but merely changed their base of operation, not their philosophy. Not only did these revolutionaries bring their socialist ideas to America, a Hungarian revolutionary, Louis Kossuth, so impressed himself upon Americans that he started a new fad in clothing. After his visit to the United States, hats, coats, and beards similar to that worn by Kossuth became very popular.[191]

About 175 years earlier than most Americans are aware, socialism had its influence in the United States. Many European socialists came to America to raise money for the ongoing socialist revolutions and to secure American military support. They did manage to obtain limited financial support, mostly from Northerners. But other than Lincoln's 1848 speech in Congress promoting the idea of revolutions, they did not secure any American political, financial or military aid.

The impact of the Forty-Eighters, as already noted, did not end with Yankee victory over the Confederate States of America. With the defeat of the Confederate military, the victorious Federal government had a relatively free hand in reconstructing the South under the new Federal government, aka, the Yankee Empire. In a letter to his communist friend and Union General, Joseph Weydemeyer, Engels noted that the outcome of the war would "doubtless determine the future of America for hundreds of years to come."[192] At the time of this writing, 2022, with Bernie Sanders, an avowed supporter of all things communist, a United States Senator, and Alexandria Ortega Cortez, a radical socialist and virtual leader of the United States House of Representatives, it appears that Engels' prediction is being fulfilled.

---

191 *Ibid.*

192 Fredrick Engels, as cited in, Marx and Engels, *Letters to Americans*, 63.

One of the last Confederate military forces to be surrendered was a force commanded by Lt. General Richard Taylor, son of President Zachary Taylor. On April 30, 1865, a meeting between Lt. General Taylor and Union commander, Major General E. R. S. Canby was held to discuss the surrender of the Confederate force under Taylor's command. At the close of the meeting, General Taylor was approached by a Union officer of German descent. General Taylor describes this German officer as a "general officer who had recently left Germany to become a citizen and soldier of the United States. This person, with a strong accent and idioms of the Fatherland, comforted me by assurances that we of the South would speedily recognize our ignorance and errors, especially about slavery and the rights of the States, and rejoice in the results of the war...I apologized meekly for my ignorance, on the ground that my ancestors had come from England to Virginia in 1608, and, in the short intervening period of two hundred and fifty-odd years, had found no time to transmit to me correct ideas of the duties of American citizenship. My grandfather, commanding the 9th Virginia regiment in our Revolutionary army, had assisted in the defeat and capture of the Hessian mercenaries at Trenton... [the German officer] assured me of his willingness to instruct me."[193] Here we see a German Forty-Eighter arrogantly lecturing the grandson of a Revolutionary War officer, the son of President Zackery Taylor, and brother-in-law of President Jefferson Davis on the "proper" duties of American citizenship. As Walter Schmidt explains in his review of *The Demands of the German Communist Party,* these radical socialists were attempting "a radical-democratic transformation of civil society in line with...the great French Revolution."[194] In a nutshell, this proves that a total reconstruction of the United States and not just the defeated South was, and is to this day, the objective of these radicals.

---

193   Richard Taylor, *Destruction and Reconstruction* (D. Appleton & Company, NY: 1879) 230.

194   Walter Schmidt, *Ibid.*

With the defeat of the Confederate military and the ending of hostilities the shooting stopped but the cultural aspects of the War have continued right down to the present. As was the case before the war, these radical European socialists known as Red Republicans and/or Radical Republicans, were very active in the Republican Party.[195] As Wittke noted, these socialist revolutionaries were also interested in "reconstructing" American cultural values. Wittke points out that "They [Forty-Eighters] hated...what they called the religious superstitions of the American people"[196] [and] "Actually dreamed of an intellectual conquest of the United States."[197]

Professor Clyde N. Wilson has duly noted: "The German revolutionaries brought with them an aggressive drive to realize in America the goals that had been defeated in their homeland. Their drive was toward 'revolution and national unification.'... The most prominent among them, Carl Schurz, expressed disappointment at the non-ideological nature of American politics and vowed to change that."[198] After the war, American politics were to become "ideological," and Schurz and his socialist friends were on hand to make sure it happened. As many Southerners understood, these Yankee victors seemed to possess a kind of hard-edged scorn for anyone who was so unenlightened as not to recognize the innate correctness of Yankee logic and utopian fantasies.

After the war ended, Schurz once again took up the practice of law, this time in Washington, D.C. He also served as a correspondent for the *New York Tribune*. The *Tribune*, it should be remembered, was the paper that Karl Marx served as a contributor; it was the *Tribune* that the radical "socialist for life" Horace Greeley owned; and it was the *Tribune* that Marx and Engels' good friend Charles

---

195   "The Story of Nine Fine Irishmen," http//www.ninefineirishmen.com.

196   Carl Wittke, "The German Forty-Eighter in America: A Centennial Appraisal," *The American Historical Review* 53, no. 4, July 1948, 714-15.

197   *Ibid.*

198   Clyde Wilson, "The Republican Charade: Lincoln and His Party." This was speech given at the Abbeville Institute Conference on "Re-Thinking Lincoln," July 7-12, 2005, Franklin, Louisiana, by Dr. Wilson, www.Abbevilleinstitue.org.

A. Dana served as associate editor. It is no surprise that radical socialists and friends of Karl Marx, and former Union general Carl Schurz, should find a home at the *Tribune!* In 1866, Schurz was sent on an investigative tour of the defeated South, ostensibly to report on conditions in the region, particularly on the work of the Freedmen's Bureau, America's first full-blown welfare scheme. By 1867, Schurz was a successful newspaper editor in Detroit and then in St. Louis, Missouri. Schurz, the Radical Republican, was launched into national politics in 1869, when chosen as a United States senator from Missouri. During the term of President Rutherford B. Hayes, Schurz served as the 13th United States Secretary of the Interior (1877-81). He ended his public career in 1901 serving as president of the National Civil Service Reform League. What a spectacular career for a man who began his life as a radical socialist revolutionary and admirer of Karl Marx's theories. One can only speculate at just how much socialist influence these radicals had in "their" day as well as the influence they are still having. When considering the influence these radicals had on the founding of the Republican Party, the election of Lincoln, and the war against the South, one should keep in mind these statements by Heinrich H. Maurer. He noted that "the fate of the Republican Party" and the election of Lincoln in 1860 were due to the support of the "German element in the Northwest." Maurer states that the election of "Mr. Lincoln would not have been possible" without the assistance of these German Forty-Eighters.[199]

With their incessant lamentations and cries for the downtrodden and abused slaves in America, it is somewhat ironic that radical abolitionist Schurz and other socialists seemed to have had little or no compassion for the American Indians. While serving as secretary of the interior, Schurz did nothing to relieve the plight of the Indians in the West. When pleas came from starving Indians on reservations, starving partly because of bad hunting and partly because of corrupt Indian agents, Schurz was almost totally unresponsive. In the book *Bury My Heart*

---

199   Heinrich H. Maurer, "The Earlier German Nationalism in America," *The American Journal of Sociology*, 533-34. The Earlier German Nationalism in America (uchicago.edu)

at *Wounded Knee* the author noted that although Schurz was appointed to the position of secretary as a reformer, all appeals for assistance for the starving Native Americans did not generate a positive response from Schurz. This man who was willing to take fire and sword into the heart of the South, ostensibly to promote the socialist values of freedom and democracy and to uplift the human condition, would not be moved to assist in the elimination of the suffering of the Native Americans. When called upon by concerned members of Congress and the public to explain his lack of action, he responded by stating, "Such details do not in the nature of things come to the knowledge of the Secretary. It is the business of the Indian Office."[200] This response was from a man who had been placed into this position to "reform" the office under his direction. Even though it was obvious that not enough money had been appropriated to secure food and supplies for the Native Americans, Schurz's only reply was to economize. Remember, the Native Americans had given up their nomadic hunting-gathering lifestyle and moved to reservations with the promise from Washington that they would be provided with food and clothing. It was the ultimate responsibility of the secretary of the interior to make sure these treaty obligations were being fulfilled and if not to report such to Congress. In total disregard for the plight of suffering humanity, this all-loving, socialist humanitarian refused to act on behalf of these Indians. Once again it must be pointed out that the history of more than one hundred years of communist and socialist regimes and nations demonstrates the total lack of concern of these people for suffering humanity. They are driven by their revolutionary desire to acquire power and will use whatever trendy slogan or popular cause to advance that objective.

With little relief coming, several Native American chiefs traveled to Washington to lobby for the cause of their starving people. Upon meeting Schurz, the Native Americans were impressed by the ample size of Schurz's eyes and named him *Mah-hah-Ich-hon,*

---

200   Carl Schurz, as cited in, Dee Brown, *Bury My Heart at Wounded Knee* (Washington Square Press, New York: 1970) 320-21.

which is to say, "Big Eyes." After appealing to Schurz, they came away from their meetings in wonder of a man possessing such large eyes and yet unable to see the needs of their people.[201]

Early in the history of the Ponca Indians, they had made a treaty with the United States in which they had retained a portion of their old lands as part of their permanent reservations. After the disastrous defeat of Gen. George Armstrong Custer at the Little Big Horn in 1876, Congress decided to include the Poncas in a list of tribes to be exiled to the Indian Territory. One fact that was conveniently overlooked was that the Poncas had taken no part in hostilities against the United States, nor had they broken their treaty with the United States in any way. The reality of the case is that it was the United States government that broke its treaty obligations with the Poncas. Dee Brown, author of *Bury My Heart at Wounded Knee,* points out that the chiefs united in their efforts to force the United States government to honor the treaty made with the Poncas. The American agent for the Ponca Indians made an appeal for the Poncas to the Commissioner of Indian Affairs in Washington, who forwarded it to the Secretary of the Interior, Carl Schurz, who in turned passed it on to Sherman. Upon receiving this report, Sherman, showing as little mercy to the Native Americans as he had to Southerners, ordered troops to force the Poncas off their land.[202]

So here is a prime example of socialist compassion for American Indians. The Poncas, who had broken no treaties with the United States, were being forced to move from their good reservation to a much worse one in the Indian Territory because of the hostilities of other Indians, who were also fighting to keep their lands. In a classic one-size-fits-all government move, the Poncas were to be swept off their land with the hostiles and moved someplace where the U.S. government felt that *it* would be safer. No doubt the land to which the Indians were forcibly moved was not worth as much as the land they were being expelled from. When the Poncas protested, the man who could do something to aid them turned the matter over to

---

201   Brown, 338.

202   *Ibid.*

General Sherman, who, in typical dictatorial fashion, determined that the Poncas should be moved anyway and urged the use of troops to accomplish such move. Sherman had the reputation of an implacable Indian hater, just as he had been an implacable hater of Southerners during the war. Remember that it was this man, William Tecumseh Sherman, who had recommended to his superiors in Washington that Southern "men, women, and children" should be exterminated in order to restore the authority of a "one nation indivisible" government to America. Rather than doing something within his power to avert an injustice to the Poncas, Schurz, in typical bureaucratic fashion, turned the whole situation over to an Indian-hating general. Schurz was probably well aware of Sherman's willingness to enforce the government's decision, right or wrong; and right or wrong seems to have made no difference to Schurz. The bureaucrat's plans were almost undone, though, in the person of Judge Elmer Dundy. When the Ponca chief, Standing Bear, was arrested for taking some of his people back North, he appeared in the court of Judge Dundy. Two lawyers, John Webster and A. J. Poppleton, then stepped forward to help Standing Bear to petition the court for a writ of *habeas corpus*. It was their position that Standing Bear and the other Poncas had not committed a crime and so should not have been arrested. G. M. Lambertson represented the Federal government against the Poncas. It was the government's position (as unbelievable as it seems today) that an Indian was not a person or a citizen, and therefore had no rights of any kind (which sounds like the Dred Scott ruling that was reviled by radical abolitionists). In other words, the Federal government could do whatever it wanted to do with the Indians because they were not human beings! Judge Dundy ruled against the government's position, declaring that Indians were human beings after all and setting Standing Bear free. This entire event caused quite a ruckus, causing President Rutherford Hayes shortly thereafter to appoint a commission to investigate. The finding of that commission was that indeed the Poncas had been treated unjustly, and some land of their original reservation was returned to them. But where was Carl Schurz, the compassionate socialist, in all of this? Recognizing Judge Dundy's order as a threat to their lucrative jobs, the political hacks in Washington who made up what was known as the "Indian Ring" voiced deep concerns about the judge's ruling; after all, a government job providing shoddy goods at premium prices is not something to give up without a fight—which is no different from what is too often the case with today's government jobs. It must be remembered that as is true in today's Washington environment (only worse now because government is bigger and has more money to dish out) anyone with connections to Federal expenditures stands a chance of making huge profits for family and friends. There was money to be made in buying and selling blankets, food, and other supplies to Indians on reservations. As is always true, it is the people close to the government and not the recipients of the aid who are best served by governmental largess. Schurz eventually acknowledged that the Ponca Indians had been mistreated. Schurz reported to Congress that the Poncas "had a serious grievance." Grievance or no grievance, Schurz remained opposed to allowing the Poncas to return to their homeland; after all, it would set a bad example to other Indians and possibly cause the downfall of the reservation system.[203]

During Ronald Reagan's presidency, James Watt, a cabinet member of Reagan's administration, made a comment about the Indian reservations in this country being a prime example of socialism. Many took him to task for that statement. Yet here we see Carl Schurz, with his socialist background, defending the reservation system that was making members of the infamous Indian Ring rich while being a total detriment to the welfare of the Indians on those reservations. Perhaps Schurz recognized the Indian reservations for what they were (socialism) and was, therefore, more than a little reluctant to do away with them, no matter whom they harmed. All of this handling of the Indian situation only points out more clearly the interesting hypocrisy of socialist compassion for the black man that did not in any way extend to the red man. Carl Schurz was probably the most prominent of the Forty-Eighters after the war, yet other Forty-Eighters also made contributions to a socialist America.

---

203 *Ibid.*

Franz Sigel, although mediocre at best and inept at worst as a soldier, possessed a strong ability to attract German recruits for the Union army. As one military historian noted, many Germans were influenced by the slogan *"I fights mit Siegel,"*[204] demonstrating the alure he had for recruiting Germans into the Union army. After the war, Sigel was successful as an editor and a publisher. Like other radicals, he remained active in politics.

August (von) Willich was the man whom Karl Marx labeled as a "communist with a heart" and other associates labeled him as "the Reddest of the Reds." Willich, rose to the rank of Brigadier General in the Union army, in January of 1866, he left the army and served three years as county auditor in Cincinnati. Returning to Europe in 1870 during the Franco-Prussian War, he offered his services to the same king he had sought to topple during his heady days as a Forty-Eighter revolt leader. Rather than having Willich measured for the hangman's noose, the king refused his offer on the grounds of Willich's age, an age not greater than the king or many officers in the king's service. Having been rebuffed, Willich remained in Europe for a while, renewing his friendship with Karl Marx. Subsequently he returned to the United States, where he settled in St. Mary's, Ohio. That is where he passed from the scene in January of 1878. Of all the communists who served in the Union army, Willich was one of the most dedicated communist revolutionaries—he was indeed, the Reddest of the Red Republicans.

A Forty-Eighter not previously mentioned is Lorenz Brentano. After the war he was elected to Congress from the state of Illinois and served as American consul in Dresden from 1872 to 1876. Brentano is just one more example of a Forty-Eighter ending up in a high governmental position.

As is demonstrated by this small representative sample, many Forty-Eighters rose quite high in positions of influence in this country after the war. These Forty-Eighters filled positions ranging

---

204   Mark M. Boatner, III, *The Civil War Dictionary* (David McKay Company Inc., NY: 1959) 718.

from secretary of the interior to important positions in journalism, teaching, governmental consuls to various countries, and even Congress. Being committed revolutionaries, these people made their political convictions and influence felt in the United States. In almost no case is there a convincing record of any of them changing their leftist viewpoint. Some of the Forty-Eighters and their American socialist allies did mellow a little as they got older and became less strident in their rhetoric and activities. Mellow or not, the socialistic mind-sets and worldviews were clearly displayed throughout the remainder of their lives. Can we, as a nation, afford to be so naïve as to think that such influence from so many sources had little or no effect on this country in the decades after the war? A socialist mind-set introduces a dangerous cancer into a free society, whether the rhetoric accompanying it is strident or subtle.

Many good and sincere Americans have imbibed socialist ideas to one degree or another and are not even conscious of that fact. In many public settings, such as public schools and universities, these institutions have become grand promoters of various socialist schemes under the guise of political correctness. At this time (2022), Black Lives Matter and Antifa radicals are acting and promoting every vestige of radical socialism and Marxism that yesterday's Forty-Eighters introduced to the United States. We can hope things will get better but recent history demonstrates the futility of hope. Shall we continue to cling to the delusion of hope until we are cold in our graves and our children's children are bound head and foot by a tyrant's rope? At what point do Americans in general and Southerners in particular answer this ancient question? "What would gentlemen wish? What would they have? Is life so dear, or peace so sweet, as to be purchased at the price of chains and slavery? Forbid it Almighty God!"[205]

---

205   Patrick Henry as cited in, William Wirt Henry, *Patrick Henry: Life, Correspondence And Speeches* (1891, Sprinkle Publications, Harrisonburg, VA: 1993) I, 266.

General John C. Fremont

The darling of most radical socialists, Fremont was the first Republican candidate for president (1856). During the War for Southern Independence, it was Fremont's camp that served as a magnet for radical socialists known as the Forty-Eighters. Early in the war, Fremont's chief of staff was a Hungarian socialist revolutionary, Alexander Asboth. (Photograph courtesy Library of Congress.)

Chapter 10

MARXISM FINDS A NEW HOME

AS A RESULT OF THE FAILURE of the numerous European socialist revolts of 1848, a wave of socialists and communists involved in those failed revolutions fled Europe. Having to flee Europe, these revolutionaries saw America as more and more promising for them and their revolutionary ideas. Many revolutionaries fled first to Switzerland, while others went to England. Some went to both countries and on to the United States.

Among the boldest and most radical socialists to emigrate to America were the German revolutionaries. Many observers of the 1848 revolutions have noted the difference between German immigrants who came to this country before 1848 as opposed to those who came afterward. The earlier German immigrants were much different both religiously and politically from those who came later. The earlier immigrants were primarily farmers and mostly Lutherans, although several smaller Christian groups were also represented. The bulk of early German immigrants entering the United States passed through Pennsylvania and slowly expanded west and south. As a general rule, they were hard-working people and expected to make their own way in the world, never expecting nor demanding other people to provide subsidies or handouts to them.

For the most part the German emigrants who came after 1848 tended to be a different breed from the earlier German emigrants. In the previously mentioned article, "The Lincoln Putsch: America's Bolshevik Revolution," the author observed that the German refugees of the failed socialist revolutions of 1848 were enticed to America by the illusion of free land for the workers as was promised by the homestead movement and other qualities that appeared to them as tending toward being friendly to their worldview. Although being favorably impressed with the promise of free land for the workers, it should be noted that these professional revolutionaries did not rush to the rural setting of America but rather huddled in the larger more urban areas of the North. They seemed to be somewhat rootless with little loyalty for any nation or area, placing their ultimate faith and alliance in their revolutionary socialist philosophy. Accordingly, as a group they tended to eschew all religion and tended toward atheism.[206]

Having made their appearance in America, the German socialist revolutionaries moved into places of influence in the German-American media; that is, newspapers and printing. It has been estimated that no less than four thousand German socialists escaped the hand of the German counterrevolutionaries by escaping to the United States. These "Forty-Eighters" wasted little time in attempting to convert their fellow German-Americans, many of whom were descendants of veterans of the American War for Independence, to their socialist worldview. Needless to say, there was a marked difference between these two groups of German-Americans; for example, the older and well-established German-Americans tended to be more rural and loyal to their church, both Roman Catholic and Protestant. The newer German-Americans, the Forty-Eighters, tended to be anti-religious, wasting no time in attacking all religious affiliations held by the older group. It is interesting to note how these "irreligious" socialist revolutionaries flocked to the new Republican Party in the 1850s, assisted in the nomination of Abraham Lincoln as the Republican candidate for

---

206 "The Lincoln Putsch: America's Bolshevik Revolution," http://www.civilwarhistory.com.

president, and filled the ranks of the Union Army in support of Lincoln's war against the sovereign states of the South; yet, the modern-day evangelical Christian movement views Lincoln as a near saint—which is somewhat ironic. The Forty-Eighters considered themselves as more cultured and refined, being freethinkers; that is, not being constrained by the limitation of religious superstition and human prejudice. As such they quickly embraced abolitionism in its most violent and extreme forms, feminism, and all other trendy reform movements.[207]

It is worth noting the anti-Christian mind-set of these socialists. They came into a society that had been predominantly Christian, although in many of the Northern states the faith had been adversely influenced by Unitarianism, and they began to be openly critical of the society they entered. Much like today's (2022) woke culture warriors, Forty-Eighters sought to remake society to conform to their own image of what they thought society could and should become. For socialists and communists, there is no "When in Rome do as the Romans do." For them it was all "Be reasonable. Do it my way!" Once the full power of the government is in their hands, the command is "Be reasonable, do it my way or else!"

These socialists have often been described as "freethinkers." In today's vernacular, a freethinker would be called a secular humanist. It would be worthwhile to take a look at the philosophy of "free thought" to see exactly what it embodied. For the average American, freethinkers are those people who reject accepted religious orthodoxy. They base their concept of life upon the ability of "rational" humans to understand all facts of life and with clear mind and human wisdom rationally set all things in proper order. According to freethinking logic, one must reject all preconceived notions of what is proper that have been handed down to man by non-freethinking individuals; thus, the rejection of orthodox Christianity.[208]

---

207 *Ibid.* Joseph R. Reinhart, "Kentucky's German-Americans in the Civil War," http://www.geocities.com/kygermans.

208 "Freethought," http://en.wikipedia.org/wiki/freethinker.

The magazine called *The Freethinker* was founded by G. W. Foote and first published in England in 1881 to promote the cause of "Freethinking." In the first issue of this publication in May, 1881, Foote wrote: "The Freethinker is an anti-Christian organ, and must therefore be chiefly aggressive. It will wage relentless war against Superstition in general, and against Christian Superstition in particular."[209] This "war...against Christian Superstition," is often displayed in the twentieth century by attacks upon traditional religious values. These attacks include but are not limited to demands for removal of Christian nativity scenes, Crosses, Ten Commandment plaques; making priests, ministers, and rabbis the objects of ridicule, scorn, and vulgar jokes. It has been noted that there are strong ties between free thought and atheism, deism, and secular humanism.

For an orthodox Christian, freethinking is nothing more than the home of both skeptics and heretics. It supposedly relies on human science, scholarship, and rationalism for its reliability and not theology. (See chapter two and addendum I for a more complete look at the humanist/socialist rejection of God and the adoption of man as the foundation of right and wrong.) It thus constitutes itself as an anti-Christian religion, supplanting Christian doctrines with its own dogma. In part or in whole, the radical Forty-Eighter socialists embraced this anti-biblical worldview. These men came to America with a worldview totally at odds with the worldview of the founding fathers of this nation. Once here, they did not adopt our worldview but sought to replace our worldview with their worldview. The radical socialist freethinking worldview springs from the fevered minds of radical socialists and would have been rejected out of hand by the founding fathers of these United States.

As has been noted, the European revolutions did not all take place at the same time, nor were those revolutions crushed by the established powers simultaneously. By the mid-1850s socialists of various stripes and nationalities had made the United States their home and had begun, each in his own way, propagandizing for the

---

209   *Ibid.*

cause they had taken up arms for in various European nations. In 1861 many of the old European socialist warriors had put on the blue uniform of "Mr. Lincoln's army" and continued the struggles for the same socialist principles they had fought for in Europe. Seeking to make the connection between the 1848 socialist revolts in Europe and "Mr. Lincoln's war," Forty-Eighter and future Union general Franz Sigel had uniforms made for his Third Regiment of Missouri (Union) Infantry that closely resembled those worn by the socialist revolutionaries in Germany in 1849.[210]

Union volunteers dressed in European socialist revolutionary uniforms are hardly something one commonly reads about in books dealing with the War for Southern Independence. The fact that the Forty-Eighters made such a connection between what they did in Europe and what Abraham Lincoln was doing in this country is a subject that, up to the present, has never been fully dealt with. It raises the whole question of what the War was really all about. It appears that these radical socialists were fighting in the United States for a Union far different from the Union established by America's Founding Fathers. It would be more correct to state that radical socialists were fighting for centralism as opposed to the separation of powers; that is, big government as opposed to small, limited government. They supposedly fought for "freedom" and "justice," yet one must remember that in the lexicon of the socialist and communist world the words "freedom" and "justice" have a different meaning from those embraced by average Americans. In the socialist and communist lexicon "freedom" and "happiness" are defined as "collectivism" and "subservience to the unitary (all-powerful, perpetual, and *indivisible*) state." Again, it must be recalled that socialists and communists never mean the same things by these terms as the average American understands them to mean.

James Neal Primm, in his introduction to *Germans for a Free Missouri,* seconded the motion regarding how the radicals from Europe viewed the war. Primm stated, "During the 1850s,

---

210 Wolfgang Hochbruck, "Forty-Eighters in the Union Armies: A Preliminary Checklist," http://www.geocities.com/kygermans.

with their ethnic consciousness raised by an assertive German-language press, Germans became a potent political force in St. Louis. Veterans of the failed political revolution of 1848 in the German states, determined to achieve their liberal agenda in America, flocked to St. Louis and other American cities, many of them as founders or editors of newspapers."[211]

Steven Rowan, co-author of *Germans for a Free Missouri,* pointed out that Forty-Eighters found in the Republican Party an outlet for injecting their socialist philosophy into mainstream American culture and politics. This is an aspect of the founding of the Republican Party that has gone unheralded and surely is an embarrassment to the present "conservative, low tax, small government" Republican Party.[212] Indeed, as we will demonstrate, the Republican Party provided these socialist revolutionaries, many of whom were close friends of Karl Marx and Fredrick Engels, a platform from which to promote their visions of a socialist America.

---

211 Steven Rowan and James Neal Primm, *Germans for a Free Missouri* (University of Missouri Press, Columbia: 1983) 6.

212 *Ibid.,* 27.

Chapter 11

THE RED ROOTS OF THE GOP

THE AVERAGE AMERICAN VIEWS the Republican Party as the party of small government, low taxes, and a bulwark against communism and socialism. Yet, until the mid-twentieth century, the red roots of the Republican Party held sway over the actions of the GOP. What most Americans do not realize is that radical socialists, Marxists, and other big government advocates were crucial in the founding of the GOP, Lincoln's 1860 GOP nomination, Lincoln's election as president, and the support for Lincoln's war against the South and, therefore, real States' Rights.

The Republican Party, organized in 1854-55, was supposedly created to prevent the spread of slavery. It must be pointed out that neither Lincoln nor the Republican Party opposed slavery "where it exists" but only the movement of slaves into the territory of the United States. In his first Inaugural Address in 1861 Lincoln stated: "I have no purpose, directly or indirectly, to interfere with the institution of slavery in the states where it exists."[213] A fact that most GOP advocates ignore is that the fourth plank of the 1860 Republican Party platform guaranteed protection for each State to "order and control its own domestic institutions."[214]

---

213   Abraham Lincoln, First Inaugural Address, March 4, 1861.

214   Republican Party Platform, 1860, *Documents of American History*, 8th ed. (New Jersey: Prentice Hall College Division, 1988), I, 22.

General August Willich

Karl Marx described Willich as a "communist with a heart." Before fleeing Europe, Willich was a member of the Central committee of the Communist League. Joining the Republican Party before the War, his fellow Forty-Eighters often referred to Willich as the "Reddest of the Reds." As with most Forty-Eighters with military experience, when the War for Southern Independence broke out, Willich offered his services to the Union.

Domestic institutions are a euphemism, i.e., code-word, for slavery. The Republican Party was the successor to the Whig Party, whose champion was Henry Clay. Clay and the Whig Party were advocates of the "'American System'" which promoted every big government scheme that Jefferson, Madison, Jackson and other Democrats opposed. The first time Lincoln ran for a public office and the first time he was elected to a public office, Lincoln was a big government Whig.[215] In the announcement of his first political campaign, Lincoln stated that he was a "Henry Clay Whig." The Whig Party was the descendant of and inheritor of the principles of America's first big government party, the Federalist Party. Like Clay, the Republican Party advocated internal improvements (little more than another method of redistributing the wealth), protective tariffs, and a strong central government. The central thread connecting all three parties, Federalist, Whig, and Republican, was their desire for a government strong (big) enough to advance the above-mentioned measures. By embracing these big government measures, the Republican Party endeared itself to newly arriving radical socialists.

It should be noted that the first Republican convention, held in Philadelphia in June of 1856, had nineteen German American delegates, most of whom were either Forty-Eighters or their sycophants. John C. Fremont became the first GOP presidential nominee at the Republican Party's first National Convention. As previously noted, Fremont was supported by the Forty-Eighters in 1856 and when war broke out, these same radicals flocked to now General Fremont's camp, filling every rank from private to general.

Before the election of 1860 many Forty-Eighters had attained positions of influence in the German-American community. Among those influential German Forty-Eighters were Frederick Hassaurek, August Willich, and Carl Schurz. In *Ethnic Voters and the Election of Lincoln,* we are informed: "In Ohio, Colonel Willich called a meeting of German voters which resolved to issue a manifesto, setting forth

215 Edgar Lee Masters, *Lincoln The Man*, (1931, The Foundation for American Education, Columbia, SC: 1997) 30-32.

the principles of the German Republicans against discrimination between native and naturalized citizens. Prominent among the out-of-state leaders at this meeting were [Carl] Schurz of Wisconsin, Nicholas J. Rusch of Iowa, George Schneider, editor of the Illinois *Staats Zeitung*, [Gustave] Koerner of Illinois, and Frederick Kapp of New York."[216] As previously noted, Schurz and Willich were Forty-Eighters, as was Kapp from New York.

The 1860 Republican Convention for nominating the GOP's candidate for president was held in Chicago. Since this area was a Forty-Eighter stronghold, this choice increased the radical socialist's influence on the Party's platform and nominee. Many Midwestern German socialists were there as delegates, credentialed from their states of residence. Johann Bernhard Stallo from Ohio was present at the GOP convention. Although he was not technically a Forty-Eighter, he was definitely one of their sympathizers. Stallo was a close friend of August Willich, an avowed communist and friend of Karl Marx and Fredrick Engels. Also attending were Frederick Hassaurek from Cincinnati and Henry (Heinrich) Bornstein from Missouri. Bornstein was another "American" friend of Karl Marx and Fredrick Engels. Bornstein's radical politics extended from socialism of the Marxist persuasion to a strongly held anti-Catholic philosophy. No lists of early Republican socialists would be complete without the name of the ever-present Carl Schurz from Wisconsin, also a delegate at the GOP convention.

Although not taking a large part of the business of the GOP on the floor of the convention, Carl Schurz and Gustave Koerner were active in the drawing up of the Republican platform. Schurz and Koerner came to the convention with a number of ideas that they were able to have placed into the platform, such as protection of the voting rights for foreign-born citizens and the promotion of the Homestead Act. During and after the convention these planks of the Republican platform were dubbed the "Dutch planks." They

---

216 Fredrick C. Luebke, *Ethnic Voters and the Election of Lincoln* (University of Nebraska Press, Lincoln: 1971) 7.

just as well could have been called the Marxist planks.[217] So here we have a case of a Forty-Eighter socialist who helped write the Republican platform in 1860. It is worth noting that the socialist revolutionaries came to the Republican Party and offered their services, but their motives were hardly altruistic. They wanted something in return, not the least of which was the political muscle to advance their socialist agenda.

As a member of the Republican National Committee, one of Schurz's functions during the election was establishing so-called foreign departments that would secure the services of foreign-speaking individuals commissioned to speak for the Republican Party and Abraham Lincoln. It was hoped, and did indeed turn out to be the case, that these speakers would secure for the Republican Party the votes of foreign-speaking voters.[218]

A short list of influential European radical socialists would include men such as: (1) Henry Ramming of Davenport, Iowa. A Hungarian, Ramming was a former officer in the Austrian military turned socialist who fled Europe for America after the collapse of the Austrian revolution. During the 1850s Ramming was an associate editor of the German-language newspaper *Der Demokrat*. It should not come as a surprise to learn that when the war broke out, he became a colonel of the Third Missouri (Union) Infantry under General Fremont. As an aside, one must wonder how a Hungarian socialist resident of Iowa became a colonel in a Missouri (a Southern state) regiment. (2) Carl Rotteck, a Forty-Eighter who fled Europe after the collapse of the German socialist revolution. (3) William Hoffbauer, a Forty-Eighter who served in the socialist parliament of the German socialist republic. Like many other Forty-Eighters, he sought refuge in America, settling in Dubuque, Iowa. Hoffbauer and Schurz were close friends.[219]

---

217   *Ibid.*, 9.

218   *Ibid.*, 11.

219   Luebke, 23-24.

Notice just how influential the radical socialists became after establishing themselves in America. For example, the German newspaper *Der Demokrat* editorialized in honor of John Brown on the day of his hanging. Many ethnic Germans wore signs of mourning and placed expressions of bereavement on their homes and businesses; one German theater showed its dismay at the hanging of Brown by lowering its flag to the half-staff position. While most modern Americans condemned Arabs for "dancing in the streets" after the tragedy of September 11, 2001, these same Americans no doubt would join with early American radical socialists and mourn the hanging of the terrorist John Brown.[220] It is interesting that the Germans should be so affected by the death of a man who has been described as America's first terrorist. Brown was a rabidly fanatic abolitionist who, like any good socialist, Marxist, and communist, believed that the *ends* justify the *means*. John Brown's method of dealing with what he considered "pro-slavery" people was to hack them to death with sabers even if these people owned no slaves. In John Brown's view, being a Southerner was evidence enough of slavery guilt and therefore deserving death. In 1856, Brown and seven other terrorists accomplished this grisly deed on the banks of Pottawatomie Creek in Kansas. In describing the death of one of those executed by Brown and his companions, four of whom were his sons, historian Otto Scott has written: "He was murdered beside the Pottawatomie with sabers. One blow severed his left hand, except for a strand of flesh, as he raised it in self-defense. His skull was opened in two places; and he fell headlong into the shallows.... Left behind were five mutilated dead men, two widows, and a number of fatherless children. And the peace of the region was in a shambles."[221]

In his murderous activities in Kansas, John Brown had the support of a group of wealthy and influential Northerners known as the Secret Six. Assisting Brown in his terrorist activities in Kansas

---

220 *Ibid.*, 38.

221 Otto Scott, *The Secret Six: The Fool as Martyr* (Foundation for American Education, Columbia, SC: 1987) 8-9.

were two radical socialist revolutionaries from Europe, August Bondi and Charles Kaiser. Without question, John Brown was a murdering terrorist. One is led to wonder why so many Germans in Iowa were disturbed at the execution of this terrorist. Were Brown's fanatical and bloody methods of dealing with Southerners so justifiable in their minds that these Germans felt compelled to mourn Brown's execution? If so, what does this tell us about the "freedom" and "democracy" these same men had supposedly been fighting for in Europe? More to the point, what does this tell us about the "freedom" and "democracy" Forty-Eighters, Lincoln, and the Republican Party were fighting to force upon the South and ultimately America? Rather than freeing the enslaved, Lincoln and the Republican Party enslaved the free by forcing the shackles of big, indivisible and all-powerful government upon all Americans. To reiterate, socialists and communists never mean the same things by their use of such terms as "freedom" and "democracy" as ordinary Americans. In our understanding of their revolutionary intentions, in the nineteenth, twentieth, and twenty-first centuries, we need to keep this fact firmly fixed in our minds. For these people, language was, and still is, a tool of propaganda.

In the book *Ethnic Voters and the Election of Lincoln,* Joseph Schafer detailed how the political refugees of the failed socialist revolutions in Europe found the United States to be not only profitable as a place to live but also advantageous for the promotion of their brand of social reform. The leaders of the failed socialist revolution were, for the most part, well-educated men, who quickly learned English and threw themselves into the political debate as advocates of the instant abolition of slavery. During Lincoln's campaign for both the Republican presidential nomination and later for the office of president, the Forty-Eighters were very influential. Radical socialists such as Carl Schurz, Friedrich Hecker, Gustave Koerner, Hoffmann, Johann Bernard Stallo, and other Forty-Eighters, without equivocation, supported Lincoln and the Republican Party.[222]

---

222   Luebke, 55-56.

As already pointed out, earlier German immigrants (pre-Forty-Eighters) displayed more religious convictions, both Protestants and Catholics, than the Forty-Eighters. Therefore, they at first looked askance at these men. Not only were the Forty-Eighters political radicals, but many were theologically freethinkers. However, as time passed, the Forty-Eighters managed to overcome this problem, eventually becoming, for the most part, the voice of the German immigrant population. It is well known that Lincoln considered the German vote in Illinois of prime importance—so much so that he secretly purchased Springfield's German newspaper, the *Illinois Staats Anzeiger*. After the election the editor of that organ was awarded a consular post in the Lincoln administration. Many historians noted that the German population of Illinois was concentrated in large cities and well-developed areas of the state. Residing in such urban areas exposed them to many ideas about the "new" and developing theories of socialism; therefore, it was not uncommon for these people to be active in various labor movements and to have a distinct left-of-center (that is, socialist) worldview.[223] Led by men like Gustave Koerner, who, in all fairness, does not appear to have been a Forty-Eighter, though his daughter ended up marrying one, and Friedrich Hecker, who was a Forty-Eighter, these men could be expected to give their support to Lincoln.

The radical communist, August Willich, was at first lukewarm in his support of Lincoln. As editor of the radical *Republikaner* in Cincinnati, he wrote, "The qualifications of the man whom we can support for President...the proper material to make a President of the People—a *Working Men's President* [has to understand that] the great struggle now going on in every civilized nation of the earth, [is] *the conflict of labor against monopoly*. [That man must] ...place himself on the side of the laborer, of the producing classes, as against the monopolist."[224] This passage demonstrates Willich's classic class struggle approach to politics and current events. And

---

223 *Ibid.*, 67.

224 August Willich, as cited in, Bruce Levine, *The Spirit of 1848* (University of Illinois Press, Urbana: 1992) 247.

to be able to do what Willich thought the ideal man should do, he observed that the candidate must be obligated to no "'political clique' organizations.... He must have laid the foundation of his own fortunes upon *his own labor*, and must never have stained his escutcheon through connivance with monopoly."[225] It is interesting, considering qualifications as these that Willich ended up supporting Lincoln's candidacy and even becoming a general in his army when the war commenced. Lincoln didn't fit any of these qualifications that Willich put forth for a candidate he could support.

Willich's desire to have a pure working-man's candidate fell upon hard times with the nomination of Abraham Lincoln, a popular and well-known lawyer who had tried thousands of cases during his practice as an attorney. As for Willich's desire to have a candidate without any connections to big business, or as Willich referred to it, "monopoly," Lincoln was a disappointment here also because he was an attorney for none other than the Illinois Central Railroad, one of the largest railroads in the world at that time.[226]

One of the first major clashes between the North and the South was over the issue of tariffs. The South, believing it was made to bear an unequal share of the tax burden due to the tariff, and receiving little of the benefit from it came to near bloodshed because of this issue. Even Northern newspapers admitted that the tariff as then constituted was nothing less than a means to plunder the South for the benefit of the North. In December of 1860, the *Daily Chicago Times* cautioned its readers of the dangers of pursuing such policies.[227] Some Northern newspapers even had the temerity to suggest that a lower tariff rate might help hold the country together. Although this seemed to be a good and logical solution, Lincoln and his supporters found such ideas to be inconceivable. It must be remembered that Lincoln was a supporter of Clay's "American System." According to this system,

---

225 *Ibid.*

226 DiLorenzo, *The Real Lincoln*, 15.

227 *Ibid.*, 242.

big government had every right and even a duty to pass laws and perform tasks that would, according to the logic of the advocates of big government, advance the national well-being. Therefore, high tariffs to protect domestic (Northern) industries, national banking and currency, and the use of Federal funds to support local industries, also known as "internal improvements," were a mainstay of Republican political philosophy.

The American System, as embraced by Lincoln and the Republicans, had more in common with the socialism of Mussolini's and Hitler's fascism than with the socialism of Marx. Nevertheless, the American System provided Lincoln and the Republican Party a means of bestowing special privileges on those wealthy men who helped to finance the Republican cause.[228] This system not only survived Lincoln and the nineteenth century but is still alive and well. The ghost of the American System today abounds in numerous Federal boondoggle payments to the Military-Industrial-Complex, Tecno-Industrial subsidies, and copious funding of Deep State sycophants. The only difference is that today *both* political parties compete to be the dispensers of power, perks, and privileges. Obviously, August Willich saw in Lincoln and the Republican Party a means by which he could push his communist ideology forward in America. What we surely know is that Karl Marx's friend, August Willich, aka "the Reddest of the Reds," supported Lincoln, the Republican Party, and the war to *prevent* Southern independence. This war not only defeated the South but destroyed America's once compound republic of limited, small government. It also secured for America Marx's and Engels' first demand of the 'The Demands of the Communist Party of Germany,' *"eine Nation unteilbar,"* one nation indivisible.

With Lincoln's political background, a career devoted to feathering the nests of the rich and influential, it is somewhat astounding that the socialists and communists of the 1848 stripe could end up supporting him both politically and in a military capacity once the war commenced, yet they did. Why were devoted

---

228   *Ibid.*, 244-45.

socialists willing and eager to support Lincoln, who was a devoted supporter of large Northern industry? Perhaps the margin of difference between the monopoly capitalists (as opposed to advocates of free enterprise) and the socialists is not as great as we were led to believe. For whatever reason, once the bandwagon got rolling, the socialists and communists enthusiastically supported Lincoln and his program. Not only did the home-grown radicals in this country support Lincoln's efforts, but those in Europe did also, especially Karl Marx and Fredrick Engels.

One somewhat well-known "home-grown" socialist is Horace Greely. In his book *Horace Greeley and Other Pioneers of American Socialism,* Charles Sotheran expresses his feeling that Greeley was a noble individual whom poet John G. Whittier proclaimed to have been a member of the quasi-New England renaissance in literature and who taught the people of the United States the truths of socialism. Sotheran's observation that Greeley never relented in his efforts of promoting the socialist agenda, confirms Greeley's status as an early American socialist. Neither his friends nor his foes ever denied the fact that Greeley was a socialist.[229] Also worth noting is that Greeley's theological worldview was largely influenced by William Ellery Channing, a unitarian minister.[230]

In and around the time of the War for Southern Independence, Horace Greely, a socialist, was the owner and editor of a newspaper in New York City. Greeley's paper routinely published articles written by the father of modern communism, Karl Marx. Marx was hired to write for Greeley's paper by a friend of Marx and Engels, the socialist, Charles A. Dana. What an interesting mix!

Let us not overlook Fredrick Engels, who was basically, Karl Marx's benefactor and ghost writer. Engels contributed much to Marx's financial support over the years and assisted him with his English language writing skills. Engels was an astute observer

---

229 Charles Sotheran, *Horace Greeley and Other Pioneers of American Socialism* (Haskell House Publishers, Ltd., New York: 1971) 1-2.

230 *Ibid.*, 238.

of the ongoing military and political maneuvers during the War. As Mayer noted, regarding the War Between the States: "As we know, this was the first war where any important strategic use was made of railways and armoured ships; at first neither side had a real army; there was an appalling lack of trained officers; and (as Engels pointed out) had it not been for the experienced soldiers who had entered America after the European revolution— especially from Germany—the organization of the Union army would have taken still longer than it did."[231] What a slap in the face to those who insist and vociferously proclaim that the War Between the States was fought by the North in defense of freedom and the Constitution—yes, with socialist and communist allies! Where in the history of socialism and communism have these people ever fought for American-style freedom and constitutional government? Socialists and communists fought then, as they do now, for the rights of big government—it was the South that was fighting for limited government, that is, American liberty.

A somewhat different group of socialist revolutionaries appeared in the United States during the 1830s and 1840s, known as "Chartists." The Chartists were a radical group in Britain which began a push for radical social reform along the lines of socialism. The Chartist Movement in England has been called "the first proletarian protest of the Industrial Revolution." It was a movement that started with a "people's charter" drawn up in 1836. As with most such movements in Europe at that time, what started as a mild reform movement with support from people across the cultural spectrum, soon morphed into a radical socialist revolution. Once the "reform" movement turned into a socialist revolution, more and more people turned against the revolt, and it failed. Even in failure, some needed reforms were instituted but unfortunately, the seeds of socialism were planted.

Richard Hinton was another English radical who was gently persuaded to leave England in 1848. He embraced the dogmas of Radical Republicanism and abolitionism and became an associate

---

231 Mayer, 175.

of the terrorist, John Brown. During the war he rose to the rank of colonel. After the war, he became a correspondent for a Boston newspaper and was said to be a "confirmed socialist."[232]

Without a doubt, the most famous of the Chartists who sought refuge in America was Allan Pinkerton, the founder of the Pinkerton Detective Agency. In his book *Desperate Men*, James D. Horan noted that Allan Pinkerton came to the United States as a result of his flight from British agents who were seeking to arrest radicals of the Chartist Movement.[233] Pinkerton settled in Dundee, Illinois, where he ran a station on the controversial "Underground Railroad" helping escaped slaves to flee to Canada. The question that begs to be asked but too often overlooked is, "Why Canada"? The reason these slaves had to go to Canada was because the people of Illinois (and most Northern States) refused to allow free people of color to move into their state. Pennsylvania Congressman David Wilmot, author of the Wilmot Proviso which would have prevented the movement of slaves into the Western territories, announced that he had, "no squeamish sensitiveness upon the subject of slavery, no morbid sympathy for the slave."[234] In 1860 Senator James Harlan of Iowa noted the feelings of the people of the Northwest when he said, "This prejudice exists in my own state. It would be impossible to carry a proposition in Iowa to educate the few colored children that now live in that State in the same schools with the white children. It would be impossible, I think, in any one of the States of the Northwest."[235] This is not to detract from people seeking to assist those desiring to be free nor those attempting to help but it is eye-opening to understand that the North was not a "safe-place" for escaped slaves or freed African Americans.

---

232 *Ibid.*

233 James D. Horan, *Desperate Men* (Bonanza Books, New York: 1949) xi.

234 David Wilmot, as cited in, Leon F. Litwack, *North of Slavey* (University of Chicago Press, Chicago: 1961), 47.

235 Congressional Globe, 33rd Congress, 2nd secession, January 11, 1860, 1679-80.

During this time, Pinkerton established a friendship with John Brown. Pinkerton assisted the terrorist John Brown by giving him money and tickets for Brown and his gang of terrorists just a few months before Brown's raid into Virginia.[236] One has to question the vaunted "love for freedom and the enslaved" when revolutionaries become involved with any seemingly altruistic efforts. Was there an ulterior motive for these efforts, such as seeking to foment a Haitian style slave insurrection in the South?

Pinkerton was not alone in his socialist and revolutionary endeavors. The socialist radical, George Julian Harney, was a contributor to a journal titled *Northern Star*. In James MacKay's book on Pinkerton, MacKay explains that Pinkerton was a devoted reader of Harney's essays. It should be pointed out that Harney was described as a man fanatically committed to advancing the socialist cause. Harney's enthusiasm for the socialist cause was one reason that Pinkerton's biographer gave for Pinkerton's admiration for Harney (remember that Harney was a friend of Marx and Engels).[237]

Pinkerton's revolutionary mind-set is clearly demonstrated after a meeting with the terrorist John Brown. During this time, Pinkerton gifted Brown and his gang with money and rail tickets. As Brown was departing, Pinkerton, speaking to his son, stated: "Look well upon that man. He is greater than Napoleon and just as great as George Washington."[238] Describing a cold-blooded murdering terrorist as being as great as George Washington is typical of those possessed of a socialist mind-set—a mind-set that allows for any action as long it is in the pursuit of what a socialist deems as a worthy objective. This philosophy has filled every socialist gulag, extermination camp, and killing field of the past one hundred years. Hitler, Stalin, Mao, and even Osama Bin Laden could not disagree with John Brown's method of promoting what he determined as just.

---

236 *Ibid.*

237 James Mackay, *Allan Pinkerton—The First Private Eye* (John Wiley and Sons, Inc., New York: 1997) 35.

238 *Ibid.*, 85.

From radical socialist refugee, radical abolitionist, Republican stalwart, and presidential confidant, Allan Pinkerton for better or worse had a great impact on American history. He established his detective agency in Chicago, which carries his name to this day. He got an early start by providing detective services to the Illinois Central Railroad at about the same time Abraham Lincoln was providing the railroad legal services. When Lincoln went to Washington to be inaugurated after his election, Pinkerton went along, and as we are told exposed a plot to assassinate the newly elected president in Baltimore. It has been asserted by some historians that the plot was invented by Pinkerton to boost his agency's status.[239] As the war began, Pinkerton served under General George B. McClellan, in the Department of the Ohio, as the chief of that department's secret service.

When McClellan went to Washington, Pinkerton went along to continue his work as a spy. Stewart Sifakis in his book, *Who Was Who in the Civil War,* has made note of the failures of Pinkerton's intelligence gathering. During the Peninsula Campaign he was responsible for identifying the placement and numbers of enemy troops. Most of his information came from runaway slaves and proved to be totally incorrect. The result was that the Union Army never had a good fix on the number and deployment of Confederate troops.[240] Over the years numerous accounts were written of how General McClellan always considered his Army outnumbered by the Confederates and was always asking for reinforcements. If these accounts are true about Pinkerton's failures in intelligence gathering, we know why McClellan's estimates were so incorrect— it was the result of Pinkerton's ineptness at gathering intelligence. Yet, inept or not, Pinkerton was yet another socialist who supported Abraham Lincoln and the Union in their war against the South.

---

239   Stewart Sifakis, *Who Was Who in the Civil War* (Facts On File, Inc., New York: 1988) 508.

240   *Ibid.,* 509.

General Carl Schurz

An active participant in the unsuccessful socialist revolution in Germany, like so many other Forty-Eighters, Schurz sought asylum in the United States. He joined the Republican Party shortly before the War for Southern Independence. At the outbreak of the War, Schurz offered his services to the Union. At the close of the war Schurz obtained the rank of major general. After the war he served as a United States Senator from Missouri and Secretary of the Interior in the Hayes administration. (Photograph courtesy Library of Congress.)

Chapter 12

LINCOLN'S GERMAN MARXIST ALLIES

IT HAS BEEN ESTIMATED that the number of dedicated socialists who immigrated to the United States were small but, like salt or yeast, a little can go a long way. Of all the Forty-Eighters, one group of radical socialists stand out, head and shoulders, over all other Forty-Eighters—the Germans. In the following chapter, we will investigate who these German Forty-Eighters were and what influence they had on the founding of the Republican Party, the election of Lincoln, and the War to Prevent Southern Independence.

Three of the most prominent and radical German Forty-Eighters were discussed previously in this work. These three are: Carl Schurz, August Willich, and Franz Sigel. Although these three were the major players in German Forty-Eighter activism, there were other German socialists who assisted in bringing socialist ideology to these United States. A short biographical list of 34 prominent European radical socialists can be found in Addendum II at the end of this book. The following is a brief summary of some of the Forty-Eighters who played a major role in Lincoln's election and the war against the South.

Carl Schurz one of the best known of the Forty-Eighters had a noteworthy military career and an even more distinguish political career. At nineteen while a university student during the turbulent time of European socialist revolutions, Schurz became radicalized while studying under Professor Gottfried Kinkel of the University of Bonn. Early in his career, Professor Kinkel was a university lecturer, theology teacher, and poet. His revolutionary activities in the '48 revolts earned Kinkel a stay in Spandau Prison awaiting his execution. Fortunately for Kinkel, his pupil, the future Union General and Republican Secretary of the Interior, Carl Schurz, helped Kinkel escape the hangman's noose.

Before leaving Germany, Schurz attended a meeting where he met and listened to a speech by Karl Marx. Here is what Schurz thought of Marx: "Marx's utterances were indeed *full of meaning, logical and clear*, but I have never seen a man whose bearing was so provoking and intolerable. To no opinion, which differed from his, he accorded the honor of even a condescending consideration. Everyone who contradicted him he treated with abject contempt; every argument that he did not like he answered either with biting scorn at the unfathomable ignorance that had prompted it, or with opprobrious aspersions upon the motives of him who had advanced it. I remember most distinctly the cutting disdain with which he pronounced the word 'bourgeois'; and as a 'bourgeois' that is as a detestable example of the deepest mental and moral degeneracy he denounced everyone that dared to oppose his opinion."[241] Although Schurz did not appreciate Marx's social demeanor, as a good socialist, Schurz *did* think Marx's ideas were, "*full of meaning, logical and clear* [emphasis added]. As noted, Schurz was offended by Marx's delivery style, not what Marx was saying.

In the summer of 1852 Schurz and his wife came to America. In 1856 he established his residency in Watertown, Wisconsin, where he immediately became active in the new Republican Party. Having been in the United States only five years, in 1857, Schurz ran for the office of Wisconsin Lieutenant Governor and lost. In 1859, Schurz was admitted to the Wisconsin bar and established his law practice in Milwaukee. Meeting Abraham Lincoln in 1858, he soon became a staunch admirer of Lincoln. In 1860 he

---

241 Carl Schurz, *The Autobiography of Carl Schurz* (1906, Charles Scribner's Sons, New York: 1961) 20-21.

was given the position as a member of the board of regents at the state university in Madison, and in that same year he was named to be one of the delegates to the May 1860, Republican National Convention. At the Republican Convention he was appointed a member of the Committee on Resolutions. We previously noted his efforts in Lincoln's election in the Midwest that year. Schurz expended much time and effort traveling and speaking to German American voters promoting the Republican Party and Lincoln. Once elected, Lincoln appointed Schurz as an ambassador to Spain over the objection of Secretary of State Seward. Seward, noting Schurz's record as a revolutionary in Europe, objected to this appointment. Apparently, Lincoln did not have the same problem with Schurz's revolutionary past as did Seward. Before his death, Schurz would become one of the most influential Forty-Eighters in the United States. Another prominent German Forty-Eighter was the man who at one time was Schurz's corps commander, Forty-Eighter Franz Sigel.

Franz Sigel has been described as one of the Union Army's most controversial generals and one of its worst. Sigel's greatest value to the Union Army was his ability in recruiting Germans into the Union Army. Born in Baden in 1824, he was a graduate of the German Military Academy. He resigned from the army in 1847, and in 1848, he began his life as a socialist revolutionary in the aborted attempt to overthrow the government. He rose to the position of minister of war in the revolutionary German republic. After the failure of the revolution, Sigel sought refuge in Switzerland and then England before emigrating to the United States. Having briefly taught in the schools of New York City, he moved west and became the superintendent of the public school system in St. Louis. Strange is it not how these revolutionaries always seem to move into areas of public influence and did so quickly after arriving to the United States. Obviously, radicals in the nineteenth century are no different than radical socialists of the twenty-first century who gravitate to areas where they can influence, that is, indoctrinate, the unsuspecting populace. Today, radicals of the left dominate public education, academia, popular entertainment, and high-tech media outlets. This should make it very clear why Marx and other socialists demanded free public education as part of their agenda. When "public" education becomes "state" education, and the state is either strongly influenced or controlled by those with a socialist worldview, education becomes a tool of the proletariat revolution— at which time the three Rs become: Red, Radical, and Revolution.

At the outbreak of the War Between the States, Sigel joined the Union Army in Missouri and was given the rank of colonel in the Third Missouri. Within a few weeks he was promoted to brigadier general. He was second in command to Nathaniel Lyon at the southwest Missouri Battle of Oak Hill, or as Yankees called it, Battle of Wilson's Creek. One of the many controversies he became enmeshed in occurred during that battle. Many Union officers, including General Henry Halleck, laid the blame for their defeat at the feet of Sigel. Not only was the battle lost, but also the able Union general Nathaniel Lyon was killed.

Although popular with his men, Sigel never enjoyed the full confidence of General Halleck. After the northwestern Arkansas Battle of Elk Horn Tavern, or as the Yankees called it, Pea Ridge, which many described as Sigel's finest hour militarily, Sigel was transferred to the Shenandoah Valley in Virginia. The victory at Elk Horn Tavern was followed by reversals in Virginia at Second Manassas and New Market. General Halleck's less than stellar view of Sigel's military capabilities was displayed when he stated, "It seems little better than murder to give important commands to men such as Sigel."[242]

Another close associate of Marx who found Abraham Lincoln and the Republican Party worthy of their support was Joseph Weydemeyer. Joseph Sullivan, in the spring 1997 issue of *Columbia Magazine,* noted that Weydemeyer was: "A refugee from the 1848 Revolt, and a particularly close associate of Marx...

---

242 General Henry Halleck, as cited in, "Battles and Battlefields of 1864 in the Shenandoah Valley," http://www.angelfire.com.

and tireless advocate of communism."[243] Sullivan also notes that Weydemeyer immigrated to the United States and established New York as his residence in 1851. Some of Weydemeyer's more notable accomplishments in New York were the publication of Marx's *Communist Manifesto,* assisting in organizing the New York Communist Club, and publishing a German-language newspaper, *Die Revolution.* Moving to St. Louis, Missouri, in 1860, at the outbreak of war, Weydemeyer offered his service to the darling of the Forty-Eighters, Major General John C. Fremont.

As was pointed out in Chapter 3, Carl Wittke confirmed that Weydemeyer was a close friend of both Marx and Engels and is lauded by America's communists as a pioneer of modern-day American communism. It is interesting to note that Weydemeyer's adoption of communism was made possible by his association with Anneke and Willich. Before being expelled from his homeland, Weydemeyer served as editor of several communist and socialist journals and newspapers in Germany. After the failure of the socialist revolution, he remained in Germany but was eventually expelled; consequently, he made his way to the United States. He arrived in New York with a letter of introduction to Charles A. Dana, the editor of Horace Greeley's *New York Tribune,* from his friend Karl Marx, and began his new life in America.[244] With the blessing of the London Marxists, Weydemeyer formed the first Marxist organization, the Proletarian League of New York, in the United States in June of 1852.[245] Communist support for Lincoln and the Republican Party cannot be hidden. Author Carl Wittke mentioned Weydemeyer's passionate support for Lincoln in his book, *Refugees of Revolution.*[246]

---

243 Joseph Sullivan, "The Blue, The Gray, and The Red," *Columbiad Magazine,* 1997, Vol. 1, No. 1, pp. 36, 37.

244 Wittke, 169, 170.

245 *Ibid.,* 170.

246 *Ibid.,* 171.

With the assistance of Dr. Grottfried T. Kellner, Weydemeyer started yet another radical newspaper in 1853. A failure in the newspaper business, Weydemeyer turned to writing and speaking about the efforts of the English Chartist. Eventually, Weydemeyer returned to New York, where he helped Frederick L. Olmstead survey Central Park. Weydemeyer's passionate support for Lincoln and the Republican Party was noted by author Carl Wittke, in his book, *Refugees of Revolution*.[247]

August Willich, or August von Willich, Karl Marx described him as "a communist with a heart" while others referred to Willich as the "Reddest of the Red 48ers." Willich was another early communist Republican! Willich was born into a family of Prussian nobility. As was the case at that time, he pursued a career in the Prussian military and was promoted to the rank of captain by 1831. Pursuing other intellectual outlets, not just military tactics and history, Willich began investigating various left-wing social causes. His pursuit of left-wing causes resulted in his meeting with Karl Marx and Fredrick Engels and embracing the ideology of communism. When Willich began expounding on the virtues of communism over the existing Prussian social order, he was court-martialed and forced to resign from the Prussian military. With the advent of the 1847 revolution in Germany, Willich quickly enlisted in the revolutionary forces. In 1849 the revolt was crushed, and Willich was forced to flee his homeland.[248]

Wandering Europe in search of a homeland, in 1853, like thousands of other Red Forty-Eighters, Willich settled in the United States. It was in the United States as an editor of a Cincinnati German-language newspaper that Willich earned the moniker "Reddest of the Red."[249] In responding to Lincoln's call for troops to invade the Confederate States of America, Willich sprang into action and proved to be a natural at raising German volunteers

---

247   *Ibid.*, 171.

248   "August von Willich, Reddest of the Red 48ers," http://www.strategypage.com.

249   *Ibid.*

who had been indoctrinated by reading his newspaper. Within a very short time he recruited more than fifteen hundred German volunteers from which the Ninth Ohio Volunteer Infantry was created with Willich as a captain in the Ninth.[250] Through various promotions Willich, who dropped the "von" from his name, rose to the rank of general. Unlike many "political" officers, Willich's deportment in battle proved that he was a hands-on commander willing to lead his men "from the front."

As previously noted, though John Brown was a terrorist and a fanatic, nevertheless the left seems to have adored him. August Willich was no exception, as demonstrated in his December 1859 speech in Cincinnati, Ohio. At that time Willich lamented the hanging of John Brown while denouncing Democrats and the institution of slavery. Not satisfied with mourning the death of the terrorist John Brown, Willich encouraged the crowd to "whet their sabers" with the blood of slaveholders and what he considered to be the supporters of the institution of slavery, the Democratic Party.[251] Notice that it was not just Southern "slaveholders" who were to be put to the sword but anyone who was considered to be a supporter of slaveholders. The threat of a Hattian style slave revolt, where all Southerners were subject to death, was a major factor why nearly 90% of non-slave-holding Southerners feared the Republican Party. Every Southerner felt threaten by the rhetoric of Radical Republicans like Willich. This fear was demonstrated in the 1860, election when out of the thirteen soon-to-be Confederate States, the Republican Party did not have enough support to be listed on a state-wide ballot. Of the two Southern States where the Republican Party was listed, Lincoln received less than 10% of the vote.

Over the years, many authors insultingly derided native-born Americans because of their "nativist sentiments." In other words, "nativist sentiments" were code words for America's lack of the sophistication, a sophistication supposedly inherent in Europeans, especially if they were Forty-Eighters. The condescending view

---

250 *Ibid.*

251 Levine, 223.

of Americans by the newly arriving "sophisticated" Germans is a form of prejudice. Willich observed: "After the first years of my stay here...in this republic a beginning is possible only through the German element...the American with his hasty action was less feeling for purposes which are less immediate and less quick to attain and bear fruits."[252] Actually, Americans seem to have done quite well for themselves before Willich and his leftist colleagues arrived from Europe. Willich was impatient with Americans because they did not share his "communist" vision for their country and for their future. It is not uncommon for radicals, especially those on the left, to be impatient with those who do not share their ideology. One point both friends and enemies have pointed out about Willich is that he was a very dogmatic socialist. Many observers of Willich have noted that he did not hesitate to express his socialist views. William L. Burton points out in *Melting Pot Soldiers* that Willich did not hesitate to sermonize on the merits of the communist/socialist system.

Willich stands out as one of the purest and most dedicated Forty-Eighters, having never sought self-aggrandizement either in the realm of politics or finance. He was a pure socialist ideologue, bent on advancing the cause of communism in the United States.[253] Looking at the lives and careers of the leaders of the Forty-Eighters, it appears that some of the socialists who commanded ethnic regiments during the war forgot their "socialist mind-set" and acted more like petty capitalists. In striving for their own ambitions their compassion for the downtrodden workers of the world seemed to have slipped ever so slightly, but this cannot be said of Willich.

Friedrich Karl Franz Hecker, was a man of the political far left. Hecker, the son of a lawyer, was born in 1811. He studied law in Mannheim and history in Heidelberg and then Munich, where he received his Doctor of Law degree. He was, even at that early stage in his life, noted for his affinity for far-left politics. Hecker was so far to the left that he became known as "Red" and "Flagrant

---

252   August Willich, as cited in, *ibid.*, 126.

253   William L. Burton, 86-87.

Friedrich." Beginning his career as a liberal, he was elected as a member of the Liberal Party to the Baden legislative chamber. As with so many zealots, Hecker began his career as a reform-minded individual seeking to introduce more freedom and liberty into society. As is so often common with zealots, he could not tame his love for revolution and reform, and evolved into a far-left ideologue. His rhetoric and wild speeches proved too much for the conservative element of Prussia; thus, in 1845 he was expelled from Prussia. Hecker's promise of freedom and justice for the people must be judged by the type of government that radicals, such as Hecker, have given the world—remember, words mean different things depending on one's worldview.

Hecker's worldview was that of a radical socialist; historically we know just how much freedom and justice exist in socialist nations.[254]Hecker's goals sound good. But as already stated, a socialist's definition of such terms (democracy, freedom, justice, and such) is usually much different from that of a non-socialist. For example, academic freedom to the socialist is nothing more than the unrestricted freedom to promote a left-wing view by whatever means possible, on and off the university campus. A leftist's view of academic freedom requires allowing all leftist views to be discussed while restricting the voice of opposition. Freedom of the press is viewed in the same vein, and freedom of conscience usually means freedom from all religious doctrines. So what Hecker was really advocating was promotion of the political leftist agenda. All men are to be free to work for the advancement of socialism; anyone questioning socialism will be condemned as an enemy of the people—this mantra should sound familiar to Americans living in the early twenty-first century.

In March of 1848, a "preliminary parliament" was formed in Frankfurt, known as the Frankfurt Parliament. Hecker and some of his associates then presented demands to this group for the immediate proclamation of the establishing of a "republic."

---

254 "German American Corner: Hecker, Friedrich Karl Franz," http://www.germanheritage.com.

This was to be done without any input whatever from any of the German princes, who held great power at that time. The Frankfurt Parliament turned down the demand of the radicals. At that time Hecker and forty comrades walked out of the legislative body with the hope of establishing a "democratic" republic by force of arms in Baden. Hecker was assisted in this effort by other radical socialists such as August Willich, Gustav Struve, and Franz Sigel, among many others. Initially Hecker was warmly received by the population as he called for an armed struggle.[255] Hecker's vision of revolution, at that point, failed to materialize because when it came time to fight, the "masses" stayed away from Hecker's revolt. Listening to and cheering emotional speeches was one thing—facing the guns of professional soldiers was altogether something else—a lesson Hecker had not yet learned.

Disillusioned, Hecker beat a hasty retreat to Switzerland, that preliminary stomping ground for failed revolutionaries. Like so many other refugees of the socialist revolution, Hecker immigrated to the United States in late 1848.[256] He purchased a farm near Belleville, Illinois. As a resident of Illinois, he took an active part in founding the Republican Party. Along with fellow Forty-Eighters like Sigel and Schurz he became a key player in the German-American community, especially in the dynamic expansion of the German newspapers and their influence. This influence was used not only in the founding of the Republican Party and the election of Abraham Lincoln, but also in propagandizing among German-Americans for volunteers for the Union Army. As war commenced, Hecker assisted in raising a regiment of German-American troops, the Twenty-fourth Illinois Volunteer Infantry, of which he later became the commander.[257]

---

255 *Ibid.*

256 *Ibid.*

257 *Ibid.*

Hecker's personality appeared to be more suited for arguing the law than leading men in battle. Although viewed as brave in combat, he did not bear criticism well. His rhetorical skills were his best asset, moving men by his skill in verbal logic. This works well on a debating team or when arguing the intricacies of the law, but not of great benefit when the bullets are flying on the field of battle. Hecker's station in the military was due to his value as a symbolic figure, despite being viewed as deficient in military skills.[258]

While still in Germany during the old revolutionary days, Hecker was influenced by and associated with Gustav Struve. Gustav von Struve, the son of a Russian diplomat and a mother who was also of noble birth, was born in Munich in 1805. He was charitably described as a "German agitator."[259] He was among the leaders in the Baden uprising in 1848, where he, along with Hecker, attempted to establish what was called a "republic." After the attempt failed, Struve lit out for France, and from there he traveled to Switzerland. But in September of 1848 he was back and, with a batch of fellow revolutionaries, sought to start a second insurrection. This one also failed, and he was arrested. In March of 1849 he was found guilty of high treason and sentenced to five years of solitary confinement. He was taken to the penitentiary on May 12, but the next day revolutionists took possession of the prison, and he was set free. After more revolutionary activity, Struve again escaped to Switzerland, from which, after a mere two months, the authorities expelled him. He then went back to France, from thence to England, and then to the United States where he arrived in 1851. In all this travel and activity, he had the support of his wife, Amelie Disar, who was apparently as much of a revolutionary as her husband.

---

258   "24th Illinois Formation," http://www.burhop.net/24illinois/formation.htm.

259   "Virtual American Biographies—Gustav von Struve," http://www.virtualology. com.

In New York City Struve edited a socialist German newspaper called the *Deutsche Zuschauer,* but he had to discontinue it after a short run for lack of support. Then, again with the help of his wife, he began work on what he referred to as a universal history viewed from the perspective of a Radical Republican.[260]

In 1861, when the war started, Struve volunteered and became a captain in the Eighth New York Infantry. His tour of duty with the Eighth New York was cut short with the appearance of a German prince, Felix Salm-Salm. One thing that most socialists do not respect is hereditary titles of nobility. After all, the princes and their allies had put the Forty-Eighters to flight after the failed revolts in Europe. Having such a person in a position of authority was something Struve could not tolerate; therefore, he resigned his commission. Prince Salm-Salm was eventually placed under another Forty-Eighter, General Louis Blenker. Obviously Blenker did not feel the same revulsion to a former adversary as did Struve.[261] It appears that among socialists, differences of opinions and conflicts did occur especially when dealing with egos.

Struve returned to Germany in 1863, taking advantage of a general amnesty that was offered in Prussia. Upon his return he devoted himself to literary projects and gave lectures on phrenology, a subject that had many devotees in that period of history.

Louis Blenker, another German Forty-Eighter, studied medicine at the University of Munich, but soon gave up that study to enter the wine business in Worms. In 1849 Blenker was among the leaders of the revolutionary government near Worms. He fought in several engagements before the revolution was completely crushed. Like so many others he fled to Switzerland but was ordered to leave that country at which time he determined to come to the United States. Studying the history of these revolutionaries, it becomes obvious that at some point in time the government of Switzerland

260   *Ibid.*

261   William L. Burton, *Melting Pot Soldiers* (Iowa State University Press, Ames, IA: 1988) 87.

began ordering the revolutionaries to remove themselves from their country. Unfortunately, the United States didn't follow the lead of Switzerland. Blenker's move to the United States resulted in his gaining relatively more financial independence and a higher social standing. As war commenced, Blenker organized the Eighth New York Volunteer Infantry and subsequently was elected its commander. Blenker, always eager to demonstrate the prowess and military training of his German-American troops, invited Mr. and Mrs. Carl Schurz to review his troops on parade. Having put on an excellent display, Blenker's troops very much impressed the Forty-Eighter couple.[262]

Over the past few years politically correct historians have informed us of the socialists' concerns for the poor and downtrodden, of their empathy for the oppressed masses, and of their desire to better the conditions of all such men. Although well known as a radical socialist, Blenker's lifestyle in the army did little to display his concern for the oppressed. Not only did Blenker maintain a lifestyle that was more fitting for a prince than a socialist defender of the poor and downtrodden, but also any German adventurer seeking a place to reside found a warm reception in Blenker's camp. If for one reason or another a commission could not be secured for one of his German "volunteers," Blenker would make a place for his unpaid nontraditional "aide-de-camp." In no time Blenker's camp took on the air of a royal court with some of the best food, entertainment, and servants then in the army. Even though alcohol was not allowed in military camps, these Germans managed to stay well stocked with beer, wine, and other spirits.[263]

Blenker's socialist "concern" for the downtrodden did not, however, appear to manifest itself in the conduct of his men in the field. In fact, it was because of him that the term "Blenkered" came into common usage. During the spring of 1862, Blenker's German-American command relocated from the command of General McClellan to that of General Fremont. Due to inadequate

---

262   "Louis Blenker," http://stonewall.hut.

263   William L. Burton, 86-87.

supplies from Army command, Blenker's 10,000-man command had to "forage" its supplies from the local citizens of Virginia as they relocated from Eastern Virginia to Western Virginia. It was during this time that the term "Blenkered" was applied to those citizens who had been looted by the German-American troops passing through their region. [264]

It seems that Blenker's men exhibited their leader's "concern" for those less fortunate than themselves right from the beginning of the war. Many historians pointed out that according to international law, the United States Constitution, and the U.S. Army's own code of military conduct, the Union Army's conduct during the War was nothing less than unlawful. Beyond that, the most fundamental concept, embraced by the citizens of the North as well as the South prior to the War for Southern Independence, did not condone the actions of the invading armies of the North. For the first time in the history of the Christian world, wholesale acts of barbarity and cruelty designed to eliminate an entire population were set afoot. Private property and life itself were no longer safe within the reach of the Union Army. This was not something that developed late in the war under Philip Sheridan and William Sherman but was instituted by men such as Louis Blenker prior to the Battle of First Manassas. These were the men who wasted no time opining on how much they "felt the pain" of the common man. As has already been pointed out, socialists view words and concepts in an entirely different light than do people with a biblical worldview. As demonstrated across the South and around the world, a socialist's compassion is a mile wide but less than an inch deep. As often is the case when a military force is unable to defeat an enemy on the field of battle, it will often turn on the defenseless civilian population. It was noted that many of the looters in Blenker's army were men fresh from the jails of

Europe. The Union Army—with the full knowledge of the military and its commander in chief, President Abraham Lincoln—turned this rabble loose on the people of the South.[265]

General Blenker's military record in the United States Army appears to be somewhat notable. During the rout of the Union Army at the Battle of First Manassas Blenker managed to maintain discipline and retire his command in good order, unlike the bulk of the volunteer army. As was the case of many of the Forty-Eighters, this was not the first time Blenker was under fire, having served as a colonel in the Baden-Palatine Army during the socialist revolution in 1848. Even though he handled his regiment well and was aggressive toward Southern civilians, his regal lifestyle in camp was the source of much conflict with most native-born Americans. This may have played a part in his terminating his commission as an officer under a cloud of suspicion of graft.[266]

Another well-known Forty-Eighter who fought under Franz Sigel was Alexander von Schimmelfennig. Schimmelfennnig, like the other Forty-Eighters, was a refugee from the failed socialist revolution in Germany. As a leader of the German-American community, he had great influence with German-Americans volunteering for the Union.[267]Although, like many of the other Forty-Eighters, he was of noble birth, when he became a dedicated socialist, he dropped the "von" part of his name. Having been an officer in the Prussian Army, Schimmelfennig had the qualifications for a military appointment in his own right. Yet, it appears that his commission was based on his political connections as much as his Prussian Army skills. After the disaster of First Manassas, Lincoln called for troops to be enlisted not for ninety days but for several years. Responding to the president's call and at the urging of the city's German-American community, the Committee of Public Safety of Pittsburgh undertook efforts to enlist several

---

265 Thomas J. DiLorenzo, "The Other Reparations Movement," http://www.lewrockwell.com.

266 Rowan and Primm, 287.

267 "German Americans during the Civil War—Freethinkers and Turners," http://www.exulanten.com.

regiments of German volunteers for the war. A subcommittee with Republican J. J. Siebnick acting as chairman was established to recruit German-American volunteers. Siebnick's committee offered the name of Alexander Schimmelfennig, whose history as a revolutionary for the radical socialist cause was no secret, for the colonel of the new regiment. Schimmelfennnig was a popular member of the German community having recently published in *Der Wecker,* a well-known abolitionist and socialist newspaper, a letter calling upon the German-American community to rally to Lincoln and the Union cause.[268] Schimmelfennig went to Baltimore, where he enlisted the support of two former Prussian Army officers, Adolph von Hartung and Alexander Theobald von Mitzel, to aid him in recruiting and organizing a regiment. The three soon began to recruit in Philadelphia. Worth observing is that when Schimmelfennig had contact with the subcommittee in Pittsburgh he urged them to seek volunteers who had previous military training such as, former ninety-day soldiers or veterans of various German and American armies.[269] There is no doubt that Schimmelfennig had in mind former revolutionary soldiers when he requested that veterans of "various German" armies be recruited.

Schimmelfennig proved himself on the field of battle to be, unlike many other "political" generals, a competent officer. His reward for his proficient service was to be awarded the commission of brigadier general. At Second Manassas, Schimmelfennig gained Sigel's recommendation for a general's star, but the authorities in Washington made no response. At that time Carl Schurz, who knew how such things should be handled, took a personal interest in Schimmelfennig's problem. Schurz interceded for Schimmelfennig by contacting the Pennsylvania congressional delegation. The Pennsylvania delegation in turn lobbied Lincoln's controversial secretary of war, Edwin M. Stanton, who apparently spoke favorably to Lincoln about a general's commission for

---

268 "The genesis of the 74th Pennsylvania Volunteer Infantry Regiment," http://www.olypen.com.

269 *Ibid.*

Schimmelfennig. Many observers noted that this was done just as much to keep the German troops happy as it was done out of the necessity for another general.[270]

Schimmelfennig made one further contribution of note to the Union war effort, during the Battle of Gettysburg. If Schimmelfennig is not remembered for his heroic war record, he has not gone unnoticed by "Civil War" enthusiasts. It was reported that during the early stages of the Battle of Gettysburg, Schimmelfennig was cut off from his command and found himself behind enemy lines. To prevent capture, Schimmelfennig hid in a ditch under the cover of a makeshift culvert until the Confederates retreated from the town. Having to hide in a ditch during the most pivotal battle of the war no doubt wounded his Prussian military pride.[271]

One rather unique family group of Forty-Eighters were the Salomon brothers. Four brothers, Frederick C. Salomon, Charles E. Salomon, Edward Salomon, and Herman Salmon, all served in or commanded German-American Union units during the War. During the war, Frederick Salomon, commanding a Wisconsin Volunteer German-American regiment, rose to the rank of brevet major general by the end of the war. Charles Salomon, like his brother, commanded a Wisconsin Volunteer regiment, and by the end of the war rose to the rank of brevet brigadier general. Edward Salomon never entered the military but was elected lieutenant governor of Wisconsin in 1861. While inspecting Wisconsin troops on the Tennessee River in 1862, Governor Louis P. Harvey of Wisconsin drowned; therefore, Edward Salomon succeeded him in April of that year and completed the remainder of his term until 1864. Herman Salomon was the fourth brother of this family to enlist in the Union Army. He was born in 1834, and so was a little too young to have fought in any of the socialist revolts in Europe. He came to the United States with his brothers and settled in Missouri along with many other Germans, settling in or around

---

270   William L. Burton, 100.

271   J. Slade and J. Alexander, *Firestorm at Gettysburg* (Schiffer Publishing Ltd., Atglen, PA: 1998) 88.

St. Louis. He did serve in a Missouri Volunteer Engineer Regiment. As with many so-called Missouri Union units, it was composed of newly arrived German recruits. Unlike his older brothers, he only rose to the rank of sergeant. All the Salomon brothers were born in Prussia and took part in one or more socialist revolts with the exception of Herman Salomon, the youngest.

Wisconsin seems to have been a haven for German Forty-Eighters who rose to command Wisconsin units: Ninth Wisconsin, Colonel Friedrich Salomon; Thirty-fourth Wisconsin, Colonel Fritz Anneke; and the Twenty-seventh Wisconsin, Colonel Konrad Krez. (Charles Salomon commanded the 5th Missouri Infantry, and later succeeded his brother Friedrich as colonel of the Ninth Wisconsin.) All of the previously mentioned regiments were volunteer infantry, not conscripts.[272]

Fritz Anneke (or Annecke, as it is sometimes spelled) was yet another Forty-Eighter well known for his politically leftward tilt. Anneke was a member of the Communist League and a veteran of the Baden revolt. Operating as a team, he and his wife, Mathilde Franziska Anneke, were European communists. As a Prussian officer Fritz was proficient as an artillery officer and as a socialist ideologue.[273] Anneke's education and training as an officer in the Prussian artillery soon collided with his ardent faith in communism. As a result of his communist connections and his willingness to advocate communist ideas, his commission in the Prussian Army was revoked, and he was condemned to a short period of confinement in jail.[274] He was later tried and condemned to death "*in contumaciam*" for his role in leading the Baden rebellion. It is of some interest to note that during this time Carl Schurz was one of Anneke's adjutants.[275]

---

272 Andrea Mehrlander, "A Review of Michael Zimmer's Diary," http:www.h-net.org.

273 http://cscwww.cats.ohiou.edu.

274 http://www.pinn.net.

275 http://www.rootsweb.com.

The Annekes moved to Milwaukee in 1849, where they lectured on the revolution and German literature. In 1852, the pair moved from Wisconsin to New Jersey. Later, he returned to Europe as a correspondent for several American newspapers. Mathilde joined him there in 1860. Anneke and his wife were both strong abolitionists and when the war broke out in America, Anneke returned to give his communist support to the Union. Modern historians push a false narrative that communists like Anneke rushed back to America to fight for freedom for the enslaved African American. We have over two hundred years of communist rule to judge what type of "freedom" exists under communist rule.

Mathilde Anneke could be recognized as one of America's original radical feminists. During the formative years of her life, she was a strong Roman Catholic. With her marriage to Fritz Anneke in 1847, with his communist views, and with the death of her father that same year, she lost her attachment to Catholicism and metamorphosed into a radical freethinker. To put it more bluntly, she apostatized from her faith, rejecting what she had been taught as true, exchanging it for the lie of communism. Her husband played a leading role in her descent from truth into socialism. Her husband introduced Mathilde to Karl Marx and other leading men of the revolution. During the revolution in Germany, she was often seen alongside her husband in the midst of many hard-fought battles.[276]

With the help of Cecilia Kapp, the cousin of Forty-Eighter Friedrich Kapp, in 1865 Mathilde opened what has been described as a progressive girls' school in Milwaukee. Doing much of the teaching herself, she managed to keep the school operating for several years. Both in her work and in promoting her socialist ideology, she was far from lazy. While attacking the capitalist system, she maintained her business and preached the glories of socialism at the same time.

---

276   http:www.pinn.net.

Like many other Forty-Eighters, Mathilde Anneke never lost her zeal for socialism. After coming to the United States, she never ceased expounding the virtues of the 1848 revolutions in Europe. An incessant social reformer, or better yet a malignant social reformer, Mathilde sought out all areas in American life that were out of keeping with her socialist worldview. Mrs. Anneke was right at home in the nineteenth-century feminist movement in this country. Most of the leading lights of that movement were apostates from various Christian denominations, and her adherence to the doctrines of freethinking would qualify her to fit right into that niche.

As previously mentioned, Mathilde Anneke's progressive school in Milwaukee was opened with the assistance of Cecilia Kapp, a cousin of Forty-Eighter <u>Friedrich Kapp</u>. Cecilia's cousin, Friedrich, was a Forty-Eighter with a bent toward writing. He earned a law degree at the University of Berlin. However, when the '48 revolution broke out, he was engaged as a newspaper correspondent. Not satisfied with reporting the events of the revolution, within a year, he traded the power of the pen for the power of the gun and was manning the barricades. Exiled to Switzerland when the revolution was crushed, he, along with most of his comrades, sought refuge in America, arriving in the United States in 1850 with two dollars in his pocket. Although he got back into the practice of law again, he still had some printer's ink in his veins as well as a love for socialist politics. Within a year of establishing residence in New York, Kapp was writing for several newspapers and journals. As editor of the *New Yorker-Abendzeitung,* he became a propaganda agent for the new Republican Party and was largely responsible for swinging the German-American vote to the Republican Party and Abraham Lincoln.[277] It should come as no surprise then that Kapp, along with the other Forty-Eighters, was a presidential elector for Lincoln in 1860. This is just one more piece of evidence of the radical socialists' love for the Republican Party. No matter how it is viewed, Abraham Lincoln had the Forty-Eighters in his corner.

---

277 William L. Burton, 7, 8.

In a meeting in Union Square in New York in April of 1861, Kapp was among the speakers. Like a true centralizer, Kapp argued in his speech that liberty was "indivisible," both Karl Marx and Fredrick Engels held this view, after all this was the first point they demanded in 'The Demands of the Communists Party of Germany.' Also, as noted in Chapter 4, this view of "one nation indivisible" was a goal of the Nazi Party in Germany. In his New York speech, Kapp, a communist, warned Americans of the danger of disunion which he proclaimed to be a curse to the people of Germany. Without any thought given to the constitutional arguments for the right of secession, as demonstrated by William Rawle in his 1825 textbook on the Constitution, these radical European socialists promoted the idea of unremitting war upon the South. Kapp expounded to his American audience that in the pending war against the South, they were "fighting the same battle in which the European nations are engaged.... The conflict on the eve of decision in the United States is neither more nor less that one of the manifold phases of the struggle between aristocracy and democracy."[278] It appears that for Kapp and other Forty-Eighters, the conflict during the War for Southern Independence was yet one more phase of the world socialist revolution. The "aristocracy" Kapp and the other revolutionaries opposed was anyone, anywhere who stood in opposition to their brand of "democracy." Their brand of democracy consisted of an all-powerful, one nation indivisible Federal government. To them America could not be divided because in division there was also a division of governmental powers, and the Forty-Eighters, true to their socialist roots, were centralizers. They wanted all power at the center where it was all the easier for them and their friends to grab power in the name of "freedom and democracy." Kapp claimed that he didn't want "the miseries of Europe" to be reproduced here, and yet that was exactly what he and his revolutionary cohorts from Germany and other countries helped to produce. They brought their socialist revolution, which failed in Europe, to America and sought to replicate it here.

---

278   Levine, 256.

By 1854 Kapp established his home in Chicago. He became active in local and state politics as well as in writing for the *Staatszeitung*. As a radical abolitionist, he showered John Brown with praise and after Brown's death wrote a poem eulogizing Brown. Kapp remained active in politics as a Radical Republican and helped to swing the Chicago German vote for the Republican Party and Abraham Lincoln.[279] As a point of clarification, it must be stressed once again that condemning radical abolitionists does not indicate a dislike for all Americans struggling for the elimination of slavery. There is a great difference between the radical bomb-throwing, saber-thrusting, murdering fanatics of the Radical Abolitionist Party and men such as George Washington, Patrick Henry, and Robert E. Lee (just to name a few) who sought a peaceful means of eliminating the institution of slavery. Opposing radical abolitionists is not equivalent to defending slavery, regardless of what neo-Marxist proclaim.

Karl Heinzen was a German journalist who often had problems with other Germans in the Union Army. When fellow German and Forty-Eighter, General Louis Blenker, was attacked and demands for his resignation were floating around in Washington, Heinzen wasted little time joining the mob demanding Blenker's resignation. Nevertheless, he was most defensive of the actions of the German-American troops when they were roundly criticized after the defeat at Chancellorsville. The idea that American troops might be superior to German troops was a slap in the face to Heinzen and his belief in German cultural superiority.[280] William L. Burton, in his book *Melting Pot Soldiers,* noted that, by the end of the war, Heinzen complained about mass immigration to this country. Of particular concern to Heinzen was the influx of Irish Catholics. So here we have a radical from Germany basically telling German immigrants that they should not seek to assimilate into American culture, which he found of less worth than German culture. Did he somehow expect that all Americans would suddenly awaken

---

279   William L. Burton, 8.

280   *Ibid.*, 207.

one day, realize how debased their culture was in the face of the "superior" German culture with which they were confronted, and from then on seek to emulate German culture?

Most biographers of Heinzen described him in rather mild terms. William L. Burton called him "a Forty-Eighter journalist," and Bruce Levine referred to Heinzen as a "radical activist."[281] While these statements are true as far as they go, they do not begin to plumb the depths of the real Karl Heinzen. Before he came to America to lend his support to Abraham Lincoln and the Union cause, Karl Heinzen, while yet in Germany, openly espoused the cause and goals of terrorism. Heinzen was described as a radical freethinker desiring to revive the tenets of a European anarchist Gracchus Babeuf. It was Babeuf who stated, "All means are legitimate in the fight against tyrants." Babeuf wrote an article in which he advocated using murder to promote what he called "democracy." Not to be outdone, Heinzen declared, "If you have to blow up half a continent and cause a bloodbath to destroy the party of barbarism, you should have no scruples of conscience. Anyone who would not joyously sacrifice his life for the satisfaction of exterminating a million barbarians is not a true republican."[282] Like Osama bin Laden and unscrupulous modern-day BLM and Antifa fanatics, Karl Heinzen saw glory and not evil in the murder of innocent people if it furthered the goals of communism because it was a "just cause." This is the same mind-set that drove two giant jets into the Twin Towers on 9-11; likewise, it was the same rationale embraced by radical abolitionists across the North while bemoaning the hanging of the terrorist John Brown. Heinzen justified the murder of "the barbarians" as long as it advanced the goal of social justice—displaying the old socialist truism of "the ends justifying the means."[283] It appears that Heinzen placed the fault for the failure of the socialist revolts in 1848 and 1849 at the feet

---

281 Levine, 84.

282 Karl Heinzen, as cited in, "Suicidal Terrorism," http.faculty.newc.edu/toconnor

283 Martin Miller and Ylana Miller, "Terrorism: The historical context and the present crisis," http://www.duke.edu/web/formums.

of those revolutionists unwilling to embrace the brutal necessity of the hour. In other words, had they been more barbaric in their attempts to destroy "the barbarians" in European governments, they might have succeeded! As already pointed out, this radical German socialist embraced the same solution to his problems as did the American terrorist John Brown; that is, just exterminate enough of one's adversaries, and the rest will cave into one's demands out of abject fear. Here is a man who, had he not been so intransigent, would really have found his niche somewhere in the Union Army—an army that had no problem treating Southerners as "barbarians."

In Heinzen we find another example of the mind-set of the freethinkers. With their aversion to anything religious and especially anything that smacks of Christianity, freethinkers are left with no sure anchor for their sense of right and wrong. This aversion to Christianity and its belief in absolute right and wrong is probably one reason that Heinzen had such an aversion to Irish Catholics. It is doubtful that his feelings toward pious German Lutherans would have differed much. The bevy of freethinkers would include but not be limited to Karl Heinzen, Franz Sigel, and Frederick Hassaurek. These men are mentioned as leaders in the "freethinking" movement. The result of such "free thought," that is, free of biblical direction and restraint, is obvious to the competent observer.[284]

Adolph Douai, with whom Karl Heinzen had major disagreements for much of his life, was another "freethinking" Forty-Eighter. Over the years he has been remembered as a leading American (though born in Germany) socialist. In 1883 Douai delivered a eulogy for Karl Marx at Cooper Union Hall in New York. His freethinking proclivities led him to author somewhat of a "people's catechism" in which he included a freethinker's parody on the Lord's Prayer. That, plus other activities, netted him an eight-month prison sentence in 1848. An ardent abolitionist

---

284   Carl Wittke, *Refugees of Revolution—The German Forty-Eighters in America* (Greenwood Press Publishers, Westport, CT: 1952) 128.

when he arrived in the United States, he went to of all places, Texas. He spent a little time in New Braunfels but eventually made his way to San Antonio where he began to edit a German-language newspaper, the *San Antonio Zeitung*, the first issue of which was published in 1853. Douai's political approach was truly revolutionary for Texas. He stated that West Texas ought to be a slave-free state. His sentiments did not endear him to most Texans, and he slept in his office at night, keeping a gun handy. At some point as an editor, he encountered Frederick Law Olmstead, the chief architect and superintendent of Central Park in New York City. Olmstead helped Douai to relocate to Boston, where the climate was much more conducive to his abolitionist and radical socialist tendencies. While in Boston he opened a kindergarten. This endeavor lasted only about a year, and then his freethinking attitudes eroded whatever support he had. Boston's Unitarians may have jettisoned the Holy Trinity, savaged Reformed Christian theology, and sought to make God conform to their own rationalist concepts, but apparently, they were not quite ready to completely deny God's existence. Moving to New York, Douai became the editor of yet another paper. During this time, he also served as the director of Hoboken Academy, a bilingual school. *His eulogy of Karl Marx in 1883 clearly demonstrated Comrade Douai's Marxist proclivities.*

In 1857 a group of Germans, disenchanted with American-style freedom, formed the New York Communist Club. This first ever Marxist club in America was established by many close friends of Karl Marx and Fredrick Engels. Men such as Joseph Weydemeyer, Abraham Jacobi, Fritz Jacobi, Adolphus Cluss, Fritz Anneke, August Willich, and F. A. Sorge were prominent communists, many of whom would take leading roles in Republican politics and were destined to have a positive impact for the cause of Marxism in the United States.[285] The Communist Club's main objective was the pursuit of what it called "nationalizing the means of production." The members of the Communist Club pledged themselves to

---

285   Levine, 100.

abolish private property, whether inherited, received for work rendered, or as interest on investment. Only by this means, so they contended, could there be any reasonable peace between people and true freedom (yes, communist freedom—somewhat of an oxymoron) for all. In other words, the communists, by seizing all private property and claiming its ownership in the name of "the people," would thereby create heaven on earth for everyone. Somehow, in all the communist dictatorships one reads about for some elusive reason, it never seems to work out that way. Whether communist or socialist, any program for the abolition of private property and/or redistribution of wealth has been nothing more than a quest for power, pure and simple. Regardless of the window dressing socialists employ to make their theories sound compassionate, despite their supposed "concern for the plight of the workers" and all the rest of the Marxist propaganda, what these people really want and seek is power. To them, centralization of all governmental into a "one nation indivisible" is the road to power and control. And so, with this mind-set, is it any wonder that Joseph Weydemeyer *et al* were "ardent supporters of Lincoln"? After all, all that big government advocates desire is to control the power of "one nation indivisible."

Fredrick Engels wrote to Weydemeyer in November 1864, regarding the war and informs the world what Marxists were seeking. Engels referred to the conflict as a "stupendous" war, as if he were somehow just delighted at the ongoing carnage of war in America. Engels informs Weydemeyer how he felt about the ongoing war to prevent Southern independence when he proclaims the war to be, "A people's war of this kind, on both sides, has not taken place since great states have been in existence, and it will, at all events, *point the direction for the future of the whole of America for hundreds of years to come*"[286][emphasis added]. Engels sounded almost like a prophet. What he wrote in this letter has come to pass. The direction the founding fathers set this nation upon was reversed 180 degrees. Thanks to "Mr. Lincoln's war,"

---

286 Engels, *Ibid.*

this nation is politically moving in a totally different direction than intended by the founding fathers. No wonder Engels labeled the war "stupendous." But he continued: "Once slavery, the greatest shackle on the political and social development of the United States, has been broken, the country is bound to receive an impetus from which it will acquire a differed position in world history within the shortest possible time and a use will soon be found for the army and navy with which the war is providing it."[287] An eye-opening comment. One almost wonders if Engels had some inkling of what the new, centralized United States was supposed to do with its military resources in the future. Contrast the prophecy of Engels to the warning of General Lee. When asked what was going to happen to the United States after the defeat of the South, Lee warned that America would become "aggressive abroad and despotic at home."[288] Interestingly, Engels was forced to admit that Robert E. Lee was a better general than any the North could field and even European leaders could learn from him. He noted U. S. Grant's tremendous loss of men around Richmond, as Lee's superior strategy and thin gray lines continued to hold him at bay. He did note, however, that in the end, all strategy would be superfluous, as Grant had so many men, he could feed into the meat grinder that superior strategy on Lee's part would make no difference. He also observed that "the army now commanded by Sherman is the best you have."[289] What a tribute to Sherman's corps of arsonists! Weydemeyer died of cholera in 1866 before he could do even more damage to America.

Lest we blame the Germans for all the 1848 socialist revolutionary activities in Europe, we shall summarize a representative sample of non-German Forty-Eighters.

---

287   Fredrick Engels, *Letters to Americans 1844-1895* (International Publishers Co., Inc., New York: 1953) 63, 67.

288   Robert E. Lee in letter to Lord Acton, www.oll.libertyfund.org/titles/acton-selections-from-the-correspondence-of-the-first-lord-acton-vol-1 #1f1480_head_058 (accessed 09/18/2018).

289   Engels, 67.

Although the most notable and numerous Forty-Eighters were German, they were by no means the only radical European socialists to seek refuge in America. The following is a short summary of non-German radicals who found a home in the United States and the Republican Party. As already noted, a more detailed list of radical socialists, communists, and Marxists is provided in Addendum II.

NON-GERMAN FORTY-EIGHTERS ASSISTING IN LINCOLN'S AGGRESSIVE WAR POLICY.

Major General Julius Stahel's career as a soldier and a revolutionary began in Hungary. Stahel was born in Szeged, Hungary, about 120 miles southeast of Budapest, Hungary. After his education, Stahel entered the Hungarian Army and rose to the rank of Lieutenant. He left the service in 1848 to join the ongoing revolt against the government of Hungary. With the collapse of the revolt, Stahel fled Hungary, reaching New York in 1859, he began working for a German language newspaper. Becoming well known among the German readership, at the outbreak of the War for Southern Independence, he and Lewis Blinker were successful in raising volunteers for the Eighth New York Volunteer Infantry. The 8th NY Vol. Infantry, was said to be the first German-American regiment in the United States Army and was dubbed, "The First German Rifles." This unit served under General John C. Freemont, the darling of the Forty-Eighters. Like so many other Forty-Eighters, after the war, Stahel served in the diplomatic corps. From 1866-68 and again in 1877-84, Stahel served in the U. S. Diplomatic Corps in Japan and in China from 1884 to 1885.

August Bondi, a Forty-Eighter from Austria was born in Vienna in 1833. At the age of 15, in March of 1848, Bondi joined the Academic Student Legion, a group that supported a well-known Hungarian revolutionary, Louis Kossuth. During this time frame, various types of socialist and quasi-democratic or liberal, revolutions broke out in many European cities, Vienna was no exception. With the failure of the revolt against established order, well known revolutionaries began seeking refuge in

General Julis Stahel

Born and educated in Hungary, Stahel joined the Hungarian Army and rose to the rank of lieutenant. Upon the out-break of the Hungarian Revolution in 1848, Stahel left the Hungarian Army and joined the socialist revolutionary army. With the defeat of the revolution, Stahel escaped first to Prussia, then England, and in 1859 to the United States. Along with Julius Blenker, Stahel was instrumental in winning the support of German immigrants to the Union cause. (Photograph courtesy Library of Congress.)

other countries. Bondi as well as other students involved in the Academic Student Legion, which supported the revolution, were expelled from school. In order to escape reprisal from the Austrian government, Bondi and his family fled the country, ending up in St. Louis, Missouri. From Missouri, Bondi moved to Kansas, where he eventually met and join the terrorist band led by John Brown. In his autobiography, Bondi wrote that he felt people in Southern Kansas regarded Brown as God's agent of retribution and revenge.[290]

Bondi offers an insight on how he felt about working alongside the terrorist, John Browns: "We were united as a band of brothers by the love and affection toward the man who, with tender words and wise counsel...prepared a handful of young men for the work of laying the foundation of a free Commonwealth."[291] What an interesting description of a group that hauled non slave holders out of their beds during midnight raids and then hacked them to death with swords in front of or near the victims' wives and children. Notice that it was not just slave holders who Brown was willing to murder. If you spoke with a Southern accent, you were guilty and must suffer at the hands of John Brown. With this thought in mind, is it any wonder Southerners lost faith in being treated as equals in the Union?

In C. Vann Woodward's book, *John Brown's Private War,* Woodward points out that Brown's use of the doctrine of the ends justifying the means was his method of mitigating charges of his being a murdering barbarian as he attempted to eliminate Southerners from the Kansas Territory. Woodward also noted that most of Brown's defenders basically overlooked the issue of Brown's

---

290   William L. Burton, 177.

291   August Bondi, as cited in, www.jewishcurrents.org.

terrorist activity. After all, he was pursuing a "just" cause.[292] In his support of his use of violence, that gentle soul, Henry David Thoreau, noted: "The method is nothing; the spirit is all."[293]

It is worth restating, that the idea of the "ends (the elimination of slavery) justifying the means (murder of non-slave holders, men, women, and children) was a significant reason Southerners lost faith with their Northern partner of government and sought safety in secession. Southerners understood that when the Declaration of Independence said people have an unalienable right to "alter or abolish" any government that no longer suits them and establish one more to their liking, they were fully within their Rights as Americans to seek safety in a new government of their own making. The problem was that Southerners were reading the Declaration of Independence while Forty-Eighters were reading 'The Demands of the Communist Party of Germany' which demanded, "one nation indivisible." Lincoln and the Republican Party holding the same view makes one wonder what were they reading?

Alexander Asboth was born in Keszthely, Hungary in 1811. He was trained as an engineer and in military science. When the 1848 Hungarian revolution broke out, Asboth joined the revolutionary army and rose to the rank of captain. Having to flee Europe, Asboth emigrated to the United States in 1851. At the outbreak of the War for Southern Independence, Asboth joined John C. Freemont in Missouri as Freemont's chief of staff and later commissioned as a brigadier general. Before the war ended, Asboth rose to the rank of brevet major general. After the war, he served as United States Ambassador to Argentina and Uruguay.

Fredrick Hassaurek was another Forty-Eighter from Austria. At 16, Hassaurek joined the leftist Student Legion based at the University of Vienna. The revolt was quickly put down and Hassaurek had to find refuge, so he fled to the United States. At

---

292   www.jewishcurrents.org.

293   Henry David Thoreau, as cited in, Rousas J. Rushdoony, *The Nature of the American System* (The Craig Press, Nutley, NJ: 1965) 19.

the age of 17, Hassaurek arrived in the United States as a seasoned revolutionary. As so many revolutionaries do, Hassaurek looked to journalism for a means of support and a means to further his revolutionary goals. He wrote articles for a radical paper detailing his view of what happened in the failed socialist revolt in Austria during 1848. The editor who published Hassaurek's articles was a radical named Emil Klauprecht, who equally detested capitalism and priests.[294] Hassaurek's descent into socialist journalism expanded, and, with the assistance of fellow radicals, he purchased the *Hochwatcher*, a weekly German paper in Cincinnati. Hassaurek's description of the *Hochwatcher* revealed that the paper was an "organ for intellectual and social reform."[295] Hassaurek's blatant anti-religious views and his often caustic attacks upon ministers and priests of all churches often set him at odds with older German-Americans. These older German-Americans were being introduced to many revolutionary ideas that had never been fashionable in Germany prior to the socialist upheavals of 1848. With the assistance of another radical extremist, Karl Obermann, Hassaurek established the "Free Men's Society" of Cincinnati. This was another quasi-freethinker organization that was committed to the promotion of the socialist virtues of humanism, rationalism, and ethical culture. Shorn of all sophistry, it was yet another leftist freethinking (that is, anti-Christian) organization. Using his own words, the "primeval forest of churches" and their attendant doctrines so common in America infuriated Hassaurek. To alleviate his hatred of Christian influence in America, Hassaurek helped to organize one of the first freethinking societies in the country in Cincinnati. Numerous freethinking opponents of orthodox Christian religion, such as Franz Sigel and Karl Heinzen, would soon don the blue coat of the Union Army and assist Abraham Lincoln in his war against the "evil" South—a South by the way that was essentially free of freethinking communists and socialists.

---

294   Morris U. Schappes, *A Documentary History of the Jews in the United States* (The Citadel Press, New York: 1950) 353.

295   Carl Wittke, "Friedrich Hassaurek: Cincinnati's Leading Forty-Eighter," *The Ohio Historical Quarterly*, Vol. 68, No. 1, January 1959, p. 1.

In 1862, when looking at the invaders of the South, Southern theologian James H. Thornwell noted the enemies were, "Atheists, Socialists, Communists, Red Republicans, Jacobins...Christianity and Atheism the combatants."[296]

Rounding out this brief survey of non-German Forty-Eighters, we now look to Prague, Czech Republic. Isidor Bush was born in 1822 near Prague, which at that time was within the fiefdom of Bohemia, now part of the Czech Republic. After his education, Bush began working in a printing establishment and became well acquainted with the publishing business. During one of the many revolts in Europe, Isidor's press was used to print revolutionary papers and handbills. Coming under scrutiny by the authorities, Bush made a hasty retreat to the United States, bringing his revolutionary zeal with him. He arrived in New York in 1849 but soon moved to St. Louis. Bush spent much time making himself known especially among the numerous Germans in and around St. Louis.

In 1861, a convention was called to determine whether Missouri would join the other Southern States and secede from the Union. Bush, as expected of all Forty-Eighters, was opposed to anything other than "one nation indivisible." Therefore, Bush became a vocal opponent of secession. When Fremont took over command of the United States military force in Missouri and made his headquarters in St. Louis, Bush was made his aide-de-camp and given a captaincy.

Early in the war, Fremont was commissioned a major general, and Lincoln appointed him to be commander of the Western Department. Outside of St. Louis, the Union Army was not overly popular in Missouri. The majority of people, even if they were not thrilled about the idea of secession, were quite unsympathetic to the Northern attempt to forcibly coerce Missouri and other Southern states to stay in the Union. When Northern armies, commanded by people associated with radical abolitionists and foreign extremists,

---

296   James Henly Thornwell, as cited in *James Henly Thornwell Collected Writings* (SGCB Classic Reprints, Vestavia Hill: 2002), IV, 405-6.

began to occupy Missouri, many Missourians felt they were being invaded. This was particularly true for the majority of Missourians who had duly elected a Pro-Southern governor. With no appreciable Confederate military to aid them, Missourians took to defending their state and they formed regular troops and partisan groups to resist the Union invasion wherever possible.

Pursuing a policy that would become typical of Lincoln's government, Fremont arrested people speaking in favor of secessionists (no freedom of speech, no First Amendment right), stopped the publication of newspapers suspected of "disloyalty," (exit freedom of the press,) and issued a proclamation declaring Missouri slaves to be free, also declaring the property of those Missourians in "rebellion" to be confiscated, (there goes the Constitutional guarantee of due process.)

This act of confiscating private property of all Southerners without regard for whether the Southerner was a slaveholder or non-slaveholder, speaks volumes as to the real objective of the invasion. Think about it. To save the Union Southerners must be killed, their property, slave or non-slave property, confiscated, and all Constitutional protections destroyed. What kind of Union is this and is this the type of Union Patrick Henry would have supported? Remember Patrick Henry's words, "The first thing I have at heart is American *liberty* the second thing is American union."[297] Obviously, Lincoln's Union is not Patrick Henry's Union.

---

297   Patrick Henry, as cited in, William Wirt Henry, 449.

Chapter 13

THE RED REVOLUTION CONTINUES

AS POINTED OUT IN CHAPTER 9, after the Confederate military was defeated the war against Southern values and culture did not end, and continues to this day. As was the case before the war, Forty-Eighters, i.e., European socialists known as "Red Republicans" and/or "Radical Republicans," were very active in the Republican Party and said activity continued after the war.[298] The activity of the socialists and Marxists continued post-Lincoln in their effort of reconstructing not just the South but all of America. As Carl Wittke noted, "They [Forty-Eighters] hated...what they called the religious superstitions of the American people"[299] [and] "Actually dreamed of an intellectual conquest of the United States."[300]

The "revolution" that Lincoln ushered in as he transformed the original republic of sovereign states into an indivisible empire was only the beginning of the triumph for big government. To complete the revolution after the death of Lincoln, Radical Republicans, led by those influenced by radical socialists and communists, imposed radical Reconstruction upon the South and the nation. As Indiana author and historian Claude G. Bowers noted in his seminal book

---

298   "The Story of Nine Fine Irishmen," http//www.ninefineirishmen.com.

299   Carl Wittke, "The German Forty-Eighter in America: A Centennial Appraisal," *The American Historical Review* 53, no. 4, July 1948, 714-15.

300   *Ibid.*

Senator John Sherman

Brother of General William Sherman, John Sherman was a zealous advocate of strong centralized government. His faith in strong centralized government is demonstrated in his statement, "Nationalize as much as possible [thereby] make men love their country before their states." (Photograph courtesy Library of Congress.)

on Reconstruction, *The Tragic Area: The Revolution after Lincoln,*
"The story of this Revolution is one of desperate enterprises by daring
and unscrupulous men.... The evil that they did lives after them."[301]
Bowers completes his introduction to his book on Reconstruction
noting that, "They [revolutionaries] changed the course of history,
and whether for ultimate good or bad is still on the lap of the gods.
The story carries lessons that are well worth pondering."[302]

In a review of Bowers' book Dr. Carl Van Doren, Board member of
the Junior Guild of the Literary Guild of America, noted that Bowers
explains how "The war itself had disturbed all the old balances and
adjustments. The conservative minority...had been tumbled out of
power and virtually destroyed."[303] Dr. Van Doren explains just how
poisonous this second revolution (Reconstruction) was for those
who held to the traditional Jeffersonian view of these United States.
Van Doren points out that Bowers was "engaged in explaining why
and how this revolution came about."[304] The revolutionary impact
which the nation had passed through is clearly stated in Van Doren's
closing remarks in his review of *The Tragic Era: The Revolution
after Lincoln:* "*The Tragic Era,* while devoted to a single revolution...
is presented with such a knowledge of human life in general that it
becomes in effect a commentary upon any revolution anywhere."[305]
The ear-mark of any communist revolution has always been the
promotion of class warfare. Marxists revolution is especially efficient
at pitting one class or group against another. Class warfare is used
to polarize groups into warring camps which will begin the process
of the destruction of the existing order. Since race relations in the
South were better than in the North, Republicans feared a racially
united South. Therefore, Republicans and radical socialists began a
process of dividing black and white Southerners into warring camps.

---

301   Claude G. Bowers, *The Tragic Era: The Revolution after Lincoln* (The Literary
Guild of America, NY: 1929), vii.

302   *Ibid.*

303   Carl Van Doren, 'Why The Editorial Board Selected "The Tragic Era'" Wings,
(The Literary Guild of America Inc., NY: 1929), Volume 3, Number 9, p. 4.

304   *Ibid,* 5.

305   *Ibid.*

This close and friendly relationship between the races in the South was noted by radical socialist, Yankee General, Carl Schurz. In late 1865 Schurz was sent on a tour of the defeated South to determine the condition of the South and report back to Washington. One of his findings as it relates to the former slaves is of interest. Schurz notes that: "Centuries of slavery have not been sufficient to make them enemies of the white man."[306]This statement does not mean that slaves liked slavery but it does point out that they never hated their white friends and neighbors. This fact became evident to Yankees when during the war and Yankee invasion black Southerners did not rise in a Haiti-style slave revolt—if that had happened, the war would have ended within weeks. Unless disturbed by invading Yankees, most slaves stayed near the only home they knew, side by side with their white friends and neighbors. Even after freedom, many freed slaves stayed on the plantations and farms of their masters and even took their masters' name as their own. Marxist revolution could not take place while such friendly relationships existed, therefore, something had to be done or the revolution would die.

Another big problem facing the Republican Party after the South was forced back into the Union was how to keep a Republican majority in Congress. As long as the South was not being represented in Congress, the Democratic Party was a minority Party. The GOP understood that once the South seated its Democratic Senators and Representatives, Democrats would become a majority party again. Added to the Republican Party's distress was the fact that all citizens of the South would be counted as full citizens, whereas before the war and emancipation each individual of the slave population was counted only as three-fifths of a person when allocating representatives in Congress. After emancipation, all of a sudden, the South gained many more Representatives in Congress—the GOP had to do something and do it fast or be relegated to minority status in Congress.

---

306   Carl Schurz, "Report of Carl Schurz," *A Just and Lasting Peace* (Signet Classics, NY: 2013), 140.

Even men such as Nathan Bedford Forrest spoke of the close relationship which existed between the races in the South and suggested that there was no reason that black and white Southerners should not work together for their common good. Speaking to black voters in Tennessee, Forrest proclaimed: "We were born on the same soil, breathe the same air, live in the same land, and why should we not be brothers and sisters...I want you to do as I do—go to the polls and select the best men to vote for... Although we differ in color, we should not differ in sentiment... do your duty as citizens, and if any are oppressed, I will be your friend." It was in response to this display of goodwill between the races in the South which drove the Republican Party, allied with Marxists and socialists, to begin the process of racial division—a division which now affects all of America.

The Republican Party's policy of racial animosity became so abhorrent that in 1875, Hiram Revels, the first Black United States Senator, resigned from the Republican Party. In a letter to Republican President U. S. Grant Revels declared: "The bitterness and hate created by the late civil strife...would have long since been obliterated in this state, were it not for some unprincipled men who would keep alive the bitterness of the past, and *inculcate a hatred between the races*, in order that they may aggrandize themselves by office, and its emoluments, to control my people, the effect of which is to degrade them[307]" [emphasis added]. Remember Senator Revels' words the next time a neo-con talking head speaks ill of the South while praising the Republican Party as the "friend of the black man."

The revolutionary drive, beyond the actual war and into Reconstruction, was noted by James S. Allen, birth name, Sol Auerbach, (1906-1986) a Marxist historian, journalist, and member of the Communist Party USA. Allen stated, "Reconstruction was the continuation of the Civil War into a new phase, in which the revolution passed from the stage of armed conflict into primarily a political struggle which sought to consolidate the Northern

---

307   Hiram Revels, "Hiram Revels Letter to President Grant," November 6, 1875 as cited in N C Pedia, http://ncpedia.org/revelsletter (accessed 4/20/ 2016).

triumph.[308]" Now compare this twentieth century communist's statement to the words of nineteenth century radical socialist and Republican, Carl Schurz. Remember that it was Schurz who advocated "revolution and national unification."

Noted historian, Dr. Clyde N. Wilson explained that: "The German revolutionaries brought with them an aggressive drive... Their drive was toward 'revolution and national unification.'... The most prominent among them, Carl Schurz, expressed disappointment at the non-ideological nature of American politics and vowed to change that."[309] After the war, American politics were to become "ideological," and Schurz and his socialist friends were on hand to make sure it happened. In modern America, this ideology is on display every time a BLM or Antifa riot takes place or every time big government uses its newfound power—thanks to Lincoln and his Marxists allies—to deny citizens their Constitutional rights or grossly overstep its Constitutional limitations.

As was stated in Chapter 9 and it is well to be restated: Too many good and sincere Americans have imbibed socialist ideas to one degree or another and are not even conscious of that fact. In many public settings, such as public schools and universities, these institutions have become grand promoters of various socialist schemes under the guise of political correctness. At this time, Black Lives Matter and Antifa radicals are acting and promoting every vestige of radical socialism and Marxism that yesterday's Forty-Eighters introduced to the United States. At what point do we say, "Hold, enough!"

---

308 James S. Allen, *Reconstruction: The Battle for Democracy* (International Publisher, NY: 1937), 175-76.

309 Clyde Wilson, "The Republican Charade: Lincoln and His Party." This was speech given at the Abbeville Institute Conference on "Re-Thinking Lincoln," July 7-12, 2005, Franklin, Louisiana, by Dr. Wilson, www.Abbevilleinstitue.org.

Chapter 14

TWENTY-FIRST CENTURY SOCIALIST GOALS

IN THE OPENING CHAPTER of *Reclaiming Liberty,* the author notes, "The twentieth century in America witnessed glorious victories for those who believe in extreme federalism, big government, central control, liberalism, and socialism. Conservatives, on the other hand, can look back with shame at one humiliating defeat after another."[210] As Ron Kennedy makes clear in *Reclaiming Liberty,* the twenty-first century displays a continuation of neo-Marxist, i.e., socialist victories. What was it that Fredrick Engels said was absolutely necessary to "promote proletarian" (communist) revolution? In his own words, Engels noted that "a single indivisible republic" was the essential element for the advancement of communism (see Chapter 3). When we place Engels' words next to the very first demand of the Communist Party of Germany in 1848, i.e., the demand for Germany to be "declared a single and indivisible republic," one should begin to understand why conservatives have experienced one hundred years of failure in fighting the growth of big government. Even after electing Ronald Reagan and Donald Trump as presidents, neo-Marxists appear to be winning.

It cannot be overstated that a <u>strong, *indivisible,* all-powerful</u> <u>big government</u> is the *sine qua non* (something absolutely indispensable or essential) of any socialist, Marxist, or Fascist government. This is

---

210   James R. Kennedy, *Reclaiming Liberty* (Pelican Publishing, Co., Gretna, LA: 2005), 15.

Ronald Reagan

"It is my intention to curb the size and influence of the Federal establishment and to demand recognition of the distinction between the powers granted to the Federal Government and those reserved to the States or to the people. All of us need to be reminded that the Federal Government did not create the States; the States created the Federal Government." Reagan's view of the Federal government is completely opposite from Lincoln's view of the Federal government. (Photograph courtesy Library of Congress.)

the very reason America's Founding Fathers feared big government and gave us a compound republic. That compound republic provided "we the people" of sovereign States the means to judge for ourselves how we were to be governed. This Jeffersonian concept of local control of all government was, and to this day is, anathema, abhorrent, and detestable to all devotees to big government.

Simply put, today's malignant growth of big government did not start with the election of Joe Biden. America's embracing the concept of an all-powerful and indivisible Federal government could not have taken place without the assistance of European Forty-Eighters.

Walter Schmidt, an observer of conditions in Germany during the tumultuous times of the 1848 revolutions noted that the radical's revolutionary intent was to rebuild society. The first object of rebuilding was to establish a socialist model state. While enlisting the aid of many middle-class liberals who desired an open and free society, the radical revolutionaries had their own agenda. The term, "liberal" is used here in its nineteenth century meaning, i.e., one that believes in government ruled by the people with respect for civil liberties—this is 180 degrees removed from the 20th and 21st century usage. In the pursuit of their agenda, radical socialists were more than willing to incorporate the phraseology (language) of liberals, but they never intended to establish a free and open liberal society. In order to have the power to implement the various social reforms desired by the radical socialists, first they needed a strong central government capable of enforcing said changes. For this goal to be accomplished, the many free and sovereign local German state governments had to be reduced and consolidated into one "indivisible" state, using the term Marx and Engels found most pleasing. By using the "democratic" method of government they hoped to unite industrial workers in urban areas with farm workers in the rural areas. In other words, using governmental tax resources, that is, dispensing governmental money and patronage, they hoped to be able to buy enough votes to gain control of the newly established all-powerful, indivisible central government. Having gained control of such a government, they could then institute their radical socialist reforms, or as Schmidt noted, "the civil democratic revolution that should lead to a radical socialist transformation.[211]"

During the 1848 revolt in Germany, the cry of big government advocates was, "All Germany is declared to be a united, indivisible republic."[212] "United" and "indivisible," those words should sound rather familiar to the reader by this time. As Schmidt pointed out, everything from the establishment of national banks to the confiscation *without* compensation of land from landowners, to the takeover of private industries such as mining and transportation was advocated as a means by which "the revolution could be advanced further into a socialist direction."[213] At one time Americans laughed at the idea of the government taking over private industries and businesses. But as the 2020 Covid 19 panic proves, the Federal government can close not only businesses but even churches. Indeed, America has taken a long walk with Marx and Engels down the road of "one nation indivisible" big government!

In a study published in 1964, Zygmund Dobbs pointed out that radical socialists fleeing Germany after the failure of the 1848 revolt reinforced the Marxist variety of socialism in the United States. These radical socialists brought more than just raw Marxism with them. They also brought the philosophies of Georg Wilhelm Friedrich Hegel and Johann Gottlieb Fichte, which laid the foundation for future Marxism. Charles A. Dana, a Fourierist socialist (see Addendum I for info on Fourierists), a close friend of Karl Marx and Fredrick Engels, and future assistant secretary of war in the Lincoln administration, along with socialist newspaper publisher Horace Greeley, helped to reinforce the "radical" wing of the radical abolitionist movement and to further move the Republican Party toward its love for big government. A leader of the radical abolitionists' "radical" wing was Thaddeus Stevens, a

---

211   Walter Schmidt, "Demands of the Communist Party," www.ohiou.edu.

212   *Ibid.*

213   *Ibid.*

powerful Republican congressman. His hatred of the South and the pursuit of militantly revolutionary policies was the keystone in creating the post-war existence of racial bigotry in the South in particular and in America in general. The mantra of the "radical" wing of the abolitionist movement was, "Down with all slavery, both chattel and wages." [214] Let us now once again reflect on the words of the father of modern-day communism, Karl Marx: *"Labor cannot emancipate itself in the white skin where in the black it is branded.*[215]*"* For the radical socialist, the abolitionist movement was never an end but rather a means of promoting the eventuality of the "Proletariat Revolution" in the United States. From promoting the Proletarian Revolution *via* the issue of slavery, modern communists, aka, neo-Marxist, now use race as a dividing issue to promote their revolution. For example, in 2019 the neo-Marxists establishment initiated the 1619 project. The purpose of the 1619 project was "to reframe the country's history." When introduced into school curriculum, parents soon discovered the project did little more than advance hatred for all white people, especially America's Founding Fathers.

The Forty-Eighters came to America with the goal of implementing the socialism that failed at that time in Europe. When the War Between the States started, they almost universally joined the Union armies, and those who did not go and fight rallied behind the Union cause in many other ways, some of them literary and some of them political. Their rallying slogan of "Union, freedom, and democracy" became their watchword. As always, one should remember that terms that sound noble and good to Americans can and usually do have a different meaning to socialists and communists.

For the radical socialists the war presented a grand possibility to put into practice their concept of class struggle—North against South, black against white, etc.

---

214   James S. Allen, *Reconstruction* (International Press, New York: 1937) 24.

215   Karl Marx, as cited in, Marx and Engels, *The Civil War in the United States*, XIV.

As Dr. Clyde Wilson observed: "The Germans brought into the American conflict and into Republican rhetoric a diagnosis of class conflict (crusade to overthrow the 'slave drivers') and a revolutionary elan."[216] These radical socialists were introducing class warfare into American politics and the war itself. The young and impressible Republican Party was also the recipient of this "class warfare" mentality. Not to be outdone, both major modern American political parties have, in one form and at some time, adopted this concept. Dr. Wilson pointed out: "Historians have long noted the influence of German refugees from the revolutions of 1848 in the founding of the Republican Party and in Lincoln's election, but usually without allowing its true weight."[217]

Dr. Wilson also noted that, because of the terror and tyranny of the French Revolution, most thoughtful Americans of the nineteenth century viewed the concept of "all men are created equal" with somewhat of a jaundiced eye. According to the Declaration of Independence, man's rights are a gift from his creator; that is, from God. This stands in direct opposition to the legacy of the French Revolution that advanced the notion that the rights of man were bestowed on him by an omnipotent government. According to Dr. Wilson, the French Revolution had the effect of creating an even more deadly and malignant form of socialism, which led to the 1848 European socialist revolts. As a result of the failure of those revolutions, "the Puritans and Forty-Eighters, along with ruthless economic exploiters, diverted politics out of its accustomed paths in the Midwest and helped elect Abraham Lincoln to the presidency by a 40 percent vote."[218] Not only did they deliver votes for Lincoln but as Engels noted, "Had it not been for the experienced soldiers

---

216 Clyde Wilson, "The Gettysburg Speech: Clyde Wilson on the Gettysburg Fraud," www.LewRockwell.com, November 2003.

217 *Ibid.*

218 Clyde Wilson, as cited in *Chronicles*, June 19, 2005.

who entered America after the European revolution, especially from the Germanies, the organization of the Union army would have taken longer than it did."[219]

The *Communist Manifesto* called for: "A heavy, progressive, graduated income tax."[220] Not to be outdone by their Marxist compatriots, the Lincoln administration gave America the Internal Revenue Service and soon began taxing everything from soup to nuts. Theodore Burton in his book *John Sherman* informed us: "The first comprehensive Internal Revenue Act became a law July 1, 1862."[221] With the fervor of the twenty-first century IRS, the "Civil War" Federal taxman levied taxes upon heretofore untaxed items such as professional licenses for many occupations, luxury items, the distilling industry, and a dividend tax was placed on many financial institutions. This coupled with a direct tax on income made this act the most expensive tax legislation ever to pass Congress since the beginning of the republic. The all-pervasive Federal taxing power and the irrepressible borrowing of funds which will have to be paid back by generations of *unborn* Americans, are signs positive that the big government lust for power now dominates the United States.

Under the enhanced taxation plan of the Republican administration, more Americans than ever in the nation's history were under the watchful eye of the Federal tax agents—a system that has grown in the twenty-first century to include virtually every working citizen. Is it not just a little ironic that a nation that fought its war for independence with Great Britain over the mother country's tax policy would allow Lincoln to introduce more strident tax policies than the King of England ever suggested? But worse still in the complacency of modern Americans whose total earned income from January to May is needed just to pay the

---

219   Engels as cited in, Karl Marx, as cited in, Marx and Engels, *The Civil War in the United States,* 243.

220   Karl Marx, *The Communist Manifesto* (American Opinion Publications, Belmont, MA: 1974) 25.

221   Theodore Burton, *John Sherman* (Chelsea House, New York: 1983) 123.

taxman! What we should learn from this fact is that living under an all-powerful, indivisible, big government, even with so-called taxation *with* representation, is more costly and harmful than it was living under King George's taxman.

With the advent of the new and improved tax measures of the Lincoln administration, every homeowner in the nation was touched either directly or indirectly by the government's tax agent. A nation that once existed on the revenue of a minimal tariff now exploited the resources of every citizen to feed its incessant desire for tax funds. Where were the men of the famed Boston Tea Party? They defied the largest and strongest empire of their day because of a minute tax on tea! Yet Lincoln's administration was foisting upon the descendants of the Americans of 1776 a tax system that was invading areas never occupied by the Federal government as well as being malignant in its very nature. That malignant tax system instituted by Lincoln and the Republican Party has grown to the point of stripping the average American working person of 25 to 50 percent of his income. As many observers of the "Civil War" have noted, the national banking system and tax system instituted by Lincoln and his Republican Party are two measures that have funneled wealth from the common man to special interest groups in and around the centers of government and finance. These measures have endured and enlarged from that time to the present and for all this the American public can thank Abraham Lincoln.[222] It almost seems as if the Lincoln administration took Marx's ideas on taxation and expanded them as far as they could be taken. No wonder Marx was in such a heat to see Lincoln reelected in 1864.

Marx's program, as outlined in his manifesto, also called for: "Abolition of property in land and application of all rents of land to public purposes." Marx wrote: "The Communist revolution is the most radical rupture with traditional property relations; no wonder that its development involves the most radical rupture with traditional ideas.... The proletariat will use its political supremacy to wrest, by degrees, all capital from the bourgeoisie;

---

222   Theodore Burton, 125.

to centralize all instruments of production in the hands of the State.... Of course, in the beginning this cannot be effected except by means of despotic inroads on the rights of property."[223]

The goals of the Radical Reconstruction faction neatly dovetailed with those of Marx. Many have noted that the goals of the radicals included: "Mandatory property taxes, determined by and payable to the government, else the taxpaying 'owner's' property is confiscated."[224] The iniquitous property tax is with us yet today, meaning that you do not own your property but are simply leasing it from the government. Don't pay your lease payment and see who owns "your" property! The enacting of the property tax has in effect done away with private property. You may well have a deed that says you are the owner of your property. You may even have a statement from the bank to the effect that your mortgage has been paid. But neglect to pay your property taxes for a couple of years, and you will find out who really owns the property. It is not you; it is the taxing body, the government, that can take it away from you should you fail to pay your yearly "rent" for your use of their land. The concept of the property tax is ultimately the idea that the state really owns all property and that you have the use of it only if you continue to pay your yearly fee for its use. Fail to do so, and the real owner will soon claim "your" property, and you will be forced to move on, only to repeat the same scenario somewhere else unless you choose to rent instead of buy. This is not what the founding fathers had in mind when they declared themselves to be free citizens. Without the right to ultimately own, unencumbered, your property, you are only as free as a medieval serf on his lord's estate—and yet Americans still proudly proclaim that they live in "the land of the free!"

At this time, many readers will protest that property taxes are usually enacted by state and county governments and not the Federal "big government." What most Americans, North or South, fail to realize is that with the defeat of REAL States' Rights, every

---

223   Marx, *The Communist Manifesto*, 24.

224   Dwyer, 609.

state government has become nothing more than an appendage of the supreme one nation indivisible Federal government. States do not possess "Rights," they only are allowed to exercise those "privileges" that Washington, D.C. thinks is appropriate. Even the constitutions of the Southern States are not legal if one judges legality upon the basis of the "consent of the governed." Remember, according to the Declaration of Independence, the only LEGITIMATE government is the one based upon the "*consent* of the governed." Did the citizens of the defeated and occupied Confederate States of America freely consent to the new state government absent any coercion? Even Northern State constitutions, post Appomattox, do not qualify as documents based upon the consent of the governed. If the citizens of the State of Wisconsin desires to remove themselves from the rule of Washington via secession, are they free to do so? The answer is NO! Troops would be dispatched to force the state back in line— so much for government by the consent of the governed. Always remember the truism, "If you can't leave, you are not free."

How can this abnormality in how we are governed be corrected? There are only two ways. Amend the Constitution to force the Federal government to recognize the inherent right of "we the people" to govern ourselves, via, nullification and/or secession, or armed conflict with the hope of a military victory over the government in Washington. Hopefully no one will ever think that the second choice is desirable. While discussing the danger of a consolidated big government as opposed to a limited small government Confederate States Vice President, Alexander Stephens, noted that with the malignant growth of government in a consolidated indivisible government, Americans will begin to understand why the South resisted Lincoln's invasion and hopefully at that time all Americans will understand that "The Cause of the South is the Cause of all!"[225]

---

225 Alexander Stephens, *A Constitutional View of the War Between the States* (1870, Sprinkle Publications, Harrisonburg, VA: 1994), II, 666.

Chapter 15

EVANGELICALS MARCHING WITH MARX

I would not have you exchange the gold of individual
Christianity for the base metal of Christian
Socialism.[311]

FOR MOST PEOPLE SOCIALISM is viewed as a political institution
that promotes a system of state-sponsored welfare. Yet, as Charles
Spurgeon points out, socialism attempted to make inroads into
Christianity as well. Spurgeon, a well-known Baptist minister,
began his attack upon Christian socialism in the last quarter of
the nineteenth century. Spurgeon viewed the concept of Christian
socialism as a form of heresy if not an outright attack upon the
Gospel. Not only were Christian socialists questioning the very
foundation of the Gospel, they were systematically substituting
the goals of socialism for the fundamentals of Christianity. The
socialists' gospel had little to do with the conversion of sinners
but everything to do with "socialist improvement" of humanity.
Thus, we see Spurgeon's warning about exchanging the "gold of
individual Christianity" for the "base metal of Christian Socialism."
Spurgeon's warning to nineteenth-century Christians is applicable
to Christians of the twenty-first century.

---

311   Charles Spurgeon, as cited in, Joel McDurmon, "Spurgeon On Socialism,"
www.americanvision.org/article/spurgeon-on-socialism/, accessed March 6, 2009.

Charles Spurgeon

Without a doubt, Spurgeon was one of the best-known Baptist evangelists of the nineteenth century. In no uncertain words, Spurgeon warned his fellow countrymen about the dangers from the neo-pagan philosophy of freethinking and its political ally, socialism. The danger of "Christian Socialism" that Robert L. Dabney and James H. Thornwell warned America about, Spurgeon fought against in Great Britain. (Photograph courtesy of Betty C. Kennedy.)

In an article posted on American Vision's Web site titled "Spurgeon On Socialism," Joel McDurmon notes that when faced with the rise of Christian socialism in the latter part of the nineteenth century, "Spurgeon sniffed out the godless, anti-biblical scheme and preached against it from his pulpit."[312] As the reader will recall, the leading element in the injection of freethinking, socialist, and communist theories into the United States were German emigrants. Note how Spurgeon identified this element as the advance guard of Christian socialism: "German rationalism which has ripened into Socialism may yet pollute the mass of mankind and lead them to overturn the foundations of society. Then 'advanced principles will hold carnival, and *free thought* [emphasis added] will riot with the vice and blood which were years ago the insignia of 'the age of reason.' I say not that it will be so, but I should not wonder if it came to pass, for deadly principles are abroad and certain ministers are spreading them."[313] Unlike Christian socialists, Spurgeon, with his biblical worldview, understood that man by his actions could not create a utopian world. Yet, this is exactly what Christian socialism was attempting to do; that is, create a world free of all negative elements such as poor housing, poor job opportunity, poor health care, and poor education. All this was to be done by the application of man's efforts. As Spurgeon points out, these radical socialists were attempting to "regenerate the world by Democratic Socialism, and set up a kingdom of Christ without the new birth or the pardon of sin."[314] Spurgeon warned the people of Britain about the danger of following the Pied Piper's tune into the dangerous waters of socialism. "Great schemes of socialism have been tried and found wanting; let us look to regeneration by the Son of God, and we shall not look in vain."[315]

---

312   McDurmon. "Spurgeon On Socialism."

313   Charles Spurgeon, quoted in, *Ibid.*

314   *Ibid.*

315   *Ibid.*

Fredrick Engels was once asked what person in his lifetime he hated most. Engels, the communist, the atheist, and the friend of Karl Marx, answered the question with one word— Spurgeon![316] Unfortunately the warnings of Spurgeon have gone unheeded not only by many average Christians but also by many Christian ministers. If people are known by the company they keep, then surely Christians would not want to be found in the company of and agreeing with the enemies of the faith. Yet, in today's politically correct (p.c.) world, it is not uncommon to find evangelical Christians standing beside Karl Marx and Fredrick Engels. Evangelical ministers are often heard parroting the very words of Marx and Engels as they kowtow to the gods of political correctness. Look at how many evangelical ministers react to the issue of Southern history. From the display of the Confederate flag, to the display of respect for Confederate heroes, to the treatment of the issue of slavery, many ministers will embrace *and* promote the very teachings of Marx and Engels. Is it possible for darkness and light to have communion? Surely not! For when darkness and light attempt to commune, one will overtake the other and have dominion over its nemesis.

As pointed out in Chapters 2 and 3, Marx promoted a particular view of the South during the War for Southern Independence. Fundamentally, Marx taught that the South was fighting to promote and extend slavery, the Confederate Constitution promoted slavery as a "good thing," and the Confederacy was more or less a despotic nation. Engels, the co-founder of modern-day communism and great friend of Marx, also believed that the destruction of States' Rights was needed to promote the cause of international communism.

Late in 2008, a well-known evangelical activist, David Barton of Wall Builders fame, wrote an article critical of anyone who rejects the idea that the so-called Civil War was fought for any other reason than ending slavery. His article was titled "Confronting Civil War

---

316   David Aikman, *The Delusion of Disbelief* (Salt River Publishers, Carol Stream, IL: 2008) 106.

Revisionism: Why the South Went To War." Although I am sure it was not the intention of Mr. Barton to sound like a sycophant of Marx, his attack upon the South runs down the same pathway as the one laid down by Marx.

It should be obvious that, using selective phrases and parsing of ideas and concepts one can prove anything about the Confederacy or even the Northern victors. For example, if one spent an inordinate amount of time studying the efforts of radical socialists and communists who were officers in the Union Army, it would be easy to "prove" that the Union Army was doing the bidding of Karl Marx. After all, General Joseph Weydemeyer was a dear friend and fellow member of the London Communist Club with Marx and Engels; General August Willich was known as the "Reddest of the Red;" and both these men and hundreds of other radical socialists and communists volunteered to help Lincoln save the Union—or were they trying to free the slaves? Here, we see a glaring problem the advocates of "the war was over slavery" must endure. If the war was being fought to end slavery, then why did Lincoln and the Republican-dominated Congress state that slavery would be safe if only the seceding states would return to the Union?[317] Why did Lincoln proclaim to Horace Greeley, a radical abolitionist, that "[m]y paramount objective in this struggle is to save the Union, and is *not* either to save or destroy slavery."[318] Cherry-picking of words and ideas is no substitute for a thorough examination of all the facts of an issue.

Since the age of political correctness, it has become fashionable for historians and political pundits to embrace the mantra of "slavery" as the cause of Southern secession. Such a narrow-minded and myopic view of history is guaranteed to lead to false conclusions about the past and political missteps in the present. The individual who looks at slavery as the sole cause of the War Between the

---

317   In 1861 both Houses of Congress passed a resolution assuring the safety of slave property, see: The Crittenden Resolution as passed by the United States House of Representatives, July 22, 1861; also see, The Johnson Resolution, United States Senate, July 25, 1861.

318   Abraham Lincoln, as cited in, Roy P. Basler, ed., *The Collected Works of Abraham Lincoln* (Rutgers University Press: New Brunswick, NJ) V, 388.

States is like a person lost in a forest who becomes so fixated upon one very large tree that he cannot see the forest. Refusing to see the forest, he is condemning himself to being eternally lost. This is an apt description of p.c. historians and commentators who see slavery as the only cause of Southern secession. Is this one-size-fits-all narrow-minded concept of slavery as the cause of the War for Southern Independence justifiable? Furthermore, is the telling of Southern history from the traditional viewpoint of the South "Civil War Revisionism?"

Any competent elementary school teacher can verify that for every fight at school, there are two sides of the story. Unfortunately for the South, the old truism that to the victor goes the spoils still holds true when looking into the facts of the so-called Civil War. As Machiavelli points out in *The Prince and the Discourses,* one thing a new ruler of a conquered people must do is shape public opinion to ensure the safe and peaceful occupation of a newly acquired territory.[319] When defending the Southern view of the War for Southern Independence, the Confederate States of America have no one to tell its side of the story. Americans who insist upon looking fairly at *both* sides of the story about the war should not be besmirched with the label of "revisionists." Is a revisionist one who defends the traditional Southern view of the war, or is someone a revisionist if he defends the Marxist view of the war? Looking fairly at *both* sides of an issue does not make one a revisionist.

Surely any opened-minded individual can understand that to have a complete understanding of this war, *both* the view from the North and the view from the South are necessary. Not only should both views of the war be studied, but it should be understood that within each view, the Northern view and the Southern view, there is no *one* view of why the war was fought. A radical abolitionist in the North may not have fought for the same reasons as his fellow Northerners. Likewise, a fire-eater from the South may have fought for a completely different reason than his fellow Southern countrymen. A Northern Democrat

---

319 Niccolo Machiavelli, *The Prince and the Discourses* (Random House, Inc., New York: 1950) 18, 182-83.

may have fought for the honor of his country and the Union, while opposing Lincoln's policies. A Southern Whig may have opposed secession as a threat to his large land and slaveholdings, but after secession, he may have supported the Southern position because of his fear of what would happen to *all* his property if the South lost the war. A Southern Democrat may have been a member of one of the many Southern abolition societies but may have favored secession because he feared that the Republican Party would pass laws that would have benefited Northerners at his expense. If a person looks only myopically at what is said and done by radical abolitionists or fire-eaters, he will never completely understand what happened during those turbulent years, 1860-65.

Any serious student of this conflict should remember one fact: there is a long history of sectional conflict between the North and the South. Furthermore, note that most of these conflicts had little or nothing to do with slavery. Ignoring this history of the war and focusing solely on slavery as the cause of the war marks one as intellectually dishonest. But more important to our present condition as a nation, by focusing upon slavery, the bona fide story of the death of *real* States' Rights and the beginning of Imperial America is overlooked.

As Robert E. Lee pointed out, with the consolidation of those powers which once belonged to the sovereign states into an all-powerful and supreme Federal government, America became "aggressive abroad and despotic at home."[320] Evangelical Christians who bemoan the inability of "we the people" to put an end to abortion on demand, the removal of Christian symbols such as crosses and the Ten Commandments from public display, or the advancement of the homosexual agenda by the Federal government, should understand that at one time (before Appomattox) "we the people" of sovereign states could limit such Federal actions. Before Appomattox and with *real* States' Rights alive and well, the Federal government could be compelled to abide by the Constitution. But after Lincoln's (and let's

---

320   Robert E. Lee, as cited in letter to Lord Acton, original on file, Washington-Lee University, Lexington, VA.

not forget Marx and Engels') war on States' Rights, "we the people" of the states stand naked before the awesome power to our Federal master—remember it was Federal agents who removed the Ten Commandments from the Alabama Supreme Court Building.

"No subject has been more generally misunderstood or more persistently misrepresented."[321] The preceding comment about slavery is as true today as when Jefferson Davis first penned it. The only difference is that in today's p.c. world, only one view of slavery is permitted. The p.c. view of slavery essentially states that the burden of slavery rests upon Southerners and that the "Civil War" was fought by freedom-loving Northerners against Southern defenders of slavery. As pointed out earlier, slavery did indeed have a lot to do with the War for Southern Independence, but it also has a lot to do with Northern history. The first law that recognized a master's right in his slave property was passed in Massachusetts; the first ship equipped for the slave trade was built in Massachusetts; the first laws to prohibit interracial marriage and establish segregated schools were passed in Massachusetts; the first fugitive slave act was passed by the United Colonies of New England; the first state laws to exclude African-Americans from voting were passed in the North, and the first state laws that were passed to exclude African-Americans from living in that state were passed by Northern states, including Lincoln's own state of Illinois.[322]

From the beginning of American history, the North and the South have been two different and distinct sections of America. This difference was not based upon slavery because slavery and the slave trade were alive and well in all the original thirteen states. States with the smallest number of slaves per capita, such as Massachusetts and Rhode Island, were the very states that were the dominant force in the nefarious African slave trade. Obviously, there was more that separated the people of the North and the South than just the issue of slavery. Many historians have explained the differences between

---

321 Jefferson Davis, *The Rise and Fall of the Confederate Government* (1881, William M. Coats, Publisher, Nashville, TN: 1998), I, 3.

322 Kennedy and Kennedy, *The South Was Right!* 59-103.

the two sections of the United States as a result of the differences in the ethnic background of the early settlers.[323] Many issues divided the two sections of America before slavery became the *cause célèbre* of radical abolitionists. Everything from the Northeast's attempt to "sell" the Mississippi River to Spain; to the Tariff of Abomination, forcing Southern merchants to use American, therefore, Northern, ships for intra-American shipping; to the establishment of a Federal national banking system; to Northerners receiving a larger portion of veterans' benefits with Southerners having provided the larger number of soldiers defending the nation. These are a few points of difference that cropped up after these two different peoples established a common government—notice that slavery was not an issue.

Yet, as pointed out, slavery has a lot to do with American history including the so-called Civil War. For example, although no more than 6 percent of Southerners held title to a slave in 1860, the institution of slavery was so pervasive that it touched most people in the South. Therefore, when John Brown, assisted by Northern ministers such as Theodore Parker, attempted to instigate a servile insurrection in Virginia, most Southerners felt attacked. On September 11, 2001, when terrorists attacked New York, every American felt a twinge of fear. Americans became fearful that if it could happen there, it could happen anywhere. Now think how Southerners felt when it became known that many Northerners were cheering for John Brown. All Southerners felt insecure at the thought of a slave insurrection because of the memory of what happened in Haiti only fifty years earlier. Non-slaveholding Southerners remembered that in Kansas, John Brown and his fellow terrorists murdered Southerners indiscriminately, not just slaveholding Southerners. Due to the low regard displayed by radicals in the North for the lives of all Southerners, the issue of slavery slowly but surely forced Southerners to "circle the wagons" to protect themselves. Remember, before the actions of radical abolitionists, Southern states from Virginia to Mississippi were

---

323   David H. Fisher, *Albion's Seed* (Oxford University Press, New York: 1989) and Grady McWhiney, *Cracker Culture: Celtic Ways in the Old South* (University of Alabama Press, Tuscaloosa, AL: 1988).

looking into ways to eliminate slavery.[324] Even under the duress of incendiary radical abolitionist activities, the states of the South nevertheless at their own expense freed and provided homes and occupations for more Africans than any European nation. Some of the most passionate Southern Nationalists, such as John Randolph of Roanoke, at his own expense, freed his four hundred slaves and provided them with homes. Not only had the South led the way in emancipating slaves, it also fought to end the African slave trade; Southerners led the way in opposing the movement of slaves into the Northwest Territory, a large land mass won from the British by Virginians, resulting in the passage of the Northwest Ordinance. It is understandable that Marx would overlook these little historical inconsistencies (inconsistent, that is, to anyone who imbibed the Marxist view of Southern history), but one stands amazed as to why any evangelical Christian would so completely embrace the Marxist view of the South.

Now, what about all those Secession Documents that allegedly state that slavery was the cause of secession? As pointed out, people should not get fixated upon one large tree while attempting to find their way out of a forest. If these documents dealt *only* with defending the right of slave ownership, they would provide some proof that secession was solely the result of a desire to defend the institution of slavery. Yet, when one considers the history of conflict between the North and the South, when one reads the words of anti-secession Southern slaveholders, and when one reads the entire state Secession Documents, it becomes clear that slavery was viewed as much as a tool used against the South as it was viewed as an economic system. As already noted, some of the largest slaveholders in the South resisted secession. For example, Greenwood Leflore owned many slaves but resisted secession and after secession flew a United States flag from the top of his mansion in Mississippi. The matter of who was and was not in favor of secession and why they were and were not in favor of secession is not as simple as "secessionists loved slavery and

---

324 John K. Bettersworth, *Mississippi: A History* (The Steck Company, Austin, TX: 1959) 194-95.

non-secessionists hated slavery." Such a narrow-minded view of the causes of historical events leads to an immature as well as an irresponsible analysis of history.

In his remarks about the so-called Secession Documents, David Barton noted that delegates from Mississippi found the claim by the Union of black and white equality to be intolerable.[325] It appears that, once again, Mississippi is being held up to public ridicule for what some believe to be its historic racism. Yet, it was none other than Abraham Lincoln who stated that he believed that the black race was inferior to the white race and that he favored maintaining white supremacy.[326] When faced with the idea of Negro equality, Lincoln responded, "Negro equality. Fudge! How long...shall there continue knaves to vend and fools to gulp, so low a piece of demagoguism [sic] as this?"[327] One is left wondering how Mr. Barton could find it so easy to condemn Mississippians of that day for holding views that Lincoln and the vast majority of Americans held at the same time. The Union *never* offered equality to slaves; most so-called free states were busy passing laws to prevent freed Southern slaves from moving into the North. These same Northern states routinely blocked African-Americans from schools, public places, and the voting booth—so much for Mr. Barton's vaunted claim of racial equality in the Union.

The issue of slavery, like the issue of race in today's world, is so politicized that anyone stating a non-p.c. position is quickly tarred and feathered as being a defender of slavery. Today, when strict constructionists demand the end of welfare payments because Congress was not granted authority in the Constitution to hand out welfare, they are tarred and feathered as racists. The same is true with any language about slavery. Slander and demagoguery are substituted for rational discussion.

---

325 David Barton, "Confronting Civil War Revisionism: Why the South Went to War," www.wallbuilders.com, accessed January 1, 2009.

326 Robert W. Johannsen, ed., *The Lincoln-Douglas Debates of 1858* (Oxford University Press, New York: 1965) 162-63.

327 Abraham Lincoln, as cited in, Basler, II, 399.

Marching along with Marx, evangelical activists also find the Confederate Constitution to be a document of unparalleled defense of slavery, something that Marx "discovered" and discussed in 1861. If people view the Confederate Constitution in the same light in which the United States Constitution is *now viewed*, thanks to Lincoln, then they are already wedded to a false premise. Today, unlike in the early 1800s, the United States Constitution is viewed as the supreme law *throughout* the land. In the beginning of this nation the Constitution was viewed as the supreme law of the land only in those areas in which it was *delegated* authority. In all other areas, "we the people," as noted in the Ninth and Tenth Amendments, were supreme. Today nothing is beyond the control of the Federal government; this was not true in the early days of these United States *or* in the Confederate States. The Confederate Constitution is the end product of the anti-federalist, strict-construction school of constitutional interpretation. Every position the Confederate Constitution takes *vis-à-vis* slavery can be found in the United States Constitution. The one fundamental difference between the Confederate Constitution and the United States Constitution, as applied today, is that the Confederate Constitution was supreme *only* in those areas where it had been delegated power. All other power was left in the hands of the people of the sovereign states.[328]

---

328 Today the United States Constitution is viewed as a document of original sovereignty, whereas the Confederate Constitution as well as the original Constitution of the United States were documents of secondary sovereignty. A document of original sovereignty is one empowered by the people such as in the original state governments. These state governments, acting by and for the people of that state, then sent delegates to a convention where a second document (constitution) was drawn up and submitted back to the states, see Article VII of the Constitution, and granted the exclusive use of certain delegated powers. As many have pointed out, a document of original sovereignty grants all power unless it is withheld, whereas in a document of secondary sovereignty all power is withheld unless it is granted. With the passage of the Fourteenth Amendment the United States Constitution was morphed into a document of original sovereignty; thus we now see judges making laws and Congress doing as it pleases, never worrying about whether an act is constitutional. See Abel Upshur, *The Federal Government: Its True Nature and Character*.

234

Looking at how similar these two documents are, let's look at the Fugitive Slave Act found in Article IV, Section 2, paragraph 3, of the United States Constitution. Please remember that this section of the Constitution is a copy of the same Fugitive Slave Act passed by the United Colonies of New England in 1664. In Article IV, Section 2, of the Confederate Constitution all property rights, including slave property, are put on an equal footing for all citizens of the Confederacy. Note that Article IV, Section 2, of the United States Constitution states that all citizens of the United States "shall be entitled to all privileges and immunities of citizens in the several states." In other words, a discrimination against a Southerner's property would be unconstitutional, as was noted in the Dred Scott case. From the beginning of the United States until around 1820, it was held that the Federal government had no role to play in ending slavery; abolition of slavery was left up to the people of each sovereign state. Thus, slavery could not be forbidden in the commonly held territory. Nevertheless, when that territory became a state, it could prohibit slavery. The Confederate Constitution deals with slavery in unorganized territory in the same manner. The only major difference between the United States Constitution and the Confederate Constitution is in the treatment of the issue of the African slave trade. Whereas the United States Constitution protects the nefarious trade for twenty years after the adoption of the Constitution, the Confederate Constitution unequivocally prohibits the African slave trade and orders the Confederate Congress to pass such laws to implement this constitutional provision.

So, we see that every measure touching upon slavery in the Confederate Constitution has an antecedent in the United States Constitution. Furthermore, the Confederate Constitution was much more aggressive in attacking the African slave trade than the United States Constitution. One very interesting point that Mr. Barton makes is that the Confederate Constitution denied the states the right to abolish slavery. Nowhere in the document is such language found. What is found is a prohibition upon the Confederate government, that is, the central government, from attempting to abolish slavery. This is not something new or invented by evil slaveholding Southerners. Northerners recognized that slavery had to be abolished by the states and not by the Federal government. Connecticut founding father Oliver Ellsworth noted that "[t]he morality or wisdom of slavery are conditions belonging to the States...the States are the best judges of their particular interests."[329] This is not a Southern defender of slavery claiming that the abolition of slavery should be left to the states, it is a Connecticut Yankee, and his view was the view of most Americans in the early years of this nation. Equally true is the fact that this is the way the Confederate Constitution dealt with the abolition of slavery. Yet, like Karl Marx, David Barton sees the Confederate Constitution as an instrument for promoting slavery.

Perhaps the most astonishing comment made by Marx about the Confederacy was his reference to President Davis as a dictator. Mr. Barton also hints at this notion when asserting that the Confederate Constitution prohibits the states from exercising the States' Right of ending slavery. As already pointed out, nowhere in the Confederate Constitution is such an act expressly stated. But what could the people of a state of the Confederate States do if they did feel they were being denied their rights or being forced to live under a dictatorship? Since this document is innately a States' Rights document and each member of the Confederation had acceded to the new government by an act of secession, the recourse of secession would always be available to the people of the Confederacy. Here we see the beauty of *real* States' Rights. If the people of a Confederate state did not like the Confederate government's removing the display of the Ten Commandments, it could fire its servant by the act of secession. If the people of a Confederate state did not appreciate the Confederate government's promoting the homosexual agenda, it could fire its servant by the act of secession. If the people of a Confederate state did not like the actions of the Confederate government as it attempted to purge Confederate society of Christian values, it could fire its servant by the act of secession. The central government of the Confederate

---

329   Oliver Ellsworth, as cited in, M. E. Bradford, *Founding Fathers* (University of Kansas Press, Lawrence: 1982) 33.

States of America understood who held ultimate power in that nation and would therefore act accordingly—too bad the same cannot be said for modern America.

The preceding narrative demonstrates what was lost at Appomattox. The founding fathers intended that the one great check upon the tyranny of the Federal government would be the undelegated powers that remained in the hands of "we the people" of the sovereign states. As they understood it, power can only be checked by an equally vigorous counter power. A few specific powers were delegated to the Federal government, but the great residual power, that is, *all* power not delegated to the Federal government, remained with "we the people" of the sovereign states. As Thomas Jefferson and James Madison pointed out in the Kentucky and Virginia Resolves, the undelegated power was to be used to defend citizens' rights against a tyrannical Federal government. The founding fathers of these United States never intended to create an indivisible all-powerful Federal government—that was the type of government they fought against in the War for American Independence. As was pointed out in Chapter 2, it was none other than Fredrick Engels who insisted that by replacing many little republics with one *indivisible* republic the foundation for the advancement of the communist world order would be established. In chapter three we noted that Adolf Hitler admired Lincoln's attack on States' Rights and emulated Lincoln by destroying the last vestiges of "statal rights" in the German Federal Republic. Lincoln, Marx, Engels, and Hitler—what a band of brothers!

Other evidence that the War for Southern Independence was not fought solely or largely over the idea of promoting and defending slavery could fill an entire book. In defense of their family's honor many Southerners point out that while their ancestors were Confederate soldiers, they were not slaveholders. They succinctly point out that it is ludicrous to think that average Southerners would die just so a rich man could own slaves. Likewise, they also pointed out that Robert E. Lee, the unchallenged leader of the Confederacy, was a practicing abolitionist, whereas, slavery existed in General Ulysses S. Grant's home well into the war. The fact that major Confederate leaders who published their accounts of the war years always insisted that the core issue between the North and the South was not slavery but what type of government the Constitution created is abundant evidence that the war was not just about ending slavery. In his article promoting slavery as the cause of the war, David Barton frequently quotes Confederate vice-president Alexander Stephens' remarks on Negro inferiority and status as slaves; yet, not one word is cited by Barton from Stephens' two-volume work *A Constitutional History of the Late War Between the States*. In these two volumes, Stephens defends the Southern states' constitutional right to secede, not to own slaves. By the clever use of sophistry and cherry-picking of words and of phrases, Barton has "proven" that the nefarious Stephens, unlike the mythological Lincoln, was a racist and dedicated only to defending slavery.

The most glaring proof that in 1861-65 the South was fighting for constitutional principles and not defending slavery is written into our present United States Constitution. After the defeat of the South slavery was abolished by the passage of the Thirteenth Amendment. Every Southern state ratified that amendment without reservation. This amendment was constitutional, and did not touch upon the nature of the Federal government, only on the right of property in slaves. When the South was faced with ratifying the Fourteenth Amendment, ratification became problematic. Southerners and many Northerners viewed the Fourteenth Amendment as totally changing the relationship between the Federal government and the states. The South understood that the Fourteenth Amendment made the states subservient to the Federal government. At that point with only one exception every Southern state refused to ratify the Fourteenth Amendment. Even under the threat of military occupation, the South refused to go along with this radical attack upon the constitution of their fathers.

If the South fought the War for Southern Independence to defend slavery and not the United States Constitution, then why did the South readily ratify the Thirteenth Amendment freeing slaves but refused to ratify the Fourteenth Amendment that radically changed the Constitution? Here again we see that the issue of why the South resisted Northern domination is not as easy to explain, as Marx and many misinformed evangelicals would have us believe. But this is how communists, socialists, freethinkers, and Christian socialists enlist otherwise good people as cohorts in their socialist struggle. Many conservatives remember the old communist adage that "the communist world must be built by non-communist hands." Evangelicals marching with Marx are the helping hands in this devilish secular humanist construction project.

As already demonstrated, there were many points of contention between the North and the South during the Republic's early history. One would have to overlook these issues in order to "prove" that slavery was *the* cause of the war. Yet, constitutional issues also divided the two sections before the war. The following are just a few examples of constitutional issues that divided the North and the South: In response to John Adams and his Federalist Party's drive for big government, Saint George Tucker of Virginia, a founding father of the republic, a Southern abolitionist, and one of the first Americans to demand an end to racial discrimination, wrote an early strict-construction treatise on the Constitution defending *real* States' Rights and the right of secession; responding to the passage of the Alien and Sedition Act, an act that made it a crime to criticize the president of the United States, Thomas Jefferson and James Madison wrote and published the Kentucky and Virginia Resolves of 1798; when Joseph Story of Massachusetts wrote his treatise on the Constitution proclaiming that the Union created the states and was superior to the states, Abel Upshur of Virginia wrote *The Federal Government: Its True Nature and Character,* offering a thorough rebuttal of Story's claim and thereby defending *real* States' Rights; when federalists sought to use the power of the Federal government to establish a national central banking system, they were opposed by States' Rights men such as Thomas Jefferson of Virginia and Andrew Jackson of Tennessee; responding to a growing number of Northern advocates of big government, John C. Calhoun wrote *A Disquisition on Government,* defending the Constitution as a document of limited, therefore, small government. Every body of water is composed of thousands of drops of rain; likewise, the stormy body of water known as the War for Southern Independence was also made of many issues, a fact blissfully overlooked by enemies of the South.

After the election of Presidents Barack Obama and Joe Biden, it should be obvious to even the most die hard Lincoln devotees that without *real* States' Rights, America is a dangerous place for liberty-loving people of the Christian faith. As a result of the loss of *real* States' Rights, a simple majority can now dictate social standards and values for everyone. At one time governmental injustice was limited by state boundaries, but no longer is that true. Today if a simple majority of Americans determines that gay rights will be the new cause to celebrate, politically there is nothing that can be done to check the Federal government from abusing our children and our rights. Unlike the citizens of a Confederate state, Americans must obey their government, and their government is Washington, D.C. With this fact in mind, it is shocking to see and hear evangelical Christians attacking the Confederate States of America, especially when they do so by parroting the very ideas and words of Karl Marx, Fredrick Engels, and innumerable freethinkers. Why should such people waste time attacking Southerners who live in what is left of the Bible Belt and are the foremost supporters of Christianity in America? Do they not understand that they are doing the devil's work of dividing fellow Christians? We should unite in the common cause of promoting moral values and constitutional government and not waste time disparaging our Christian forefathers. Perhaps these evangelicals are misled into embracing that form of American nationalism that puts government above liberty. If so, perhaps a quick reminder of what Patrick Henry said about American government would be helpful: "The first thing I have at heart is American *liberty*; the second is American *union*." For Henry, liberty trumps government, but of course that is the same argument our Confederate forefathers used against Lincoln and his love of union *first*. Following Lincoln and Marx is tantamount to exchanging the gold of constitutionally limited government for the base metal of Federal Empire.

Chapter 16

THE ABRAHAM LINCOLN BRIGADE

Self-motivated and ideological, the Lincolns attempted to create an egalitarian "peoples army."[330]

FEW AMERICANS HAVE EVER HEARD of the Spanish Civil War, and fewer yet have any knowledge of American socialists, communists, and other left-wing ideologues fighting in that war. Just a few years before the commencement of World War II, the forces of fascism, led by Benito Mussolini in Italy and Adolf Hitler in Germany, and the forces of international communism, led by Joseph Stalin in the Soviet Union and other international Marxists, struggled for control of the government of Spain. In defiance of fascism and with an eye at promoting Marxist ideology, socialists, Marxists, and other "progressives" eagerly contributed to the "Republican" war effort in Spain. Seen through the eyes of those who believe in limited government and local control of government, the Spanish Civil War appears to be nothing more than a struggle between two advocates of *big* government. While proclaiming that it was fighting for freedom and progress, each side was wedded to an ideology that runs counter to the idea of freedom and progress that the founding fathers of these United

---

330   Sam Sills, "The Abraham Lincoln Brigade of the Spanish Civil War," www.writing.upenn.edu/~afilreis/88/abe-brigade.html, accessed March 3, 2009.

John Brown

The notion that "the ends justify the means" led John Brown to massacre non slaveholding Southerners in Kansas and murder a free man of color in Virginia. It was the same notion that "the ends justify the means" which drove Osama Bin Laden's sycophants to fly planes into the Twin Towers in New York. Radicals always attempt to justify their hideous acts by stating that the greater good necessitated their monstrous acts. (Photograph courtesy WiKi Media.)

States held dear. To a Fascist, freedom may mean the freedom of action of government to promote the well-being of the state; whereas, to a Marxist, freedom may mean freedom of the state to prevent unemployment or freedom from homelessness. While the objectives of these advocates of big government may be worthy in and of themselves, there looms a greater question. How do Fascists and Marxists provide *their* form of "freedom?" Fascists and Marxists do indeed promote their form of freedom; they do so using big-government policies—unfortunately, these policies destroy freedom as announced by the founding fathers of these United States. One should always remember that the word "freedom" has different meanings to Fascists, Marxists, and the founding fathers of these United States.

As we noted throughout this book, radical socialists and communists seem to have had an affinity for the Republican Party and Abraham Lincoln. As demonstrated in previous chapters, the radical socialists and communists were active in many areas of American life. These leftist radicals were active in attacking established religion, promoting the concept of "freethinking," advancing the concept of radical abolitionism, assisting in the formation of the Republican Party, the election of Abraham Lincoln, and, of course, the war against the South. America's homegrown utopian dreamers, that is, socialists and communists, were soon joined by European radical socialists known as the "Forty-Eighters," and together, they worked for socialist progress. Socialist progress is the key element in the word "progressive," which so many leftists use to describe themselves. When a leftist announces that he is a "progressive," every freedom-loving American should inquire of him, "In which direction are you progressing?"

After the defeat of the South, the struggles for a socialist world order in America were carried on by the ideological descendants of these homegrown socialists and their Forty-Eighter allies. Men such as Francis and Edward Bellamy propagandized for their concept of a socialist America right into the beginning of the twentieth century.

Is it any wonder then that when volunteers were being recruited in America to defend the "progressive," that is, leftist, government in Spain, the name of Abraham Lincoln was chosen for these volunteers? Lincoln was and remains an idol of the radical left; therefore, it made sense to use his name to promote recruitment into this left-wing volunteer military unit. Interestingly at the time of the Spanish Civil War (1936-39) there were two names associated with these American leftist volunteers, the Abraham Lincoln Brigade and the George Washington Brigade. Nevertheless, within a few years, Washington's name was slowly phased out. Today, the Abraham Lincoln Brigade is the customary name for all leftist American volunteers who served in the Spanish Civil War. Also, note that the designation "brigade" was inaccurate. Usually, a brigade is composed of several battalions. The total number of American volunteers in this unit was no more than 2,800 during its entire history. After dividing these volunteers into various groups, both combatant and non-combatant, at best they would be described as a battalion, not a brigade.

As stated, the Spanish Civil War took place from 1936 to 1939. Although the main combatants were the followers of Marxism or Fascism, the war itself began with the downward economic spiral known as the Great Depression. After the end of World War I, the Spanish military imposed a dictatorship in Spain under the leadership of General Primo de Rivera. As the effects of the Great Depression reached Spain, its economy staggered to a near halt. As a result of the economic crisis, the dictatorship under Rivera was replaced with a weak republic. With pressure from left-wing ideologues for the redistribution of property, the weak republic soon faced collapse. In the election of 1936, a left-wing coalition of socialists, communists, and liberals won control of the government. With the reintroduction of a radical leftist government, traditional forces under the leadership of General Francisco Franco, aided by European Fascists, attacked the leftist republic.

As in most civil wars, atrocities abounded on all sides, but it was the socialists and their allies who took great pleasure in attacking religion in general and the Catholic Church in particular.

In 1936, Santiago Carrillo, leader of the Spanish Communist Party and chief of police of Madrid, oversaw Cheka death squads. This Russian terrorist group supported the Republican cause. These death squads were responsible for the murder of 2,800 people in one weekend.[331] The "crime" these people committed was the crime of being a "bourgeois." As is usual during any Marxist revolution, the Church and its clergy were prime targets of the leftist brigades. During the Spanish Civil War hundreds, if not thousands, of priests, nuns, brothers, and other servants of the Church were murdered because of their religious faith.[332] It should not be overlooked that advocates of the so-called freethinker societies laid the groundwork for hatred of religion and people of religious faith. In the early part of the nineteenth century America, freethinkers were the first to assault the Church and people holding strong religious convictions. This freethinking attitude of disrespect and loathing of religion is typically displayed in many modern-day Hollywood movies and TV productions. In today's America, religious people are often ridiculed as those who "cling to guns and religion."

Remember that fascists, socialists, and communists are all equally guilty of atrocities whenever they gain control of an all-powerful, indivisible government. This is the primary reason why limited government in which the people at the local level can restrain the abuses of the central government is the best choice of government for those loving freedom. As already stated, neither side in this war should have been supported by Americans who love freedom and liberty as won for us by our founding fathers. The Spanish Civil War also points out why we should fear big government regardless of what type of big government it purports to be. Big government is the problem, not the label we attach to it.

As part of the effort to support the leftist republic in Spain, many communists, socialists, and anarchists, supported by the Soviet Union, organized an international brigade of volunteers.

---

331 Andrew Cusack, "Martyrs of Spain, Pray for Us!," www.andrewcusack.com/2007/06/13/martyrs-of-spain-pray-for-us/ accessed March 9, 2009.

332 *Ibid.*

The so-called Lincoln Brigade was part of the international brigade in Spain. The international brigade consisted of 50,000 volunteers from many nations; the Abraham Lincoln Brigade counted 2,800 volunteers from the United States. Ideologically, most of these volunteers were politically left of center. For the most part, the politically active members were communists, both followers of Joseph Stalin and Leon Trotsky, socialists, anarchists, liberals, and other "social activists." The desire to defend the socialist republic of Spain from attack by fascist "counter-revolutionaries" was no doubt the driving impulse of the volunteer spirit of most of these people. Many chroniclers of the Lincoln Brigade's history noted the extent of left-wing mind-set of the vast majority of the Lincoln volunteers. For example, Sills states that no less than 60 percent of the Lincoln Brigade volunteers were members of the Communist Party or the Young Communists League, Marxist labor unions such as the International Workers of the World, also known as "Wobblies," or unaffiliated socialists.[333] As evidence of the "progressive" mind-set, the Lincoln Brigade was the first United States military unit to be racially integrated. Not only were Americans called upon to volunteer for the Lincoln Brigade, but many Americans assisted in raising money and medical supplies for the brigade. Among those donating money and medical supplies to the Lincoln Brigade were Albert Einstein, Gene Kelly, A. Phillip Randolph, and Gypsy Rose Lee (for the younger readers, Gypsy Rose Lee was a one-time famous stripper and actress).

In his profile of the Lincoln Brigade, Stephen Lendman notes that the major focus of the Lincoln Brigade was to see the establishment of "[a] radical working-class movement."[334] In Lendman's view, with the assistance of the Soviet Union, oppressed workers, peasants, and left-wing intellectuals stood against Spanish middle- and upper-class bourgeois, the Catholic Church, and European fascists. Although many European nations did not

---

333 Sills, "The Abraham Lincoln Brigade of the Spanish Civil War."

334 Stephen Lendman, "The Abraham Lincoln Brigade: A Profile in Courage, Honor and Hope," http://rense.com/general79/abra.htm, accessed March 2, 2009.

aid the fascist element in Spain, by their very unwillingness to fight fascism in Spain, they assisted in its final victory. Yet, when two tyrannical systems fight for control of a foreign nation, why should freedom-loving people (by this term, I mean freedom as defined by America's founding fathers, not Marxist freedom) aid one side or the other? Remember, we believe in freedom of association, freedom of action, small limited government, republicanism, and respect for private property—which makes us advocates of free markets, not government-controlled markets. As freedom-loving Americans, we should defend our chosen way of life and not get involved in the struggles of big governments—no matter who wins the victory, freedom and liberty are the losers.

The Lincoln Brigade was organized primarily in New York and Chicago. The majority of recruits were from large cities with a large percentage of African-Americans from Southern states. Most white recruits from the South stated that they moved to the North or to the West early in their lives. For the most part, the recruits were Northerners or from the West Coast. As already pointed out, these recruits were overwhelmingly left of center in their political views. Surely not all members of the Lincoln Brigade held these views, but as its supporters and chroniclers point out, these views were held by the vast majority of its membership. The following short list demonstrates the leftist ideology of members of the Abraham Lincoln Brigade:

1. Milton Wolff (1915-2008): Wolff was reported to have been the last living commander of the Lincoln Brigade. During the Great Depression Wolff worked in the Civilian Conservation Corps. Upon returning home to New York, he joined the Young Communist League and subsequently volunteered as a member of the Lincoln Brigade.[335] During the Spanish Civil War Wolff served first as a medic then as a combatant. His leadership skills put him in line to become the ninth and final commander of the Lincoln Brigade.

---

335 W. T. Whitney, Jr., "Milton Wolff, Last Lincoln Brigade Commander," People's *Weekly World Newspaper*, 01/29/08, http://pww.org/article/view/124121/, accessed March 2, 2009.

When the international brigade was forced out of Spain at the end of the Civil War, Wolff made his way back to the United States. According to the" People's Weekly World Newspaper," Ernest Hemingway proclaimed Wolff to be as talented a commander as any battalion commander at Gettysburg. (It is likely that Hemingway was thinking only of Yankee commanders.) Hemingway also proclaimed Wolff as "tall as Lincoln and gaunt as Lincoln."[336] Wolff served with Army Intelligence (U.S.) during World War II and after the war always did his part to protest American involvement with Franco's regime in Spain. After World War II, Wolff commenced a life of radical leftist political activism. Wolff was active in the civil rights movement, was called before the House Committee on Un-American Activities investigating whether the Abraham Lincoln Brigade or the Abraham Lincoln Brigade veteran's organization was a communist-front organization. Wolff led the Veterans of the Abraham Lincoln Brigade as they protested America's involvement in the Vietnam War, worked to send ambulances to Sandinista-ruled Nicaragua, and organized donations for Cuban hospitals in his later years.

2. John Gates, aka Solomon Regenstreif (1913-92): Gates was introduced to radical politics while studying at City College in New York. His interest in radical politics led to his joining the Young Communist League while still a student. At the outbreak of the Spanish Civil War, Gates volunteered with the Lincoln Brigade. A strict disciplinarian, Gates advanced to the position of commissar of the Lincoln-Washington Brigade. From 1938 until 1958 Gates worked for the Communist Party, first as leader of the Young Communist League, then as editor of the *Daily Worker*, the journal of the Communist Party. In 1958 Gates resigned from the Communist Party citing many personal disagreements

---

336   *Ibid.*

with communist tactics. In a 1958 interview with Mike Wallace, Gates noted, "I am not ashamed of my 27 years in the communist party."[337]

3. Abraham Osheroff (1915-2008): Osheroff was born in New York to immigrant Russian-Jewish parents. He became a leftist social activist as a teenager resisting the removal of tenants who refused to pay rent. As police removed the tenants' belongings, Osheroff would take them back into the dwelling. Becoming irritated with the youthful interference a policeman caught him and, according to Osheroff, beat him and called him a "dirty Communist Jew bastard."[338] Osheroff said the policeman was correct except that he was not a bastard. In 1937, he volunteered in the Lincoln Brigade. He took an active part in the fighting in the last year of the war and was wounded in the leg rallying a company of troops. Back in the United States, Osheroff ran unsuccessfully for the New York state legislature as a communist. Osheroff served in the United States Army during World War II. At the close of the war, he again joined the Communist Party and hid for several years from the FBI. Stating that he thought communism was no longer "radical or humanist," and after the ruthless suppression of the Hungarian revolt by the Russians in 1956, Osheroff left the Communist Party.[339] Osheroff remained active in left-wing politics and causes. He worked in the civil rights movement in Mississippi, helped build villages for the Sandinistas in Nicaragua, and won an award at the East German (Communist East Germany) film festival. Throughout his life, he pursued an ideology he called "radical humanism."[340]

---

337   John Gates, as cited in, interview with Mike Wallace, January 15, 1958, http://solstice.ischool.utexas.edu/tmwi/index.php/John_gates, accessed March 9, 2009.

338   Abe Osheroff, as cited in, Gregory Roberts, "From Spanish Civil War to Iraq, activist Abe Osheroff looks back," Seattle Post-Intelligencer, January 13, 2004, http://seattlepi.nwsource.com/local/156359_osheroff13.html, accessed March 2, 2009.

339   Ibid.

340   Ibid.

4. Harry Haywood, aka Haywood Hall (1898-1985): The child of former slaves, Haywood was born in Omaha, Nebraska. Haywood's revolutionary career began with his joining the African Blood Brotherhood in 1922, the Young Communist League in 1923, and the Communist Party USA in 1925. Haywood has the distinction of being a member of the Communist Party USA and the Communist Party of the USSR.[341] In 1925, Haywood moved to Russia and attended two communist universities. While there Haywood worked with fellow communists on issues of race for the United States and South Africa. As a delegate to the 1930 Communist International he helped draft the Comintern (Communist International) Resolution on the Negro Question. The main thrust of this resolution was that black people of the South constituted a "captive nation" within the United States and had all rights to free and independent status, that is, independence. Back in the United States, Haywood continued his work as a communist organizer, working to organize Marxist labor unions, promoting civil rights, and sharecropper unions. With the outbreak of the Spanish Civil War, Haywood joined the Lincoln Brigade. After Stalin's fall from grace and Haywood's refusal to accept the new Communist party line about Stalin, he was expelled from the Communist Party USA. Not to be outdone, Haywood joined with other faithful followers of Stalin and worked for traditional Stalinist policies. In later years he would ally himself with various communist groups that followed in the footsteps of Mao Tse-tung of China.

As noted, this is only a small sample of left-wing ideologues who joined the Lincoln Brigade. This small sample is representative of the radical ideologues at the center of the leadership of this unit. As stated, not all volunteers of the Lincoln Brigade were radical left-wing ideologues, but the leadership as well as the vast majority of the members of the Lincoln Brigade were radical leftists. The point being made is that these groups of radical socialists and communists were happy to embrace the name of Lincoln as they charged off to Spain to fight fascism and advance the cause of socialism. And why

---

341 Mari Jo Buhle, Paul Buhle, and Dan Georgakas, ed., *Encyclopedia of the American Left* (Garland, New York: 1990) 750.

should they not be happy to embrace the name of Lincoln? Their socialist and communist forefathers had equally embraced Lincoln and the Republican Party in 1856, only eighty years earlier.

The formation of the Lincoln Brigade took place approximately seventy years after the death of Lincoln. In no way can nor should we attach a sense of odium to Abraham Lincoln because communists, socialists, and other freethinkers used his name. Nevertheless, it is worth noting why these radical leftists were so enchanted with Lincoln. Obviously, it was a smart move by the left to identify the cause of defending the leftist government of Spain with the name of one so well respected as Abraham Lincoln. Making it easier to gain recruits was one reason the names of Lincoln and Washington were misappropriated. The notion of fighting for freedom, notwithstanding the fact that socialist freedom has little to do with traditional American freedom, was also a motivating factor for choosing the name the Lincoln Brigade. There is also one other factor that may very well explain why the name of Lincoln played such a role with this group of Marxists.

Karl Marx and Fredrick Engels admired Abraham Lincoln and did all within their power to assist Lincoln during the War for Southern Independence. In a congratulatory address to President Lincoln on his reelection, Marx made the following statement: "[I]t fell to the lot of Abraham Lincoln, the single-minded son of the working class, to lead his country through the matchless struggle for the rescue of an enchained race and the reconstruction of a *social world*."[342] [Emphasis added]. Marx, speaking of Lincoln as the "single-minded son of the working class" and champion of "the reconstruction of a social world," points out what Marx desired for America. For Marx, every twist and turn in history was viewed as one more step toward the successful conclusion of the communist or proletarian revolution. The building of a new *social world* had to begin somewhere and somehow, and a good Marxist would do anything to advance the communist cause. As Fredrick Engels pointed out to future Lincoln

---

342 Karl Marx, "Address of the International Workingmen's Association to Abraham Lincoln," as cited in, Marx and Engels, *Letters to Americans*.

supporter and Yankee general, Joseph Weydemeyer, the forging of a strong *indivisible* republic would lay the groundwork for the advancement of communism (see Chapter 2).

From the beginning of these United States, utopian dreamers sought to build a *social world* in America. Surely, they all did not have the same idea of a social world like the one envisioned by Marx and Engels. Still, they all did have a few things in common: (1) They believed that man was capable of creating a "brave new world" free of injustice; (2) They believed that by cooperative labor *man* could fulfill every need for himself and his fellow man; (3) Slowly as time passed, these homegrown American utopian dreamers began to believe that in the pursuit of their *social world* they were justified in the use of whatever force deemed necessary to achieve their objective. These utopian dreamers demonstrated this determination first and foremost in the form of radical abolitionism. When John Brown murdered non-slaveholding Southerners in Kansas, radical abolitionists excused his exuberance because, after all, he was fighting slavery. When John Brown raided Harper's Ferry, killing a free man of color and inciting a slave insurrection, an act which if successful would have led to the murder of innocent men, women, and children; his acts were excused because, after all, he was fighting slavery. Thus, man freed from the moral limitations of Christianity is allowed to "make up the rules as he goes," which is the benchmark of freethinking philosophy. A quick look at the record of violence of men such as Stalin and Hitler demonstrate the deleterious results of following such a philosophy.

The tracks of freethinkers, socialists, and other humanists are visible across the pages of American history. From the early sectarian and secular socialists, the Forty-Eighters, the freethinkers, the Bellamy Clubs, to the formation of America's first socialist and communist political parties, the footsteps of these utopian dreamers lead us to modern America. Along the way, we see footprints leading us to the Abraham Lincoln Brigade and on to Spain. These left-wing Americans of the Lincoln Brigade happily adopted other names identified with American history such as: the John Brown Anti-Aircraft Battery and the Yankee Aviators. For those who understand the neo-pagan ideology of these utopian dreamers, it is easy to understand why there is no record of a Robert E. Lee or Jefferson Davis unit in Spain.

As demonstrated throughout this book, it was Abraham Lincoln and the Republican Party's attack on States' Rights and their advocacy of a strong *indivisible* (big) government that attracted early American communists, socialists, and freethinkers to Lincoln and the Republican Party. No one can better point out why socialist, communist, and freethinkers flocked to Lincoln better than Robert G. Ingersoll. Ingersoll was a freethinker, a radical abolitionist, a prominent Republican, and a colonel of the Eleventh Illinois Cavalry during the War for Southern Independence. Beyond those facts, Ingersoll is viewed as an idol by followers of the American freethinking philosophy. In an address given in honor of Abraham Lincoln, Ingersoll noted, "The great stumbling block, the great obstruction in Lincoln's way *and in the way of thousands,* was the old doctrine of States Rights" [emphasis added].[343] Likewise, modern-day communists and socialists, like their counterparts of the Lincoln Brigade, still hate the concept of "the old doctrine of States Rights," but they still find much in Lincoln to appreciate.

---

343   Robert G. Ingersoll, "Abraham Lincoln, a Lecture," speech given by Ingersoll, New York City: 1894, as cited in, http://www.archive.org/stream/abrahamlincolnle00inge/abrahamlincolnle00inge_djvu.txt, accessed March 16, 2009.

Edward Bellamy

Author of the utopian communist novel, Looking Backward, Bellamy bridged the gap between the radical socialists/ communists of the early nineteenth-century and the late nineteenth-century America. Bellamy and his cousin, Francis Bellamy, author of the pledge of allegiance, continued their work of promoting big government via socialism through the twentieth century. (Photograph courtesy of the Library of Congress.)

Chapter 17

LOOKING BACKWARD

The parties in this conflict are not merely Abolitionists and Slaveholders; they are Atheists, Socialists, Communists, Red Republicans, Jacobins on one side and friends of ordered and regulated freedom on the other. In other words, the world is the battleground, Christianity and Atheism the combatants, and the progress of humanity at stake. [344]

JAMES HENLY THORNWELL, a noted Presbyterian theologian from South Carolina, understood the conflict between the North and the South, commonly known as the "Civil War," as a conflict between two different and distinct worldviews. He was not alone in viewing the war as a conflict between two ideas of how a society should be organized. Reverend Basil Manly, an Alabama founding father of the Southern Baptist Convention, also insisted that the conflict between the North and the South was not so much a rebellion against legal authority as it was a Christian reform movement.[345] Before socialism or communism took root in America, these noted

---

344   James Henly Thornwell, as cited in, *James Henly Thornwell Collected Writings*, (SGCB Classic Reprints, Vestavia Hills, Al: 2002), Vol. IV, pp. 405-6.

345   James Fuller, *Chaplain to the Confederacy* (Louisiana State University Press, Baton Rouge: 2000) 292.

theologians, among numerous others, warned Americans of the tragic consequences awaiting America when it rejected a society framed by a biblical worldview and reordered that society along the concepts embraced by sycophants of humanism. Looking back over the years of American history, one is compelled to admit that Thornwell, Manly, and other such men were painfully accurate.

In the early part of the twentieth century, utopian dreamer Edward Bellamy's socialist novel *Looking Backward* became a best seller, selling more than a million copies. Many influential men of the twentieth century proclaimed this work as one of the most significant works in their lives following the works of Karl Marx and Fredrick Engels. Edward and Francis Bellamy are but two of thousands of utopian dreamers who sought to impress upon the general public of America their socialist worldview. The deleterious results of socialism in America would be hardly noticed if we were only dealing with two men and their willingness to promote socialism in the United States. As should be clear by this point, the infection of American society with the poison of socialism was the work of an innumerable number of socialist utopian dreamers who would stop at nothing in their pursuit of a socialist paradise.

Pursuing a socialist utopian dream world was not something unique to socialists in America. Around the world and especially in Europe, more and more people were ingesting the hallucinatory drug of socialism. Taking leave of fundamental Christian theology, Europe embraced the socialist fantasy that man, by his own wisdom and power, could create a perfect world *via* the means of socialism. The consequences of the rejection of a biblical worldview and the embracing of a socialist worldview can be measured by the amount of innocent blood spilt and the number of tyrannical governments established during the years of the twentieth century. Observing this deleterious result of embracing socialism during the past century, a noted economist, Llewellyn H. Rockwell, Jr., stated: "The 20th century was a time when the world sang the praises of despots and despotism. The more wars government leaders fought, the more they hobbled the economy, the more liberty they stole, the more they cut off trade and exchange with other nations, the more their gain was our liberty lost, the more these very government leaders have been celebrated by historians and pundits of all stripes."[346] Whether looking at Communists, Fascists, Nazis, or any other big government advocates, it soon becomes obvious that each one in its own way has roots that extend back to some utopian dreamer— who only wanted to usher in a better society and a better world. Although dreaming of a better world, one brought into being by man's own wisdom and power, we are forced to face the reality of mountains of human corpses and rivers of human blood brought to us by so many utopian dreamers. The one key element that permeates the philosophies of all the aforementioned utopian dreamers is their reliance upon big government. As surely as Hitler destroyed the remnants of "statal" sovereignty when his Nazis took control of Germany; as surely as Lenin concentrated all power in his government in Moscow; and, as surely as Lincoln denied the sovereignty of the states of the American Union, liberty became less important than the well-being of government—ostensibly a government dedicated to the well-being of "its" citizens. Let us state this point once again: *Whenever utopian dreamers seize control of government, liberty becomes less important than the well-being of government.* In the world of utopian dreamers, there is little room for States' Rights because States' Rights is *the* bulwark between the liberty of local citizens and the growth of central governmental power.

The nature of States' Rights is counterproductive in a society bent on producing a utopian perfect society. Establishing a utopian dreamer's perfect world requires a tremendous amount of effort. After all, every person in the less than perfect society will not fully or quickly embrace the utopian dreamer's concept of a perfect world. This being the case, an all-powerful and indivisible central government is needed to gently, or if necessary, not so gently, persuade the less sophisticated plebeians of the nation to fall in

---

346   Llewellyn H. Rockwell, Jr., "Heart of a Fighter," The Free Market, July 2005, Vol. 23, No. 7, p. 1.

line with the desires of the anointed and highly sophisticated socialist leadership of the nation. Thus, we see why States' Rights cannot be allowed in such a situation.

When explaining their view of States' Rights, many opponents of States' Rights will contend, "A state can be just as tyrannical as a large central government." In dealing with the States' Rights issue in the reality of these United States, remember, that it is impossible for a state to be "just as tyrannical" as the Federal government. The very size and *power* of the Federal government allows for far more intrusions upon individual liberty by the Federal government than a state government can exercise. Nevertheless, every true States' Rights advocate concedes the point that *any* government can, and left to its own volition will, abuse its citizens' rights. True States' Rights advocates do not trust government regardless of size. The point we make is that it is easier to control a small, limited government than it is to control a large, indivisible government. Furthermore, when a state government, as opposed to the Federal government, tramples upon liberty, the effect is limited to one of many states; whereas, when the Federal government tramples upon liberty, that act is transmitted to the whole of the nation—and without true States' Rights, there is no way to call the Federal government's hand in its usurpation of the rights of the citizens. Given these points, is it not understandable why Socialists, Fascists, Communists, and Nazis (of course, it must be remembered that all the previously mentioned groups are at bottom, socialists) hate the very idea of local control of government? States' Rights must be attacked and destroyed or these utopian dreamers will never gain what they desire, that is, the power to build *their concept* of a perfect world.

Likewise, the advocates of big government in these United States had dreams of building a "brave new world" for the American people. But one thing stood in their way—States' Rights. How could Washington become the tool of social reform and political change if the unsophisticated people at the local level, that is, the state level, retain the ability to negate the actions of the Federal government? If the states of this Union were recognized as sovereign, real States' Rights stood as a bulwark against the growth of big government. Thus, the attack upon States' Rights became the centerpiece in a Herculean effort to increase the power of the government in Washington. As Lincoln's chief justice of the United States Supreme Court jubilantly announced in 1866, "State sovereignty died at Appomattox." From that day to this, the growth of the scope and power of the Federal government has done nothing but increase each year. Even under the influence of the most "conservative" president in the twentieth century, Ronald Reagan, only the *pace* of the growth of the Federal government decreased, but never has there been a decrease in the ultimate *power* of the Federal government. Ten years after the Republican takeover of Congress, two consecutive Republican presidents (Reagan and Trump) and a Supreme Court filled with Republican justices, the growth of the Federal government continues unabated. Is it not time for Americans to stop and ask the obvious question: "Why are we still living with more government and less liberty?"

To answer the question, "Why are we still living with more government and less liberty," we must revisit the founders of the Republican Party. Again, we must ask the question that was first posed at the beginning of this book: "Why did radical socialists view the Republican Party and Abraham Lincoln as worthy of their support?" No, the authors of this work are not contending that the Republican Party is a socialist party, nor that Abraham Lincoln was a communist or fascist. Yet, fundamentally, the Republican Party and Abraham Lincoln offered a means for introducing into these United States a system that no one less than Karl Marx's philosophical twin, Fredrick Engels, referred to as absolutely essential to the promotion of the proletariat struggle—one strong national and indivisible government.[347] The power of this "new" Federal government cannot be checked by anyone other than the Federal government itself, something every American has had to live with since Appomattox. With the realization of this fact, the Federal government cannot be limited if "state sovereignty," or as Hitler called it, "statal sovereignty," is dead; Americans and surely

---

347   Fredrick Engels, as cited in, Marx and Engels, *Letters to Americans*, 57.

conservative Americans must question their long-held view that the so-called "Civil War" promoted freedom! No, the legions of radical European socialists in collaboration with their homegrown American socialist allies did not fight the "Civil War" to increase American freedom. In reality they did not so much free enslaved men as they enslaved free men. As pointed out throughout this book, with the growth of government, liberty is the ultimate loser. Today, average Americans will pay 25 to 50 percent of their income to government *via* direct and indirect taxes—a gargantuan amount for a "free" people to pay. Before Appomattox, the average American paid less that 5 percent of his income to government, and his sovereign state had the ability to interpose its power between the citizens of that state and the power of the Federal government. Since Appomattox, the average American stands alone before Federal power, and as a sheep, he is annually sheared of his tax wool, all the time being thankful that his master desires only wool and not mutton.

America's homegrown socialists and the radical European socialists saw a chance to advance their concept of a utopian paradise by waging war upon those who stood in their way, the advocates of States' Rights. Lincoln and the Republican Party were more than willing to accept this assistance because Lincoln and the Republican Party represented what was known as the "American System" under the Whig Party; that is, big government involvement in perfecting society. The Democrats, especially Southern Democrats, since the days of Jefferson and Jackson, stood in the way of the drive for big government solutions for social and business problems. This "big government" legacy haunts the GOP to this day. It is one reason that some conservatives do not feel that the Republican Party, as it is now constituted, can ever return these United States to the kind of liberty-based society that our founding fathers established.

The specter of early American socialists will continue to have an adverse effect upon the nation until they can be exposed and dealt with by a people who, like Patrick Henry, place more faith in liberty than in Union (government). As Henry stated: "The first thing I have at heart is American *liberty*; the second thing is American *union.*" In a liberty-based society, liberty always trumps government. A society in which liberty is first and foremost is indeed the object that our founding fathers sought in 1776 and one which we should be willing to contend for in our lifetime.

Abraham Lincoln

Admired by Karl Marx, Fredrick Engels, and Adolph Hitler, Lincoln fulfilled the desire of those who wanted the United States to become "one nation indivisible" with an all-powerful central government. Lincoln is the only United States President to had friendly communications with Karl Marx as well as the first United States President to have a communist in his administrated. As Engels predicted, because of Lincoln's war the nature of America would be changed forever. (Photograph courtesy Library of Congress.)

CHAPTER 18

THE GODFATHER OF BIG GOVERNMENT

Fredrick Engels, in a letter to fellow communist
and Union General, Joseph Weydemeyer, stated his
belief that the war would "doubtless determine the
future of America for hundreds of years to come."[348]

DURING THE FIRST 72 YEARS of these United States, the average
American's only contact with the Federal government was a monthly
or weekly visit to the post office. Unless a citizen was a member
of the military service, the Federal government had virtually
no direct control of his life. Today, few activities of the average
citizen are not impacted by some form of Federal tax, regulation,
or supervision. From birth to death, a plethora of Federal rules
and regulations hovers over and around every citizen. Where once
the Federal government was under the supervision of the citizens
of the sovereign states, today, the people of the states have been
reduced to living as subjects of the Federal government. How did
these United States morph into a super-intrusive all-powerful

---

348   Fredrick Engels, as cited in, Marx and Engels, *Letters to Americans*, 63.

state? The overturning of state sovereignty by Lincoln and the Republican Party made the growth an all-powerful, indivisible big government not only possible but inevitable. Of course, making such a statement lays one open to the charge of being a "neo-Confederate." Conservatives, the supposed defenders of limited government, are the most vociferous and determined individuals screaming that charge. Historical facts may be drowned out or veiled by screaming "neo-Confederate" at the truth but it will not overturn facts.

The most important and deadly change in American politics, which made big government possible, was the simple act of pronouncing the Federal government as the agent of American sovereignty rather than viewing the states as sovereign. As noted above, Fredrick Engels understood that indeed, the war would change America "for hundreds of years to come." Many High Federalists, such as Hamilton, Marshall, Story and others were vigorous advocates of this theory of American government. Yet, as history proves, although very prominent and loud, they were advocating a view that was never accepted by the majority of Americans. The standard view, that is, the Jeffersonian view, of the Federal government was held by the vast majority of Americans. As Jefferson noted, the Federal government (Union) was a compact among sovereign states which created the Federal government. This government was delegated authority in a few areas but the vast number of rights and power was retained by the sovereign states. "We the people" of each sovereign state had the ultimate authority to judge how they were to be governed. This Jeffersonian philosophy prevented the uncontrollable growth of big government for 73 years. The Jeffersonian system worked well until the election of the sixteenth president, Abraham Lincoln.

Lincoln had a very strange if not mystical view of the Union. According to Lincoln, it is this mythical Union that created the states and the Federal government: "The Union is older than the States and, in fact created them as States. The Union, and not themselves separately, procured their independence and their liberty. [T]he Union threw off their old dependency for them and made them States, such as they are."[349] [Emphasis added] The notion that the Union created the States makes as much sense as saying that the members of the Sons of Confederate Veterans begot their Confederate ancestors! Yet, the concept of the Union as some type of supernatural, mystical force that predates the founding of the thirteen original states and acted as the new states' midwife as they were "born" into the Federal Union is the very foundation upon which the war against the South was based. According to Lincoln, before South Carolina or Massachusetts could act in its own benefit, the Union, like an unseen mystical force, took them by their juvenile hand and assisted them into the safety of the arms of a benevolent supreme and indivisible Federal Union. It is on this point that Lincoln makes his claim that the states of the American Union were never sovereign. According to Lincoln, the Union had existed before the states and therefore the Union is sovereign not the individual states.

Here is Lincoln's view of state sovereignty: "Having never been States, either in substance, or in name, outside of the Union, whence this magical omnipotence of 'State rights,' asserting a claim of power to lawfully destroy the Union itself? Much is said about the 'sovereignty' of the States; but the word, even, is not in the national Constitution; nor, as is believed, in any of the State constitutions." Notice here that Lincoln is pushing again the idea that these "states such as they are," only exist because of the efforts of the Union. Lincoln goes on to make two rather odd statements about sovereignty: (1) "...the word, even, is not in the national Constitution;" and (2)," nor... in any of the State constitutions." According to Lincoln's logic, if a word or idea does not exist in the "national Constitution" it does not exist in the governmental relationships within these United States. Lincoln is correct when he states that the word sovereignty does not exist in the Constitution. But does that mean that sovereignty cannot belong to "we the people" of the states? The word marriage cannot

---

349   Patrick Henry, as cited in, William Wirt Henry, *Patrick Henry: Life, Correspondence and Speeches*, (1891; Sprinkle Publications, Harrisburg, VA: 1993), I, 449.

be found in the Constitution but does that mean that marriages do not exist in these United States? A quick reflection upon what is said in the Constitution will destroy Mr. Lincoln's premise. The Ninth Amendment of the Constitution informs us that, "The enumeration in the constitution of certain rights, shall not be construed to deny or disparage others retained by the people." The Ninth Amendment tells us that just because some rights are named in the Constitution that does not mean that other UN-NAMED rights or ideas do not reside with the people of the states. Furthermore, the Tenth Amendment proclaims, "The powers not delegated to the United States by the Constitution nor prohibited by it to the States, are reserved to the States respectively, or to the people." If sovereignty has not been delegated to the United States nor prohibited to the states by the Constitution, where does it reside? The Tenth Amendment of the Constitution makes it clear that sovereignty belongs to "we the people" of the sovereign states. In his second attack upon the principle of state sovereignty, Lincoln states that sovereignty does not exist "...in any of the State constitutions."

Was Mr. Lincoln correct in asserting that the word 'sovereignty' does not exist in any state constitution? Unfortunately for Lincoln (and the nearly one million Americans who died as a result of Lincoln's war) the answer to his statement is; no he is not correct. Just three years after the adoption of the Federal Constitution, the State of New Hampshire adopted her Constitution. Notice the strong language the people of New Hampshire placed in their Constitution: "The people of this Commonwealth have the sole and exclusive right of governing themselves as a free, sovereign, and independent State; and do and forever hereafter shall exercise and enjoy every power, jurisdiction, and right which is not, or may not hereafter be, by them expressly delegated to the United States." [Emphasis added] When petitioning Congress for admission to the Union, Louisiana's Constitution stated that Louisiana would be "a free and independent state." A sovereign state is "free and independent" and a "free and independent" state is sovereign. The state constitutions of both New Hampshire and Louisiana were recognized as valid for people of a republic and both states were admitted into the Federal

Union proclaiming their independent status. Pointing once again to the Ninth and Tenth Amendments, these two state constitutions clearly demonstrate that the people of these United States believed themselves to be members of sovereign states. The people were right, Lincoln was wrong.

As just demonstrated, Lincoln's contention is that states cannot be sovereign because the word "sovereignty" is not found in the Constitution. The notion that states cannot be sovereign because the word sovereignty is not in the Constitution is absurd. Using Lincoln's logic if states cannot be sovereign because the word sovereignty does not appear in the "national Constitution," what does that say about Federal sovereignty? Since this is the Federal Constitution, we are discussing and the word "sovereignty" does not exist in this Federal document, can we therefore say that the Federal government is not a sovereign government? Mr. Lincoln's logic would leave us with a nation where no sovereignty can be found, state or federal! Such a "nation" has never and will never exist.

The discussion of state sovereignty verses Federal sovereignty is not just an exercise in academic Constitutional theory. The concept of "we the people" of the states being sovereign as opposed to the Federal government (Union) being sovereign points to where the ultimate power to govern belongs in these United States. If the ultimate power of government belongs to "we the people" of the states and NOT the Federal government then the Federal government cannot be the final or exclusive judge of how much power it has been delegated. If the states are sovereign then the states must judge if and when the Federal government is acting incorrectly and rebuke, chastise, or (in the words of the Declaration of Independence) alter or abolish the offending government. Under the system of REAL States' Rights, the Federal government is under the control of "we the people," whereas under the system of Federal sovereignty (Federal supremacy) the people of the states are under the control of an all-powerful, indivisible Federal government.

Lincoln also stated that the Union created the states. Is there evidence to prove that the states existed before the Union? Here, according to James Kent of New York, are the basic functions of a sovereign state: (1) Conducts war or pursues peace, (2) Makes laws to regulate society, (3) Taxes and spends tax funds, (4) Raises military forces, (5), Conducts relationships with sovereign nations. These functions were being performed by each of the Thirteen Original Colonies before and during the War for American Independence. These acts of a sovereign nation began when the colonies expelled all Royal authority from their colony. This act of expelling Royal authority from their colonies transformed colonies into sovereign states. This transformation was performed without the assistance of some mystical union. The very first battles of the War for American Independence were fought by state troops without any assistance from Lincoln's omnipotent ever-present union. It should be noted that each colony was acting for its own benefit when expelling Royal authority from their colony. There was never a "master plan" laid out by a mystical union force for the colonies to follow. Acting for their own interests and benefit without assistance from Lincoln's "mother hen" union, former colonies became thirteen sovereign states. These states raised taxes, organized and equipped troops, and conducted foreign affairs with other sovereign nations, including enforcing the rule of international law. James Kent noted particularly that when it came to enforcing international law the only thing the Colonial Congress could do was "...to have infractions of it punished in the only way that was then lawful, by the exercise of the authority of the legislatures of the several states." Taken together the above-mentioned evidence points out that Lincoln was most incorrect when he stated that the Union created the states and that the states were never sovereign.

As already noted, the war against the South was predicated upon Lincoln's assumption that the Federal government was sovereign and that the only way to "save the Union" was to use military force to compel the "rebel" states back into the Union. Nevertheless, as Edmond Burke so correctly pointed out to his fellow members of Parliament in 1775, when the application of force is used to maintain a relationship, everything changes. In an address to Parliament entitled "Conciliation with the Colonies" Burke stated that the use of force to bring the colonies back into the British Union was wrong because, "you impair the object by your very endeavors to preserve it. The thing you fought for is not the thing which you recover, but depreciated, sunk, wasted, and consumed in the contest." Burke goes on to state that to prove that the colonies should not be free, "we are obliged to depreciate the value of freedom itself."

In his effort to "save the Union," Lincoln trampled upon the Constitution. Members of opposition parties in the North were tried and jailed by military courts for speaking against Lincoln's war policy. Francis Scott Howard, grandson of the author of the Star Spangled Banner, was jailed by Lincoln's military police for speaking and editorializing against Lincoln's war policy. Francis Scott Howard was thrown into prison at Fort McHenry, the very Fort which his grandfather watched the British bombard, inspiring him to write what became our National Anthem. The irony was not lost on Key's grandson! Lincoln refused to abide by a Supreme Court order to obey a writ of habeas corpus; opened the private mail of citizens in the North; and closed down many Northern newspapers. All this Lincoln did in the name of "saving the Union."

According to Lincoln, the government of the United States came first and then Constitutional rights came second. Most modern neo-conservatives agree with Lincoln's view of saving the Union at any cost. Is this what our founding fathers fought for in 1776? Did they contend with the tyranny of an all-powerful central government in London just so they could live under the domination of an even more tyrannical central government in Washington? Patrick Henry answers this question for all Americans when he states, "The first thing I have at heart is American liberty, the second is American union." For Patrick Henry and the vast majority of our founding fathers, liberty always trumps government. Unlike other nations of the world where people existed for the benefit of government or the governmental elite, in America liberty, NOT union, was the sine qua non (the essential element) of government. Without liberty, there is no real American government, only an empire where freedom has been, "depreciated, sunk, wasted, and consumed in the contest."

In order to force Southerners to live by the Yankee Empire's dictates, the United States has done to the South what Burke warned Great Britain was doing to America in 1776, it had become an empire that is now, "obliged to depreciate the value of freedom itself." Is it any wonder that men such as Marx and Engels were so enthusiastic in their support of Lincoln and the Republican Party's war upon the Confederate States of America? As communist advocate, James S. Allen, AKA, Sol Auerbach, noted in his book *Reconstruction: The Battle for Democracy*, "Modern Socialism in the United States found its start in the Civil War decade. The forerunners were organizations of German émigrés such as the Communist Club of New York, and the General German Labor Association.... They also laid the foundation in this country of scientific socialism."[350] Socialism cannot be imposed upon a free people without an indivisible, all-powerful big government. Thanks to Mr. Lincoln, America now suffers under that which is the *sine qua non* of all socialists' governments, an all-powerful and indivisible union. This is the very reason that extreme socialists such as Edward and Francis Bellamy were so determined to indoctrinate America's children into the notion of the United States as being "one nation indivisible" [see Chapter 17].

---

350 James S. Allen, *Reconstruction: The Battle for Democracy*, (International Publishers, NY: 1937), 175-76.

John Tyler   Franklin Pierce

John Tyler, 10th president of the United States was a member of the Whig Party and a strong supporter of States' Rights. Tyler held office from 1841 to 1845. At the beginning of the secession crisis, Tyler was opposed to secession and was a member of the Peace Commission seeking to resolve the conflict between the States. When Lincoln called for 75,000 troops to invade the seceded States, Tyler then understood that Virginia had no choice but to secede. Tyler voted for secession. Before his death, Tyler was elected to the Confederate House of Representatives. Tyler is the only former United States President to lie in state under a flag other than the United States Flag. His coffin was draped with the National flag of the Confederate States of America.

Franklin Pierce, 14th President of the United States, serving from 1853 to 1857. Pierce, a New Hampshire native, was a lifelong Democrat with very strong States' Rights view of the Constitution. Pierce served as a United States Congressman from New Hampshire as well as a United States Senator from New Hampshire. During the Mexican War, Pierce served as a brigadier general. During his presidency, Jefferson Davis served in his cabinet as Secretary of War. Peirce and Davis remained close friend during and after the War for Southern Independence. It is even reported that Peirce offered Davis and his family a home in New Hampshire after the war. Peirce was known as a vocal opponent of Abraham Lincoln which has led many modern historians to downplay his role as President.

[Photographs courtesy Library of Congress.]

CHAPTER 19

LINCOLN REJECTED: FIVE TO ONE

The whole of Germany shall be declared a single and indivisible republic.

—Karl Marx and Fredrick Engels, 1848.

The preliminaries of the proletarian revolution, the measures that prepare the battleground and clear the way for us, such as a single and indivisible republic...are now convenu [taken for granted].

—Fredrick Engels, 1863,
in a letter to Union General Joseph Weydemeyer.

MOST MODERN AMERICANS do not understand the tremendous change in the nature of the Federal government which the election of Lincoln and defeat of the Confederate States of America brought about. The nation established by America's founding fathers which held to the Jeffersonian concept of government has been replaced by an all-powerful and indivisible federal system. This new post-Lincoln federal system has more in common with an empire than a federal system of government. Before Lincoln, it was not uncommon for United States presidents to refer to the Federal government as a "confederacy." Federalism is a system of government where several republics "federate" or unite for a common purpose without destroying the inherent rights of the member republics. An empire does not allow "federated" provinces of the empire the freedom of action that was once so commonly exercised by the sovereign states of the United States.

As pointed out in chapters II and III, both Marxists and Nazis embraced the concept of an indivisible national government. As early as 1848, Marx and Engels, writing at the behest of the Communist Party of Germany, were advocating replacing the weak government of the German Federation with a strong, central "indivisible" government. As has been noted, all communist, socialist and fascist nations require a strong and indivisible government. Lincoln, a follower of Henry Clay's concept of a powerful central government, advocated a government which uses its unquestioned power to promote desired economic and political outcomes. Lincoln, a disciple of Clay, pursued similar policies. From his election, Lincoln proclaimed that these United States was indivisible and the Federal government, not the states, were sovereign. In other words, the Federal government's actions were always supreme. Lincoln, unlike any previous president, even proclaimed that the Union created the states and that the states of the United States were *never* sovereign. According to Lincoln, the Federal government had both the power and right to invade and overturn the action of the people of any state which did not comport with Federal policy. It was upon the concept of total Federal sovereignty that Lincoln and the Republican Party inaugurated war upon the Confederate States of America.

Although Lincoln's concept of an indivisible and sovereign Federal government is embraced as absolute fact today, the questions that must be asked are: Was Lincoln's view of Federal and State sovereignty accepted by the fifteen presidents that preceded Lincoln; did previous presidents believe that the States of the Union could not withdraw from the union; and, how did the five living presidents in 1861 react to Lincoln's war?

Nowhere in the inaugural addresses of the fifteen presidents who preceded Lincoln will any of Lincoln's absurd theories be found. On March 4, 1797, John Adams of Massachusetts became the second president of the United States. In his inaugural address he does not even hint at the concept of the Union creating the States, the Federal government being sovereign, or the Union being indivisible. Adams does note that the Constitution created the foundation of "a plan to form a more perfect union." "More perfect union" does not mean "indivisible" union. A more perfect union of free people is one that protects the rights of the citizens of a free society.

In 1793, after an open attack upon state sovereignty was made by the Federal Supreme Court, Massachusetts Representative Theodore Sedgwick, introduced a resolution to amend the Constitution. His proposed amendment would prevent a sovereign state from being compelled *against its will* to appear before a Federal Court. Here are the words of a Massachusetts Representative as he speaks to the issue of state sovereignty: "I rise to protest in the name of Massachusetts against this decision. It gives a new and wrong construction of the character of this Government. It reduces free and independent sovereignties to the rank of mere provinces. It contradicts the Declaration of Independence, which solemnly declares, 'That these united Colonies are, and of right ought to be, free and independent States.' Nor can the United States lawfully rob them of their rights as sovereign States until the Tenth Amendment... is repealed.[351]" Rep. Sedgwick's resolution began the process of amending the Constitution, giving us the Eleventh Amendment, the very first amendment add after the adoption of the Bill of Rights. It should be noted that thirteen of fourteen states ratified the Eleventh Amendment.

---

351 Theodore Sedgwick, as cited in, J. A. Richardson, *A Historical and Constitutional Defense of The South* (1914, Sprinkle Publication, Harrisonburg, VA: 2010), 266.

The preservation of the union was indeed very important to all presidents. Lincoln chose war to "preserve" the union, which had the deleterious result of destroying the union as described by Adams and Rep. Sedgwick. Adam's plan for the union's preservation is much more conciliatory: "If national pride is ever justifiable or excusable it is when it springs, not from power or riches, grandeur or glory, but from conviction of national innocence, information, and *benevolence*" [emphasis added]. How is the union to be maintained? Not "from power or riches... but from conviction of national innocence, information, and benevolence." Twenty-nine years later James Kent, a New Yorker, stated that the union was to be maintained by "the concurrence and good will of the parts, the stability of the whole depends."[352] Both of these Northerners insist that for a union of free men to be maintained, it must be done by the free and unfettered action of the parts of said union. This idea is completely and totally opposite of the actions of Lincoln and the Republican Party in 1861.

In 1825 President John Adams' son, John Quincy Adams, became the 6th president of the United States. In his inaugural address, Adams pays homage to the "confederated representative democracy" that the Constitution created. Note that Adams, as well as many other pre-Lincoln presidents referred to the Union as a "confederation" or a "confederacy." Adams also noted that it was necessary "To respect the rights of the State governments is the inviolable duty of that of the Union.[353]" According to Adams, it is the DUTY of the Union to respect the rights of the States. Where the 6th president sees a duty to respect the rights of the States, Lincoln saw only the right to invade and conquer any State that did not obey his decrees. Adams also informs the world how the union was to be maintained: "The harmony of the nation is promoted and the whole Union is knit together by the sentiments of mutual respect, the habits of social intercourse, and the ties

---

352   Kent, 196.

353   John Q. Adams, as cited in, Masters, p. 336.

of personal friendship formed between the representatives of its several parts....[354]" Mutual respect and personal friendship are the bonds that holds together the union, not bloody bayonets.

Reviewing the inaugural addresses of the fifteen presidents that preceded Lincoln will demonstrate similar language about the nature of the Union formed by the Constitution. That document is referred to as a "compact," a "confederacy," and bond of mutual respect but nowhere is it deemed perpetual, indivisible, or forming an agent to police the actions of "we the people" of the sovereign States. Yet, Lincoln and the Republican Party asserted that no State was ever sovereign and that the union was indivisible and therefore, the use of bloody bayonets were necessary and proper in order to maintain the Union.

At the time of Lincoln's war upon the sovereign States of the South, there were five living former United States Presidents. If indeed Lincoln and the Republican Party were correct in their view of the use of bloody bayonets to preserve the Union, surely these former presidents would go on record supporting Lincoln. Of the five living presidents, Martin Van Buren of New York was the oldest. In his 1837 inaugural address Van Buren notes that at the time of the adoption of the Constitution, the States were, "Distinct sovereignties...in actual existence, whose cordial union was essential to the welfare and happiness of all." That these States were "left unimpaired their sovereign power over the innumerable subjects...excepting such only as necessarily appertain to the concerns of the whole confederacy or its intercourse as a united community with the other nations of the world." Notice that Van Buren recognizes that the States enjoy all the sovereign rights that they have not voluntarily granted to the Federal government—such as foreign diplomatic relations and that this union was a "cordial" i.e., mutually beneficial, association. Van Buren also emphasizes that the "perpetuity of our institutions depends upon ourselves;

---

354   *Ibid.*

that if we maintain the principles on which they were established...."
Again, the maintenance of the mutual benefitable Union depended
not upon brute military force but upon "ourselves."

Holding such views, is it any wonder that in 1861, Van Buren
suggested to Franklin Pierce, the 14th United States President
and close friend to Jefferson Davis, that Pierce call a meeting
of all living former presidents to seek a peaceful solution to the
secession crisis. Without a doubt, Van Buren's deeply held, strict
construction, States' Rights view of the Constitution were 180
degrees removed from the views of Lincoln.

Another living former president during the Lincoln era was
New Yorker Millard Fillmore, the 13th United States President and
a member of the Whig Party. Unlike most Northern Whig Party
members, Fillmore never joined the Republican Party. Although
the Whig Party was a proponent of a vigorous and strong Federal
government, Fillmore was strongly attached to the idea of States'
Rights. In his 1850 inaugural address he stated, "The powers
conferred upon the [Federal] Government and their distribution
to the several departments are as clearly expressed in that sacred
instrument...I deem it my first duty not to question its wisdom, add
to its provisions, evade its requirements, or nullify its commands.
The Government of the United States is a limited Government.
It is confined to the exercise of powers expressly granted and
such others as may be necessary for carrying those powers into
effect; and it is at all times an especial duty to guard against any
infringement on the just rights of the States."

Other than his rather strong States' Rights view, how did
Fillmore believe the Union could be preserved? Fillmore opposed
radicals who were seeking to destroy "those fraternal sentiments
which are the strongest supports of the Constitution. I can not
doubt that the American people, bound together by kindred blood
and common traditions, still cherish a paramount regard for the
Union of their fathers." Once again, we see "fraternal sentiments,"
not marching armies, that are the glue that maintains the Union.
This Union is "bound together by kindred blood and common

traditions" not invading armies with bloody bayonets. Is it any wonder then that according to the official White House Website, Fillmore opposed Lincoln's war policy and was not a strong supporter of Lincoln and the Republican Party?

John Tyler was the 10th President of the United States, a Virginian and a member of the Whig Party. As was the case with Fillmore, Tyler rejected the Republican Party. When it became clear that Lincoln, with 39% of the popular vote, won the 1860 presidential election, Tyler noted, "We have fallen upon evil times...madness rules the hour, and statesmanship...gives place to a miserable demagogism which leads to inevitable destruction.[355]" Tyler, originally opposed Virginia's act of secession and remained an opponent of secession until Lincoln called for troops to invade the seceded States of the South. At that point, Tyler remarked, "In a choice of evils, war may not always be the worst.[356]" Understanding the danger to his home State, Tyler wrote home to his wife, "I think only of you and our little one...I shall vote secession.[357]" John Tyler, the 10th President of the United States, was elected as a Representative from Virginia to the Congress of the Confederate States of America. Tyler died in 1862 and became the only United States President whose body would lay in state under a flag of a nation other than the United States.

Franklin Pierce, the 14th United States President was from New Hampshire, a Democrat, and close friend of Jefferson Davis. Like Davis, Pierce was the son of a Revolutionary War Veteran. Pierce's strong States' Rights feelings were displayed in his inaugural address when he stated, "The dangers of a concentration of all power in the general government of a confederacy so vast as ours are too obvious to be disregarded.....If the Federal Government will confine itself to the exercise of powers clearly granted by the Constitution, it can hardly happen that its action upon any

---

355   John Tyler, as cited in, Gary May, *John Tyler* (Times Books, NY: 2008), p. 136

356   *Ibid.*

357   *Ibid.*

question should endanger the institutions of the States or interfere with their right to manage matters strictly domestic according to the will of their own people." No former United States President opposed Lincoln more than Pierce. After Lincoln's call for troops to invade the South, Pierce noted that Lincoln's aim appeared to be the "subjugation" of the South. Pierce also stated that this odious scheme would not be assisted, "through any aid of mine." Even after the defeat of the South, Pierce remained a loyal friend of Jefferson Davis, even offering him a home in New Hampshire. Although Tyler, who voted for secession and Pierce who verbally opposed Lincoln's war plan and remained a friend of Jefferson Davis, are despised and ridiculed by modern historians, no former president receives more scorn than James Buchanan.

James Buchanan, the 15th United States President was a Democrat from Pennsylvania. As a Democrat, Buchanan was a supporter of the Jeffersonian States' Rights tradition. In his 1856 inaugural address Buchanan clearly announced that, "The Federal Constitution is a grant from the States." He acknowledged his belief in the strict construction view of the Constitution. Buchanan pointed out that the grant of power from the States to the Federal government should be "strictly construed." He boldly proclaimed this strict construction view by affirming, "I desire to state at the commencement of my Administration that long experience and observation have convinced me that a strict construction of the powers of the Government is the only true, as well as the only safe, theory of the Constitution." As did most if not all previous presidents, Buchanan refers to the Union under the Constitution as a "Confederacy." Buchanan understood, even if Lincoln and modern neo-conservatives don't understand, that a federal government and/or a confederate government is not an empire. An empire *is* indivisible and *is* all-powerful, whereas a government of free republics "federated" together for their MUTUAL benefit is very much a government of limited power and a divisible government.

In his textbook on the Constitution, William Rawle of Pennsylvania proclaimed that the right of secession of an American State was essential to free government. Speaking of the right of an American State to secede, Rawle declared, "To deny this right [secession] would be inconsistent with the principle on which all our political systems are founded, which is, that the people have in all cases, a right to determine how they will be governed.[358]" As has been noted, Rawle was a friend of George Washington and Benjamin Franklin and his textbook was well received when published (1825) and recommended for students of the Constitution up unto the election of Lincoln.

In the face of the secession crisis, Buchanan held firm to his States' Rights view of the Constitution. Buchanan would not agree with any plan of waging war upon sovereign States of these United States. Lincoln held no such guiding principle. Lincoln's stated objective was the preservation of the Union. But how can a union of friendship, mutual benefit and *goodwill* be maintained by a war of aggression, spoilation, and conquest? Such a war would not only present the most effectual means of destroying the Union of friendship and mutual benefit but would totally destroy that union. Not only would that union be destroyed but in such a conflict a vast amount of blood and treasure would be expended, rendering *future reconciliation* between the States impossible. Buchanan noted this when he stated: "Suppose such a war should result in the conquest of a State; how are we to govern it afterwards? Shall we hold it as a province and govern it by despotic power?" Such a conflict renders the old Union D.O.A. The Union that Lincoln created is, as Buchanan predicted, a government "by despotic power." Lincoln's war did NOT save the Union! Lincoln and the Republican Party murdered the Union of America's Founding Fathers and gave the world a Yankee Empire that was, as General Lee predicted, "aggressive abroad and despotic at home."

---

358   Rawle, 235.

Buchanan's opposition to using force against a sovereign State was not something he pulled out of thin air, as modern neo-conservatives and other Lincoln sycophants would have one believe. Buchanan was a Jeffersonian Democrat and followed that tradition. When faced with the possibility of some New England States seeking secession, Jefferson wrote that they should "call a convention of their State, and to require them to declare themselves members of the Union...or not members, and _let them go_. Put this question solemnly to their people, and their answer cannot be doubtful"[359] [emphasis added]. Here Jefferson is referring to the idea that the American people, via their sovereign State, have the right to "alter or abolish" their government. Jefferson rejects the idea of coercion or war to force people back into a union in which the people feel that they are being oppressed. If forced back into such a union Jefferson warns that, "near friends falling out, never reunite cordially."[360] Lincoln's use of force to "save the Union" is opposite from Jefferson's view of the Union.

But Jefferson was not the only former president who believed that waging war upon sovereign States was un-Constitutional and destructive to ends of a mutually beneficial union. The Union of States united by a "fraternal spirit" was so important to President John Q. Adams, that he advocated peaceful secession rather than war to keep states in a union of discontented members. Adams said, "If the day should ever come...when the affections of the people of the states shall be alienated from each other; when fraternal spirit shall give away to cold indifference...far better it be for the people of the disunited states, to part in friendship from each other, THAN TO BE HELD TOGETHER BY CONSTRAINT"[361] [emphasis added]. Lincoln did not get that memo!

---

359   Thomas Jefferson, as cited in, William B. Parker and Jonas Viles, eds., _Letters and Addresses of Thomas Jefferson_ (National Jefferson Society, Buffalo, NY: 1903), 231.

360   _Ibid_, 68.

361   John Q. Adams, cited in Joshua Horne, "John Quincy Adams on Secession," discerning History, 27 July 2013, tinyurl.com/yywbqmok (accessed 7/4/2020).

Buchanan refused to wage war and not one American death, due to that War, can be charged to his account. Once Lincoln and the Republican Party took control of these United States, over one million Americans died—military and civilian, black and white, during and after the war. Afterall, Reconstruction was just another form of war, both active 1865-75 and passive, 1875 to the present day.

But Lincoln did fulfill the desires of Karl Marx, Fredrick Engels and other communists and radical socialists by making the United States the type of nation Marx and Engels demanded for Germany in 1848: *"Germany shall be declared a single and indivisible republic."* Even Adolph Hitler praised Lincoln for this very act. Fredrick Engels, the co-founder of modern-day communism, correctly observed the real meaning of the defeat of the South when he proclaimed that the results of the war would "doubtless determine the future of America for hundreds of years to come." Americans, North and South, are living within that nation proclaimed by Engels. Col. Robert Ingersoll, U.S., a freethinker (today's secular humanist) and lackey of Lincoln, noted the results of the War upon States' Rights when he opined, "The great stumbling block, the great obstruction in Lincoln's way and in the way of thousands, was the old doctrine of States Rights." Real States' Rights was a barricade which prevented these United States from becoming what Marx and Engels understood to be the bedrock of any authoritarian government, "a single and indivisible republic."

CONCLUSION

CHINA—LINCOLN—TAIWAN AND SECESSION

While recognizing the historic significance of the War for Southern Independence in American history, most Americans do not believe that this history has much bearing upon modern America. Nevertheless, Communist China's Defense Minister, Wei Fenghe, does understand the importance of Lincoln and the building and maintaining of an empire. Fenghe noted that China's policy toward Taiwan simply follows in the footsteps of Abraham Lincoln. Fenghe stated, "American friends told me that Abraham Lincoln was the greatest American president because he led the country to victory in the Civil War and prevented the secession of the U. S. The U.S. is *indivisible,* so is China"[362][emphasis added].

As noted throughout this book, Karl Marx and Fredrick Engels believed that the creation of an *indivisible* central government was essential for advancing the communist revolution. Marx and Engels' adherence to the concept of an *indivisible* central government was displayed in 1848 when they authored the 'Demands of the Communist Party of Germany.' Of the seventeen "Demands" of the Communist Party that Marx and Engels wrote, the very first Demand was the formation of an *indivisible* German government. While waving the Red Banner of Marx and Engels, Communist China is following the trail blazed by Lincoln and the Republican Party in their effort to make these United States, "one nation *indivisible.*" Fenghe succinctly noted that as a result of Lincoln, "The U. S. is *indivisible.*"

Communist China is so dedicated to keeping its empire *indivisible* that in December of 2004 China adopted its "Anti-Secession Law."[363] Taiwan is not the only "region" in China that is being warned about any idea of seceding from the not so tender grasp of the *indivisible* Communist empire of China. This law was enacted as a "shot across the bow" of any people, region, or culture in China that may be thinking of following the path blazed by men such as George Washington, Thomas Jefferson, & co. Following the Lincoln model, any attempt by citizens of the empire of China to live under a "government by the consent of the governed" will

---

362 Wei Fenghe, China invokes Abraham Lincoln in justifying push to take Taiwan, 'Hindustan Times' 6/02/2019 China invokes Abraham Lincoln in justifying push to take Taiwan | World News - Hindustan Times pulled, 7/02/2022.

363 William R. Stimson, China and Taiwan: The Anti-secession Law, 'The Peking Duck' 1/4/2005, China and Taiwan: The Anti-secession Law » The Peking Duck pulled 7/2/2022.

be put down by whatever force necessary. Empires, including the Yankee Empire, do not take lightly the actions of its subjects when they become "uppity" and choose to "alter or abolish" an existing government that they no longer respect and attempt to "establish one more to their liking." Note that these terms come from America's most fundamental document, The Declaration of Independence. Americans in 1776 understood that "If you can't leave, you are not free."

As proclaimed by Communist China's Defense Minister, today "The U. S. is indivisible." The America that this communist is describing is NOT the <u>America</u>, the <u>Union</u>, or the <u>Federal government</u> that was given to us by America's Founding Fathers. Patrick Henry noted that liberty always trumps government "liberty first...Union second." Patrick Henry was not shy about announcing his belief in liberty over government: "The first thing I have at heart is American *liberty,* the second thing is American *Union.*"[364] Likewise, James Madison, in the Federalist No. 43, proclaimed his love of freedom over government when he declared: "the safety and happiness of a society are the objects at which all political institutions must be sacrificed."[365]

As pointed out in chapter 19, before Lincoln was inflicted upon these United States, America was a very different nation. Before Lincoln, Real States' Rights existed wherein "we the people" of each sovereign state were the final judge of how we were to be governed and "we the people" were the final judge of the actions of our agent, the Federal government. In other words, "we the people" ruled the Federal government, the Federal government did not rule "we the people." As proclaimed in the words of the Declaration of Independence, the "consent of the governed" is *the* bulwark against a tyrannical government. In modern America,

---

364 Patrick Henry, as cited in, William Wirt Henry, *Patrick Henry: Life, Correspondence and Speeches* (1891, Sprinkle Publications, Harrisonburg, VA: 1993), III, 449.

365 James Madison, as cited in, George W. Carey and James McClellan, *The Federalist* (Kendall/Hunt Publishing Co., Dubuque, IA: 1990), 228.

the Federal government can and has, (1) closed down churches, (2) moved against and stifled freedom of expression, i.e., free speech, (3) used the power of the Federal police to intimidate political opponents, (4) harassed parents who dare to speak against racists ideology (CRT) being forced on their children, (5) used the IRS to stifle political opponents of the deep state, and (6) unlawfully incarcerated citizens who question the validity of elections. Conservative "talking heads" on radio and TV have vociferously cried out against these actions of the establishment—an establishment which consists of both Republicans and Democrats—but these same "talking heads" kneel before the icon of Lincoln, the man who made these tyrannical acts possible.

Conservatives, better identified as "neo-conservatives or neo-cons," have a very large Achilles heel that makes their above mentioned denunciations fall apart. The very same neo-cons who are enraged by the tyrannical actions of the present Federal government, virtually fall down and worship before the icon of Lincoln. Yet, it was Lincoln who did much worse, it was Lincoln who made it impossible for "we the people" to hold the Federal government accountable to the people of once sovereign states. Neo-cons will quickly come to Lincoln's defense by declaring that he only committed unconstitutional acts because it was "necessary" to save the Union. As has been pointed out throughout this book, Lincoln did not "save the Union," he destroyed the Union of sovereign states and replaced it with an empire which, as the Defense Minister of Communist China noted, "The U. S. is indivisible, so is China." Lincoln (1) un-Constitutionally suspended the writ of habeas corpus and authorized U.S. military authorities to ignore writs of the Supreme Court; (2) Lincoln opened private mail and shut down opposition newspapers; (3) Lincoln arrested elected members of the Maryland legislature and a former Ohio congressman and had them tried in a military court; (4) Lincoln had Northern ministers arrested if the military felt their sermons were not loyal to Lincoln's policies; and yet, neo-cons still kneel before the icon of Lincoln. None of the above-mentioned tyrannical acts, and there are more, could have happened without the support of the Republican Party and its communist and radical socialist allies.

At this time in America's political history, the South is crucial for the Republican Party's power in Washington. Yet, it was the Republican Party with its invasion of the South which made Deep State Constitutional abuses of today not only possible but inevitable. Lest the reader thinks that the author is over-stating the issue of the *revolutionary* change Lincoln and the Republican Party inflicted upon America, we offer the words of Lincoln's longtime friend and law partner, William H. Herndon: "We, America, the people of America, have just passed through the greatest rebellion the world ever saw, *ending is a sublime Revolution*."[366]

Until Americans recognize the fundamental damage done to these United States by Lincoln's revolution, more tyrannical government will be our lot. Where once America was a "compound republic" as described by Madison and Hamilton, or a "confederate" federal government as described by virtually every United States president prior to Lincoln, or a "republic of free independent and sovereign states" as proclaimed by every one of the original 13 states of this union, that system of government was destroyed by Lincoln's revolution. The original Republic of America's Founding Fathers has become a federal empire. Like the Roman Republic when it became an empire, America has become an empire and will continue down the road of authoritarian government, due to Lincoln and the Republican Party's Lincoln Revolution. Only a *fundamental change* in the nature of the present government will alter the current course toward total tyranny. That change can happen if Americans will embrace the idea of returning to REAL States' Rights and not accept the current system of state privileges — privileges that can be revoked at will by the Federal government. The future belongs to those who are brave and bold.[367] Passive acceptance of the current reality only assures serfdom for us and slavery for our posterity.

---

366   William H. Herndon and Jesse W. Wick, *Herndon's Lincoln* (Chicago: University of Chicago Press, 2006), 266.

367   For more information of how to regain that which Lincoln and the Republican Party have destroyed, see: James R. Kennedy *Dixie Rising: Rules for Rebels* (Shotwell Publishing, Columbia, SC: 2019).

Addendum I

Early American Socialists and Communist's Communes

FOR MOST MODERN-DAY CHRISTIANS it is very difficult to think of anyone being a socialist, let alone a communist, and a Christian at the same time. These very same Christians will dutifully place their right hand over their heart and repeat the pledge of allegiance to the United States flag, a pledge that was written by one of America's most notable Christian socialists, Francis Bellamy.[368] In the early history of American socialism, it was small sects of "nominal" Christians who made up the bulk of the socialist movement in America. Arising in the late 1880s, Christian socialists were responsible for scattering far and wide the essential points of socialism. For example, most Christian socialist ministers attacked capitalism as if it were the embodiment of sin and offered socialism as a form of earthly salvation.[369] Although Christian socialism arose in the latter part of the nineteenth century, it was the descendant of many early nineteenth-century quasi-Christian

---

368   James R. Kennedy and Walter D. Kennedy, *Jefferson Davis: The High Road to Emancipation and Constitutional Government* (Shotwell Publishing LLC, Columbia SC: 2022) 364.

369   Draper, 14.

socialist groups.[370] The socialist Christian ministers' attacks upon capitalism as a prime sin of man and their offering of socialism as a substitute for salvation parallels the activity of earlier radical abolitionist ministers. Radical abolitionist ministers assured their followers that slavery was *the* sin from which only they could "save" America. Both radical abolitionists and Christian socialists placed more reliance on the wisdom of man than on the teaching of the Holy Bible in their pursuit of their objective—the building of a perfect society or a heaven on earth. Once again it must be pointed out that the worthy objectives of these various groups are not being condemned, but it must also be pointed out that how an objective is pursued is just as important as the objective. The old truisms, "The ends do not justify the means," and, "Might does not make right," are still very correct. These truths are something those utopian dreamers have never understood.

In his history of socialism Morris Hillquit identified six major groups of sectarian socialists. Hillquit noted that "the theories of utopian socialism frequently led to experiments in communistic settlements and we may add here that these theories gained more or less popularity in the United States as the scheme was associated with such experiments."[371] Hillquit stated that the total of all "communistic and semi-communistic colonies founded in this country" during the nineteenth century was around seventy-eight.[372] Many of the seventy-eight colonies were from one of the following six sectarian societies: (1) the Shakers, (2) the Harmony Society, (3) the Community of Zoar, (4) the Amana Community, (5) Bethel and Aurora, (6) the Oneida Community.

---

370   These early sectarian socialist groups are herein referred to as "nominal" or "quasi" because their doctrine runs counter to accepted Church dogma. These early socialists did indeed claim the name and mantra of Christianity but were far outside normally accepted principles of the Church, either Catholic or Protestant.

371   Hillquit, 23.

372   *Ibid.*, 24.

Each of these sectarian societies was founded as a "Christian" socialist community. Although their brand of Christianity was far removed from that of their fellow nineteenth-century Christians, Christianity formed the original glue that held these groups together. No doubt, the most common of the six named sectarian groups are: the Shakers and the Oneida Community. A quick look at the history of these two sectarian groups will help us understand the mind-set of early American socialists. After all is said and done, it must be remembered that it was our own homegrown variety of early American socialists/communists who blazed the trail for the radical European socialists of 1848. Proceeding hand in hand with these early American socialists/communists, the utopian dreamers of Europe continued in their attempt to build a heaven on earth. Although we are more than 150 years removed from these socialists/communists, the legacy of these "American" utopian dreamers intrudes upon our lives today in the form of modern political correctness and liberalism.

I. The Shakers

"The causes which contributed to make this country [United States] the chief theater of experiments of the utopian socialists of all nations were many."[373] Noting that the United States was a magnet for experimenters in socialism, the socialist historian Morris Hillquit revealed just how much influence these utopian dreamers did have upon early American life. While operating outside the mainstream of American political philosophy, these dreamers had a rather large influence for such a small group. Theodore Draper in *The Roots of American Communism* noted the paradox of these groups, isolated from American life, yet having great influence far out of proportion to their size.[374] One of the first foreign utopian dreamers to make America their new home was "Mother" Ann Lee, founder of the Shakers.

373   *Ibid.*, 23.

374   Draper, 3.

Escaping religious persecution at home, "Mother" Ann Lee, an illiterate Englishwoman with a number of followers, immigrated to the New World in 1774. From that time until the early 1800s the Shakers grew into a society of up to 5,000 members. Slowly declining, that number was reduced to around 2,500 by 1874 and 500 by 1910.[375] Today there are no active Shaker societies.

In today's world where everything from cars to ice cream is advertised by some sexual innuendo, the one most notable aspect of Shaker society was its abolition of sexual activity for its members. The abolition of sexual activity was a precept that flowed from an even more bizarre creed of the Shakers. According to Shaker ideology, God is a dual being. This dual being exists as both male and female, Jesus representing the male portion of God, and Ann Lee representing the female portion of God. Shakers taught that man was also created in the image of God with a dual sexual nature. Man's original sin was asking God for a companion, at which time God cut out Eve (the female portions of man) from man. Following the logic of Shaker ideology, from that time onward humanity has existed as both male and female. Since marriage seeks to maintain the "companion" status of women, Shakers therefore prohibited marriage and any sexual activity. The idea of God as a dual male/female being would therefore demand a society of absolute equality for men and women; therefore, both male and female members held administrative and other positions in total equality throughout Shaker society. This being the case, we can say that "Mother" Ann Lee, the "female portion of God," was the first American feminist.

Shakers divided the history of man since Adam into several "cycles" or dispensations: (1) from Adam to Noah, (2) the time of the Jews to the coming of Jesus, (3) the time of Jesus to the birth of Ann Lee, (4) heaven or the last dispensation. The fourth dispensation according to the Shakers included all Shakers and would expand to create the perfect society. Deriving their religious creed from communion with the spirit world, which was heralded

---

375   Hillquit, 29.

by violent contortions of their bodies, the Shakers shared with the radical abolitionists the characteristic of using extra-biblical sources as a foundation for their ideology.[376] The wild contorting and shaking of their bodies as they "communed" with the spirit world ultimately led to their name "Shakers."

The basic unit of the Shaker society was the "family." A family was composed of male and female members living together from a few members to many hundreds. Each family was more or less independent of other families of Shakers. Within each family of Shakers all property was held in common, and absolute equality of members regardless of sex was the norm. All meals were eaten in common with separate eating and sleeping sections for male and female members (absolute equality seems to have ended at meals and bedtime). According to Hillquit "The communism of the Shakers is part of their religious system, but it extends to the family only."[377] Although each Shaker family held all property in common, the collectivism of the Shakers extended only to the family. One family might be rather rich while their neighboring family was relatively poor. Yet, the Shakers held ideals in common with other early American utopian dreamers: (1) the use of extra-biblical sources for supporting their dogma, (2) the belief that man could create by his own effort a "heaven on earth," (3) the belief that socialism, i.e., communal ownership of all property, was a means of achieving a more equal and equitable society. These ideas coupled with the notion that the state could be used as an instrument of human betterment were the foundation stones from which the edifice of modern American socialism/communism was laid. Understanding these points will better equip modern Americans to defend their liberties from the abuses of an all-powerful state. Better yet, understanding these concepts will better equip modern Americans to reestablish a liberty-based society,

---

376   Walter D. Kennedy, *Myths of American Slavery* (Pelican Publishing Company, Gretna, LA: 2003) 80.

377   Hillquit, 31.

rather than having to live in a society based upon the impulses of utopian dreamers. If we are to be dreamers, let us be dreamers of liberty and not dreamers of utopian socialism.

II. The Oneida Community

The other major "Christian" socialist community we will examine is the Oneida Community. According to Hillquit, the founder of this "communistic" community was John H. Noyes. "The first historian of communism in the United States was himself the founder of one of the most noteworthy of communistic societies."[378] John Humphries Noyes was born in Brattleboro, Vermont, in 1811; he was educated at Dartmouth College where he studied law. He soon took up the study of theology at Andover and Yale. During this time he evolved the doctrine of "Perfectionism." Perfectionism taught that man could become perfect and live a life above the power of sin. John and Charles Wesley, the founders of the Methodist movement, also advocated a similar doctrine. The clear difference between Noyes and the Wesleys was that perfection, as taught by the Wesleys, was a gift of God to his people and not something *gained* by man's own ability. Here we see the specter of socialism/communism injecting itself into the debate of how to perfect society—by the power of God, or by the power of man. In reality the theology of John and Charles Wesley was closer to that of John Calvin than that of John Noyes. Those with a biblical worldview will of necessity come down on the side of Calvin and Wesley. Both Calvin and Wesley would teach us that there is much that needs to be corrected in the world, and man must of necessity be the instrument of that work. But, it is man as God's instrument and not man *himself* who is the one who will correct all of the ills of the world. Here we see the fundamental difference between orthodox Christianity and Christian socialism. For the orthodox Christian it is God who is the center, the power, and the means for all positive change; whereas, for the Christian socialist, it is man, *inspired* by the teaching of Jesus, who will correct all the faults of mankind. Is this not the same argument that we saw between

---

378 *Ibid.*, 42.

Pelagius and Augustine? Pelagius argued that man is capable of doing good, and Augustine argued that man, without the grace of God, cannot do anything that would be denoted as good.

In 1847, Noyes began his movement as a purely religious sect. But by 1848, and after reading *The Harbinger,* among other socialist documents, Noyes' group slowly moved from a purely religious sect to an openly communistic society.[379] In that year Noyes established a communistic society at Oneida, New York. The bulk of the members of this sect was from New England and was on the average above the norm in education. The sect was governed more or less in a democratic fashion. The most striking features of the Perfectionists of the Oneida Community were their religious doctrines, their views on marriage, and their belief in and practice of "mutual criticism." Noyes' Perfectionists believed that the second coming of Christ happened at the fall of Jerusalem in A.D. 70; that the final kingdom of God began at that time; that a church on earth was rising to meet the approaching kingdom; that these two bodies (church and kingdom) by inspiration and communion lead to a perfect sinless life; thus, the term "Perfectionism." The following is a definition of Perfectionism as given by a follower of Noyes: "As the doctrine of temperance is the total abstinence from alcoholic drinks, and the doctrine of antislavery is immediate abolition of human bondage, so the doctrine of Perfectionism is immediate and total cessation of sin."[380] Once again it must be noted that the abolition of drinking alcohol, the abolition of slavery, or the refraining from sin is not an evil within itself. But Christianity looks not to the power of man but to the power of God to perform these and other worthy goals—man is the agent of God's providence, not the agent of worldly change. Also, as has been stated by early American constitutional scholars, one must not in

---

379   *Ibid.,* 43.

380   *Ibid.,* 44.

the pursuit of worthy objectives violate other noble principles.[381] In the pursuit of a better world, early American socialists were violating the noble principles of the Holy Bible. In pursuit of a worthy objective, they were willing to ignore or circumvent biblical authority—something those with a true biblical worldview would not countenance.

The Oneida Community's view of marriage was probably considered the most deplorable aspect of the society's lifestyle. Hillquit gave the following account of the Oneida Community's view of marriage:

> Their communistic theories extended to persons as well as to property, and they rejected monogamous marriage just as vigorously as they rejected individual ownership of property. Their marriage system was a combination of polygamy and polyandry. They pretended to secure the propagation of children on a scientific basis, preferably pairing the young of one sex with the aged of the other. This system they styled the "complex marriage" system. They strongly resented the charge of licentiousness, and exacted "holiness of heart" before permitting "liberty of love."[382]

Children of these "complex marriages" were left with mothers until they were weaned. At that time they were placed in a general nursery and cared for by specially trained nurses. The community

---

381 James Kent, *Commentaries on American Laws*, Kent, from New York and an opponent of slavery, noted that in the pursuit of the worthy objective of ending the African slave trade the United States could not act in an unlawful manner. In other words, the ends did not justify the means. Not only Kent from New York, but John Q. Adams, as secretary of state, noted that America could not, without lawful authority, impede the movement of African slaves from Africa to the Western Hemisphere.

382 Hillquit, 44-45.

provided an excellent education system, educating the children according to the dogma of the Oneida Community—not unlike modern American public education.

To promote their communistic system the Oneida Community published several books and periodicals. The most popular of these was a weekly publication, the "Oneida Circular." As stated in one of its columns it was clearly a communistic tome:

> The Circular is sent to all applicants, whether they pay or not. It costs and is worth at least two dollars per volume. Those who want it and ought to have it are divisible into three classes, viz.: 1, those who can not afford to pay two dollars; 2, those who can afford to pay only two dollars; and 3, those who can afford to pay more than two dollars. The first ought to have it free; the second ought to pay the cost of it; and the third ought to pay enough more than the cost to make up the deficiencies of the first. This is the law of communism.[383]

"This is the law of communism." These words are not the words of Karl Marx or an expatriate of Europe's failed socialist revolution of 1848 but the words of a New England political journalist—the toddling steps of infantile American socialism. Those who follow these steps must of necessity walk away from individual liberty as conceived and established by the founding fathers of this nation. One cannot follow those who possess the worldview of Marx and the worldview of the founding fathers of this nation at the same time. As the Bible teaches, light and darkness can have no communion (2 Corinthians 6:14). For us, the authors, and hopefully for most Americans, the choice is clear: We prefer to follow the biblical worldview of the founding fathers of this nation. Once again it must be stressed, socialism only makes the rich poor and the poor poorer. While promising freedom, socialism delivers free men into slavery.

---

383 *Ibid.*

Another aspect of life in the Oneida Community of the nineteenth century that will sound familiar to modern man is the concept of "mutual criticism." One hallmark of most Marxist societies is the process of self-criticism and group criticism. Every Marxist state has utilized the concept of self-criticism and group criticism to promote uniformity of action within the commune. Joseph Stalin, Fidel Castro, Pol Pot, and Mao Tse-tung among scores of other lesser-known communists have used this method as an agent of terror to maintain a harmonious communist state. How ironic, here in America more than a hundred years before these communist dictators existed, early American socialists/communists were using the same method to enforce group unity.

During his college years, Noyes is said to have invented the concept of "mutual criticism." Members of the Oneida Community embraced this concept from the beginning of the community. Mutual criticism replaced trials and punishment and was considered a remedy for all moral delinquencies and some physical ailments. The individual seeking the expunging of a character flaw could initiate the "criticism," or it could be administered without his solicitation. Charles Nordhoff, author of *The Communistic Societies of the United States,* gave the following account of a "mutual criticism" secession:

> One Sunday afternoon a young man, whom we will call Charles, offered himself for criticism. A committee of fifteen, Mr. Noyes among them, assembled in a room, and the procedure began by Mr. Noyes inquiring whether Charles had anything to say. Charles said he had recently been troubled by doubts, that his faith was weakening, and that he was having a hard struggle to combat the evil spirit within him. Thereupon the men and women present spoke up in turn. One man remarked that Charles had been spoiled by his good fortune, that he was somewhat conceited; another added that Charles had no regard for social proprieties, that he had recently heard him

condemn a beefsteak as tough, and that he was getting into the habit of using slang. Then the women took a hand in the criticism, one remarking that Charles was haughty and supercilious, another adding that he was a "respecter of persons," and that he showed his liking for certain individuals too plainly, calling them pet names before the people, and a third criticizing his table manners. As the criticism made progress the charges accumulated. Charles sat speechless, but as the accusations multiplied, his face grew paler and big drops of perspiration stood on his forehead. The criticisms of his comrades had evidently made a strong impression on him.[384]

This display of group criticism by a voluntary society is not in itself dangerous. Yet whenever socialists or communists are in control of the power of a government, Mao, Stalin, or Pol Pot are good examples, such exercises as these very often end in up in the killing fields. Regardless of how innocuous this little exercise by the Oneida Community was, it is somewhat disconcerting to realize that these methods have been adopted *in toto* by modern-day communists. Twentieth-century communists and socialists caused rivers if not oceans of blood to flow as a consequence of their various "criticism" techniques. This is not an attempt to blame the communists at the Oneida Community for the excesses of latter-day communism. But it must be pointed out that modern-day communism did not spring from the earth full grown in the twentieth century. The foundation for modern-day communism, with all of its faults, was laid by many nineteenth-century communists; among them were America's socialist/communist communities.

The Shakers and the Oneida Community are two of the most notable of the sectarian or religious communistic societies in early America, but there were many other such groups. The Harmony Society in Pennsylvania and Indiana, the Community of Zoar in

---

384   Charles Nordhoff, as cited in, *Ibid.*, 46-47.

Ohio, the Amana Community in New York and Iowa, and Bethel and Aurora in Missouri and Oregon are other such groups that existed in the early nineteenth century. The Shakers were the most extensive of these sectarian communistic groups, having "families" in the following states: Maine, New Hampshire, Massachusetts, Connecticut, New York, Ohio, Kentucky, and Florida. This is not an exhaustive list of sectarian communistic societies, but it does cover the bulk of members of such societies. Yet, the aforementioned list does not cover all utopian communistic societies or experiments in early America.

SECULAR SOCIALISTS

Paralleling the growth of Christian socialism was an equally diverse group of followers of various utopian dreamers, the secular socialists. These socialists were inspired not so much by religious or spiritual idealism as by altruistic idealism. The practitioners of this form of socialism viewed capitalism as the prime source of all human suffering and misery. According to this view of human suffering and misery, capitalism must be replaced by a more "humane" economic system. Perceiving capitalism as an unjust economic system, socialism offers itself as an alternative to the injustice of capitalism. As many economists will testify, rather than being the source of human degradation, true capitalism raises the standard of living for all those willing to work.[385] Under socialism, the state controls the means of production and sets quotas and limits on production, whereas in a free-market system the consumer ultimately determines what and how much of a commodity is produced. Under socialism there is little or no economic freedom and therefore little political freedom; under a free-market system there is absolute freedom of economic activity and, of necessity, freedom of action in general. Nevertheless, in the late eighteenth and early nineteenth century there were numerous inequities in society that drove many altruistic people to seek a

---

385 Thomas J. DiLorenzo, *How Capitalism Saved America* (Crown Forum, New York: 2004) 8.

better system of ordering society. For such men, active reformation of society along the lines of a socialist society was very appealing. One such man was Robert Owen.

I. Owenite Communities

One of the most notable secular utopians and ultimately socialist activists was a man from the Welsh village of Newton, Robert Owen. Owen was born in 1771 to an impoverished family. He received limited education but appeared to be of such mental agility as to impress those for whom he worked. By skillful application of his talents, he became a rather prosperous stockholder and owner of several companies. Never forgetting his humble background, Owen held firm to the conviction that man was the creature of his surroundings and circumstances. Furthermore, Owen believed that man's character was not the product of man's soul or spirit but was the product of his environment. According to Owen, "Man becomes a wild, ferocious savage, according to the circumstances in which he may be placed from his birth."[386] As has been stated before, orthodox Christianity teaches that man's inner nature, i.e., sinful nature must be changed before any real outward change can be made. Owen's system did not see man the person as a problem but saw man's environment as being the basis of man's misery. Owen's system did not seek God's assistance in improving man's lot, as was seen in the Christian socialist movement. In Owen's worldview the only way to improve the character and habits of mankind was by improving the conditions (environment) in which man lived. Here we clearly see that Owen saw man as the ultimate means of improving his lot.

Let it be stressed once again that according to orthodox Christianity man is the instrument of God's providence. Inspired by the grace, mercy, and love of God, Christians always seek the improvement of their fellow man, but God and not man is

---

386   Robert Owen, as cited in, Hillquit, 49.

the center of this action. This dichotomy of worldviews, God as the center of man's improvement and not man, is the one great difference between Christian activism and utopian activism.

Initially Owen's reforms were centered on the improvement of working conditions, health, and education for workers in local factories. Up to this point most rational people could not find much to disagree with Owen. But for utopian dreamers mere reform is never enough—society must be perfected. It is at this point that Owen began to think and act more like a communist than a liberal reformer. Owen soon embraced the notion that if all men lived in a society of total equality of goods and services where all property was held in common, a high and equal degree of morality and happiness would reign supreme. By embracing this idea, Morris Hillquit, a socialist historian, stated, "Owen had developed from a mere philanthropist into a full-fledged communist."[387] It was with this idealistic thinking that in 1824 Owen brought his system of communism to the United States. Although many of the reforms he championed became a reality, his dream of a communistic utopian society did not take root in America. In his day no other utopian dreamer had the influence that Robert Owen enjoyed. Owen influenced even Southerners such as Jefferson Davis and his brother Joseph. After studying the reform efforts of Owen, the Davis brothers instituted changes on their plantations. These improvements led to a happier and more educated workforce among the slaves of the Davis brothers and have been cited by many as the reason that their slaves fared so well after emancipation.[388]

Bemoaning Owen's success as a reformer, Hillquit stated, "[T]he other side of Owen's activity in this country, *his personal propaganda for the theories of communism,* has been too

---

387 Hillquit, 52.

388 Kennedy and Kennedy, *Jefferson Davis: High Road to Emancipation and Constitutional Government* (Shotwell Publishing LLC, Columbia, SC: 2022) p. 57-59.

often overlooked"(Emphasis added.) Hillquit continued, "That propaganda has, however, had a powerful influence on many of his contemporaries."[389]

In 1858 Robert Owen died. Owen's son, Robert Dale Owen, became one of the foremost exponents of his father's communistic ideas. Robert Dale Owen became a citizen of the United States and publisher of a magazine titled *Free Thinker*. He was twice elected to Congress and was responsible for the enacting of much liberal or "progressive" legislation including women's rights and the introduction of a free state school system. According to Hillquit, Owen's personal letter to Lincoln was very influential in Lincoln's issuing of the so-called Emancipation Proclamation.[390]

II. THE FOURIERIST

Charles Fourier of France was responsible for the establishment of the communal system that carries his name. Fourierism has the distinction of being the first socialist system in America to gain the status of a national movement.[391] Like many modern liberal ideologues, Fourier was not from the lower social and economic class; rather, he was the son of a wealthy French merchant. Being somewhat financially secure, early in life Fourier began studying social problems. Although his family had become wealthy by commercial ventures, Fourier embraced the teaching of utopian ideologues and embraced communism as a remedy for all social ills. In 1803 he published his first essay, "The Continental Triumvirate and Perpetual Peace Within Thirty Years." In this essay Fourier announced a theme that has been constant with most communist/socialist groups up until this day—big government as the agent of universal peace. It may go by different names depending on which brand of socialism is in charge—United Nations, NATO, New World Order, or Communist International—but all such groups

---

389 Hillquit, 54.

390 *Ibid.*, 56.

391 *Ibid.*, 26.

advocate big government as the agent of world peace. The reality of the twentieth century proves that big government is the one sure source of war and not peace, but utopian ideologues are never troubled by facts.

Albert Brisbane of Batavia, New York, brought Fourierism to the United States after a somewhat extended stay in Europe. Publishing *Social Destiny of Man* in 1840, Brisbane introduced Charles Fourier's brand of socialism/communism to America. Consisting of about one-half of Charles Fourier's teachings and one-half of Brisbane's commentaries, this book was an early "best-selling" work on how to build a utopian society. It was well received in certain parts of the United States and had a rather large impact upon those who were seeking redress of many social problems of the day. One very influential convert to this socialist system was Horace Greeley, abolitionist and founder of the influential newspaper, the *New York Tribune*. Here is the way Brisbane described Greeley's conversion:

> I engaged Park Benjamin to look over the proof-sheets of 'Social Destiny of Man," he being a practical journalist of wide experience. Talking over the subject together one day, and of the probable effect of the book on the public, he suddenly exclaimed: 'There is Horace Greeley, just damned fool enough to believe such nonsense.' 'Who is Greeley?' I asked. 'Oh, he is a young man up-stairs editing the *New Yorker*.' I took my book under my arm and off I went to Greeley. As I entered his room I said, 'Is this Mr. Greeley?' 'Yes.' 'I have a book here I would like you to read.' 'I don't know that I can now,' he replied; 'I am very busy.' 'I wish you would,' I urged; 'if you will, I will leave it.' 'Well,' he said, 'I am going to Boston tonight, and I'll take it along; perhaps I'll find time.' Greeley took the book with him and read it, and when

he came back, he was an enthusiastic believer in Industrial Associations."[392] [Industrial Associations was a euphemism for a collectivist industrial society.]

Overstating the significance of recruiting Horace Greeley to the Fourier movement is difficult. Not only was Greeley an active radical abolitionist but, also, his newspapers had a wide American readership. As editor of the *Tribune* he gave men such as Albert Brisbane, Charles Dana, and Karl Marx an opportunity to spread their communistic views to a wide American audience. Unlike some youthful communists, Greeley, one of Brisbane's converts, "remained true to the ideas of his youth to the very end."[393] Although many people do not recognize Fourierism today, one branch of Fourierism is well known to many Americans—Brook Farm.

Brook Farm did not begin as a Fourierist society but slowly evolved into one. It is without a doubt the most notable of all American communistic societies. Brook Farm began as a unique New England semi-communistic society. Members of Brook Farm believed they could better the lot of man by establishing a society on the basis of "wisdom and purity...to substitute a system of brotherly cooperation for one of selfish competition [and] diminish the desire of excessive accumulation by making the acquisition of individual property subservient to upright and disinterested uses."[394] The society gained a boost in its reputation due to its association with New England notables such as: Ralph Waldo Emerson, Henry David Thoreau, Nathaniel Hawthorne, and Elizabeth P. Peabody. All of these personalities were movers and shakers among those pursuing various utopian goals. The idealistic founders of Brook Farm were the ardent social, political, and religious utopian reformers of Massachusetts known as the

---

392   Albert Brisbane, as cited in, *ibid.*, 81.

393   Hillquit, 91.

394   Articles of Association, The Brook Farm Institute for Agriculture and Education, as cited in, *Ibid.*, 97.

"Transcendentalists." Transcendentalists believed in "an order of truth that transcends the sphere of the external senses. Our leading idea is the supremacy of mind over matter."[395] The Transcendental Club purchased a parcel of land near West Roxbury, Massachusetts, in 1841, which subsequently became known as Brook Farm.

The members of the Transcendental Club/Brook Farm were some of the most outspoken antagonists of the South up to, during, and after the War for Southern Independence. From their ranks came many soldiers, administrators, and politicians who led the attack upon all things Southern. Ralph Waldo Emerson, a very well-known member of this group, made his contempt for the South clear when he stated, "If it cost ten years, and ten to recover the general prosperity, the destruction of the South is worth so much."[396] Much of the hatred of the South centered upon the issue of slavery. Yet, New England's hands were not clean *vis-à-vis* the issue of American slavery. While heaping praise upon New England's efforts in freeing Southern slaves via the Underground Railroad, New England and obviously Emerson also remained silent on the issue of the African slave trade. The Underground Railroad "freed" approximately 54,000 Southern slaves during its forty years of existence, yet Massachusetts and Rhode Island slave traders in *one* year, 1754, brought an equal number of African slaves into the Western Hemisphere.[397] Ralph Waldo Emerson's great-grandfather Cornelius Waldo was himself an active member of the New England slave trading cabal. Yet, it is the South that Emerson and other New England utopian socialists targeted as America's ultimate demon.

Uniting with their ideological brothers from Europe, the various utopian socialists joined hands in 1861 as the North rallied the troops for its invasion of the South. Brook Farm sent no less than two notable officers to the Union Army: Gen. Francis Channing

---

395 George Ripley, as cited in, Hillquit, 96.

396 Ralph Waldo Emerson, as cited in, *Otto Scott, The Secret Six* (Times Books, New York: 1979) 319-20.

397 Walter D. Kennedy, *Myths of American Slavery*, 137.

Barlow and Col. George Duncan Wells. Either as members of the society, or educated in the Brook Farm education system, these men and their socialist/communist cohorts neither limited their labors nor recognized any constitutional limit in their efforts to destroy the South.

These are just a few of the more prominent groups of utopian socialist/communist societies in early America. A summation of their beliefs would include the aforementioned belief in man as the architect of his life and world—of course placing God in at best a support role, much like a divine cheerleader; rejection of free markets with the elimination of private property; ultimate faith in big government as a tool of social justice, as long as it is in the hands of socialists; and, faith in the absolute equality of all men and women. During the early nineteenth century many novels were written glorifying the socialists' dream of a utopian society. One such novel by French communist writer, Etienne Cabet, *Voyage to Icaria,* published in 1839, described the prominent measures communists had to pass into law in order to advance their drive for a communist utopian world: (1) progressive income tax, (2) abolition of the right of inheritance, (3) state regulation of wages, (4) national workshops, and (5) free public education.[398] With the exception of "national workshops," it appears that the communist/socialist dreamers of the nineteenth century have been rather successful in their efforts to transform these United States from a republic of liberty to a utopian socialist society.

Many nineteenth-century utopian novels were written in the United States, but the most important nineteenth-century utopian tome was *Looking Backward* by Edward Bellamy of Chicopee Falls, Massachusetts. By 1900 Bellamy's book had become a best-selling novel behind *Uncle Tom's Cabin* and *Ben-Hur*, selling several million copies in the United States alone.[399] Bellamy's communist utopian influence on the twentieth century is measured

---

398 Hillquit, 111.

399 Erich Fromm, as cited in, Edward Bellamy, *Looking Backward: 2000-1887* (1888, The New American Library, New York: 1960) V.

not only by the volume of readers of his book but also by the type of people who were influenced by his work. The following three significant American personalities, all leaders in their respective fields, named Edward Bellamy's book, *Looking Backward*, as the second most influential book at the turn of the nineteenth century: John Dewey, educator; Charles Beard, political scientist; and Edward Weeks, author and publisher. As stated, these men said Bellamy's book was for them the second most important book published; more interesting is their choice for the number one most important book published—Karl Marx's *Das Kapital*. John Chodes in his book, *Destroying the Republic: Jabez Curry and the Re-Education of the Old South,* made the following observation about Dewey: "John Dewey hated the America that he grew up into.... He was called a Socialist or a Communist, based on his own statements which often mirrored Karl Marx. Dewey saw education as a way to create the revolutionary common man for the new millennium's Utopian social order."[400] In Charles Beard's neo-Marxist theory of the United States Constitution, he attempted to show that it was a document drawn up by rich Americans for the benefit of the rich. Beard's work has been the basis for much of the judicial activism that has placed tremendous unconstitutional powers into the hands of the Federal government. Fortunately, Forrest McDonald's work, *We the People: The Economic Origins of the Constitution,* published in 1992, served to rebuff Beard's neo-Marxist interpretation of the Constitution.[401] Edward Weeks was a prominent writer, journalist, and editor during the early to mid-portion of the twentieth century. As with Dewey and Beard, Weeks' life's work was well tainted with utopian socialist dogma, much of it inspired by Edward Bellamy.

---

400   John Chodes, *Destroying the Republic: Jabez Curry and the Re-Education of the Old South* (Algora Publishing, New York: 2005) 272.

401   Forrest McDonald, *We the People: The Economic Origins of the Constitution* (Transaction Publishers, New Brunswick, NJ: 1992) XXII.

Bellamy's book was so influential that one year after his death more than 165 "Bellamy Clubs" had been established in the United States for the purpose of advancing his communist utopian ideas. In the foreword of the 1960 edition of Bellamy's book, Erich Fromm noted that this utopian society would be the handiwork of man. Fromm noted, "[T]he brotherhood of man is to be achieved by man's own efforts to attain enlightenment within historical time."[402] At least the early American "sectarian" socialists kept God around as their unofficial divine cheerleader, but it appears that both Karl Marx and Edward Bellamy removed God from even this marginal roll in the improvement of man's life. Here again we see a sharp contrast between early Americans (not the early American secular socialists) with their biblical worldview, and communist utopian ideologues with their humanistic worldview. This contrast is as real and even more acute in today's politically correct society; thus, we see the adverse effects of following the lead of America's early communist/socialist utopian dreamers.

Of all the followers of Edward Bellamy, his cousin, Francis Bellamy, has had more lasting impact upon Americans than any other nineteenth-century utopian socialist ideologue. Each time an American place his hand over his heart and recites the so-called pledge of allegiance, he is repeating a pledge inspired by and written by a utopian socialist ideologue.[403] Francis Bellamy, not unlike his cousin, Edward Bellamy, was a proponent of "Christian Socialism." Francis Bellamy's denial of the deity of Christ, his rejection of the resurrection of Christ, and his rejection of the Bible as the infallible Word of God was justification of his removal as a Baptist minister. Born and raised in Massachusetts, a short stay in the South was enough to convince Bellamy that the South was hopelessly tied to orthodox Christianity even to the point of rejection of such "modern" and progressive theories as evolution.[404] Francis Bellamy

---

402   Erich Fromm, as cited in, Bellamy, viii.

403   Margarete S. Miller, *Twenty-Three Words* (Printcraft Press, Inc., Portsmouth, VA: 1976) 49.

404   *Ibid.*, 351.

believed that the defining event in American history was the "Civil War," and he admitted that he desired that his pledge would reinforce everything that the arguments of "Hamilton, the Webster-Haynes debate, the speeches of Seward and Lincoln, [and] the Civil War"[405] had accomplished. Alexander Hamilton, Daniel Webster, Abraham Lincoln, and William H. Seward were all advocates of big government—the antithesis of States' Rights.

As with all good socialists/communists, Bellamy had ultimate faith in man and big government. All major socialist political leaders in the twentieth century, Vladimer Lenin, Joseph Stalin, Adolf Hitler, Benito Mussolini, Mao Tse-tung, and their sycophants have been advocates of big government—none have advocated a government organized along a States' Rights concept. The mad rush to join the Union Army by radical European socialists, the strident condemnation of the South by America's homegrown socialists/communists, Karl Marx's own cheer leading for the Union cause during the war, and Francis Bellamy's desire to have a pledge that would solidify the victory of the Federal government over the South is proof positive that the South stood in the way of America's utopian socialist ideologues.

405   Francis Bellamy, as cited in, *Ibid.*, 121.

ADDENDUM II

PROMINENT EARLY AMERICAN SOCIALISTS AND COMMUNISTS

AS DEMONSTRATED in the first three chapters of this work, the United States has a long and somewhat extensive history of socialist and communist activity in the early history of this country. At the time of the founding of this nation the terms socialism and communism were virtually interchangeable. Also, at that time the term communism did not carry the same political connotation as it does for those living in the twenty-first century. Communism was simply a term applied to a communal lifestyle in which all property was held in common. A communist was one who lived or advocated living in a communal society. After the Russian Revolution and the establishment of the communist regime in that nation, the world has had more than eighty-nine years to see what "communism" really means. The harsh reality of a secret-police state with its numerous killing fields and gulags has caused the term communism to mean much more than just "collective ownership of private property." Nevertheless, as the historians of American socialism and communism have pointed out, it was these embryonic collectivist and communal societies that led to the formation of modern socialism and communism in the United States.

The very first British settlers in the American colonies, both those landing in Virginia and those landing in Massachusetts, experimented with communal, that is, communistic, living arrangements. To their credit they both soon recognized that socialism/communism does not work—something modern American political leaders appear to have overlooked. As has been stated numerous times in this work, socialism makes the rich poor and the poor poorer. After the rejection of communal living arrangements, both Virginia and Massachusetts began experiencing an ever-growing and prosperous style of living. Both Virginia and Massachusetts were well established, having passed through their communist failures by 1620, when in 1776 one of the first proponents of a "new" style of living, "Mother" Ann Lee, an illiterate English utopian dreamer, reintroduced the communal societal lifestyle to America. Ann Lee introduced to the United States a communal society that many socialist and communist historians indicate as being the first attempt at establishing a communist society in the United States. She and a host of other utopian dreamers would "collectively" inflict upon the American public the economic philosophies espoused by men such as Marx, Engels, Lenin, Mussolini, and Hitler.

Most utopian dreamers do not advocate socialism in order to establish the now all too typical tyrannical mega-state. As has been noted, most advocates of socialism are "utopian dreamers." A utopian dreamer is one who enthusiastically and sincerely desires the betterment of his fellow man. His mistake is not in the dream of healing a sick world, thereby making his fellow man healthier; his mistake is in the choice of the wrong medicine to cure his patient. Collectivism, socialism, communism, and all other forms of "big governmentism," destroy the very mechanism that creates a more prosperous and healthy society: free market capitalism. As the size and scope of government increases, the amount of freedom left to the individuals of that society is directly diminished, and equally the ability of the free market to produce wealth is reduced. The failure of socialism to produce is a lesson learned the hard way by the settlers of Jamestown, Virginia, and Plymouth, Massachusetts.

Unfortunately for Americans who are almost four hundred years removed from the experiences of the settlers of Virginia and Massachusetts, the lesson of socialism's failures may have to be relearned the hard way.

The following is a partial list of some of the more influential socialists and communists in early American history. The list is by no means exhaustive, but it will help the reader to understand the scope and influence of these early American socialists and communists.

1. Anneke, Friedrich (1817-66): Anneke was born into an aristocratic family in Germany. He was trained in a Prussian military academy and commissioned as an officer in the Prussian Army. Due to his strong communist sympathy, he was forced to surrender his commission as a Prussian officer. On leaving that service he joined in the effort to overthrow the government of Baden and establish a socialist government. Anneke was a member of the Communist League in Germany, and after the failure of the socialist revolution he immigrated to the United States. When Abraham Lincoln called for volunteers to "put down the rebellion," Anneke offered his service to the Union and was commissioned a colonel of Wisconsin volunteer infantry. Anneke was an associate of Karl Marx and Fredrick Engels while in Europe.

2. Anneke, Mathilde Franziska: Wife and fellow socialist radical of Friedrich Anneke. After rejecting her Roman Catholic childhood faith, Mathilde embraced the philosophy of freethinking. Her husband introduced her to Karl Marx before they departed from Europe for the United States after the failure of one of the socialist revolts in Germany. Mathilde became an early feminist and played a role in most "progressive" movements, especially if they offered her a chance to advance her utopian socialist dream for America.

3. Bellamy, Edward (1850-98): A latter-nineteenth-century socialist utopian dreamer whose influence extends into the twenty-first century. Born in Massachusetts, Bellamy earned his claim to fame by his best-selling book, *Looking Backward*. Within twenty years of its first publication, *Looking Backward* had sold more than one million copies. *Looking Backward* is a socialist polemic advocating a communistic society in America. This book has been cited by many notable Americans such as Charles Beard and John Dewey as the second most important book of the nineteenth century. The book cited by Beard and Dewey as the most influential book of the nineteenth century was Marx and Engels' *Das Capital*.

4. Bellamy, Francis: Cousin of noted socialist author Edward Bellamy, Francis was also born in Massachusetts. Following in his cousin's footsteps, Francis, a Baptist minister, embraced a concept known as "Christian socialism." As a follower of Christian socialism, Francis rejected the biblical concept of Jesus Christ as the Son of God and redeemer of lost mankind. His rejection of the deity of Christ resulted in his removal from the ministry. Francis's chief claim to fame is as author of the pledge of allegiance to the United States flag. Francis believed that the "Civil War" was the defining event of American history and desired a pledge that would reinforce the meaning of the North's victory over the South. His pledge was designed to incorporate into the mind-set of all Americans the views of Abraham Lincoln, Daniel Webster, and the radical abolitionists, who he believed held the correct view of what America should be.

5. Birney, William (1819-1907): Born in Alabama, Birney, a radical abolitionist, moved to Europe. Embracing radical socialism, he participated in the Paris socialist revolution of 1848. After the failure of the socialist revolution, Birney returned to the United States. At the commencement of

war, Birney offered his service to the Union, commanding a regiment of African-American troops and attaining the rank of brigadier general.

6. Cluseret, Gustave Paul (1823-1929): Trained as an officer in the French Army, he left that service to become the chief of staff of the Paris Commune during the socialist revolt of 1848. Cluseret immigrated to the United States with the collapse of the revolt. At the outbreak of war in 1861, Cluseret offered his services to the Union Army and subsequently accepted a commission as a Union officer. Returning to France, he proclaimed himself a socialist. In March 1871, with the communist revolt in Paris, Cluseret rushed to Paris and was elected as a member of the Commune of Paris. With the failure of the communist government he fled France.

7. Dana, Charles A. (1819-97): A member of the Fourier communistic society, Dana was well acquainted with Karl Marx, Fredrick Engels, and many other prominent European radical socialists. It was Dana to whom Karl Marx addressed a letter in 1851 on behalf of Joseph Weydemeyer. Weydemeyer was a close friend of Marx and Engels and a fellow communist. Marx's letter to Dana in New York was an effort to gain assistance for Weydemeyer as he arrived in the United States. Dana was also a close friend of Horace Greeley, editor of the *New York Tribune.* It was with Dana's assistance that Greeley hired Marx as a contributor to the *Tribune.* During the war, Dana served as assistant secretary of war, becoming the first high-level communist in an American administration.

8. Devoy, John (1842-1928): Fenian and socialist Irish-American, Devoy represented the Irish contingent at the First International (communist) in New York. He was the editor of an Irish-American newspaper and author of *Recollections of an Irish Rebel,* a book detailing his efforts in freeing Ireland of English domination.

9. Douai, Adolph (1819-88): One of the few European socialists who immigrated to a Southern state before the war. Douai was an active participant in the socialist revolution in Germany in 1848. As a result of the failure of the socialist revolt, Douai immigrated to San Antonio, Texas, and established an abolitionist newspaper. Douai and his message were not well received by the general population of San Antonio. During his life he was the editor of several newspapers promoting various socialist causes such as the newspapers of the Working Men's Party.

10. Foster-Avery, Rachel: A socialist activist, Foster-Avery helped in the publication of Fredrick Engels' American edition of *The Condition of the Working Class in England.* She was active in the early feminist movement, serving as secretary of the National Women's Suffrage Association.

11. Greeley, Horace (1811-72): Radical abolitionist and dedicated socialist. Like his assistant editor, Charles A. Dana, Greeley had a warm relationship with Karl Marx and other radical socialists. It was Greeley who first hired Charles Dana as assistant editor of his *New York Tribune,* and it was also Greeley, via the efforts of Marx's friend Dana, who hired Karl Marx as a contributor to his New York daily paper.

12. Harney, George Julian (1817-97): Member of the Communist League of London and the leftist Chartist Movement in England. Harney was an editor of several newspapers and a representative at the First (communist) International. Harney immigrated to the United States in 1860 and served as a mid-level bureaucrat in the state of Massachusetts.

13. Kapp, Friedrich (1824-84): A participant of the 1848 German revolution. Upon the collapse of the socialist republic, Kapp sought asylum in the United States. Kapp returned to Germany after serving for the Union cause during the War Between the States.

14. Kelly, Florence (1859-1932): Kelly was an activist in the American socialist cause. Her major claim to fame appears to be in translating a work of Karl Marx's good friend and fellow communist, Fredrick Engels, *The Condition of the Working Class in 1844,* and in serving as executive secretary for the National Consumers League.

15. Luning, Otto (1818-68): A German publicist and physician known as a "true socialist." This "true socialist" was the brother-in-law of Union general Joseph Weydemeyer and a close friend of Karl Marx and Fredrick Engels.

16. McDonnell, J. P.: In 1833 McDonnell organized the New Jersey State Federation of Trades and Labor Unions. He was an Irish-American with strong attachments to the Fenian movement and served as a member of the General Council of the First International.

17. Meyer, Siegfried (1840-72): Immigrating to the United States in 1867, this German socialist and engineer assisted in the founding of the General German Working Men's Union and served as a delegate to the First International.

18. Most, Johann J. (1846-1906): After being expelled from the German Social-Democratic Party because of his anarchist views, Most immigrated to the United States in 1883. After the publication of *Die Freiheit,* Most became known as the leader of the anarchist movement in the United States.

19. Rosenberg, William L.: A German-American writer, Rosenberg served as secretary of the National Executive Committee of the Socialist Labor Party. Rosenberg's brand of socialism did not endear him to the more radical Marxists within the Socialist Labor Party, and subsequently he was forced out of the party.

20. Sanial, Lucien (1837-1920): French-American radical socialist. Relocating to the United States, Sanial became active in the socialist labor movement. He was an active member of both the Socialist Labor Party and the Socialist Party.

21. Schurz, Carl (1829-1906): Schurz was active in the socialist movement in Germany and participated in the socialist revolution in Germany. After the failure of the socialist republic, Schurz sought asylum in the United States. At the outbreak of war in 1861, Schurz joined in the Union's effort to suppress the independence of the Confederate States, attaining the rank of brigadier general. After the war and during Reconstruction he served as senator from Missouri and, under the Hayes administration, secretary of the interior.

22. Seiler, Sebastian (1810-90): A radical socialist German-American journalist, Seiler was a member of the League of the Just, a communist/socialist organization, and the Communist League. He was active in communist and socialist organizations in the United States.

23. Sherman, William T. (1820-91): While doing research for this book, the author came across this name in a list of "approved" socialists/communists in America. The press of the Communist Party of the United States published the book from which this name, as well as the names of other leading socialists/communists, was taken. The editor of this communist book noted that Sherman was an "outstanding" general of the Union Army. It should be noted that the co-founder of modern-day communism, Fredrick Engels, also held this opinion. Both Gen. William Sherman and Sen. John Sherman, his brother, believed in a strong indivisible central government.

24. Sigel, Franz (1824-1902): Commander of socialist troops in the Baden (Germany) revolt in 1849. With the failure of the socialist revolution, Sigel sought asylum in the United States. At the outbreak of war, Sigel volunteered for service in the Union Army and rose to the rank of major general.

25. Swinton, John (1830-1901): A journalist and a socialist, Swinton served as the managing editor of the *New York Times* during the War Between the States. Swinton was a founding member of the Socialist Labor Party and served as editor for several workers' journals.

26. Tucker, Benjamin R.: Founder of the *Radical Review and Liberty,* Tucker was an avowed anarchist.

27. Van Patten, Phillip: An activist in socialist causes in New York, Van Patten served as secretary of the New York Central Labor Union, secretary of the Working Men's Party, and secretary of the Socialist Labor Party.

28. Vogt, August (1830-83): A member of the Cologne (Germany) Communist League and the General Association of Workers of Berlin, Germany, Vogt moved to the United States one year after the defeat of the South. He served as a correspondent for the General Council of the First International for the United States.

29. Walther, Otto: Walther was a German-American socialist leader, a member of the Executive Council of the Socialist Labor Party of New York, and the editor of several socialist labor journals.

30. Weitling, Wilhelm (1808-71): German-American socialist labor leader described as a "Utopian Communist." In 1837 Weitling joined the League of the Just, a utopian socialist/communist organization. Between 1835 and 1841 he was an active propagandist for communist ideas in France and

Switzerland. Taking flight to the United States in the early 1850s, he lived in New York City where he edited several socialist/communist newspapers.

31. Westphalen, Edgar V. (1819-90): Karl Marx's brother-in-law. As a young man Westphalen and Marx were schoolmates. Joining the Communist League in 1846, he began his lifelong association with Marx and Marx's system of socialism. Westphalen moved to and lived in the United States, bringing with him his love for socialism.

32. Weydemeyer, Joseph (1818-66): Brigadier General Weydemeyer of the Union, that is, United States, Army has been described by a communist publication as a "pioneer American Marxist." Weydemeyer was active in the socialist revolution in Germany, and as a result had to flee his homeland. He was a close friend of Karl Marx and Fredrick Engels. While in London Weydemeyer was a fellow member of the London Communist League with Karl Marx. In 1851 Weydemeyer moved to the United States, and a close relationship was maintained between Weydemeyer, Marx, and Engels. Weydemeyer founded and edited several radical socialist journals both before and after the War Between the States. Weydemeyer was active in Republican Party politics, supporting both John C. Fremont in 1856 and Abraham Lincoln in 1860. With his socialist faith in strong central government, Weydemeyer had little problem in supporting the Union cause during the war.

33. Willich, August (1810-78): Brigadier General Willich of the Union Army (United States Army) was a German-American often referred to as "the Reddest of the Red '48ers" by the observers of that group of socialist activists and a "communist with a heart" by Karl Marx. A Prussian officer, he left the service of the Prussian government and embraced the ideas of socialism. When the socialist revolution broke out in Germany, Willich joined the revolutionary effort as a corps commander of the revolutionary army. Willich was

a member of the Central Committee of the Communist League until his flight from Europe to the United States in 1853. A lukewarm supporter of Abraham Lincoln, Willich did not appreciate Lincoln's close ties with big-business interests; nevertheless, he supported the Republican Party, Lincoln, and the Union's war effort against the South.

34. Woodhull, Victoria C. (1838-1927): Early American feminist and social reformer. Woodhull was a delegate to Section 12 of the First International in New York City. With the assistance of her sister, Tennessee Claflin, she founded and edited a social activist journal, *Woodhull and Claflin's Weekly*. In 1872 she was nominated for president by the Equal Rights Party, thus becoming one of the first women to be nominated and to run for president of the United States.

About the Authors

WALTER D. (DONNIE) KENNEDY is a life member of the Sons of Confederate Veterans and is best known as the author and co-author of several pro-South books. The most notable book the Kennedy Twins have written is 'The South Was Right' which has sold over 150,000 copies.

Many in the media have noted the Kennedy Twins advocacy of limited government, that is, real States' Rights, which have led to several interviews and TV appearances. The Kennedy Twins have been interviewed by numerous local and national talk radio shows including Col. Oliver North's radio show, Alan Comes radio show, Bill Maher's show Politically Incorrect, BBC, and French National TV.

From 2018 to July of 2022 Donnie served as Chief of Heritage Operations and Ron Kennedy as Deputy Chief of Heritage Promotions for the Sons of Confederate Veterans (SCV). In July of 2022 Donnie was elected Lt. Commander-in-Chief of the SCV and Ron was appointed as the Chief of Heritage Operations for the SCV. Both have served as Commander of the Louisiana Division SCV. They have received special recognition awards from the SCV's Commander-in-Chief, including the Robert E. Lee Medal and (Donnie) the Jefferson Davis Medal. Both have been awarded the Jefferson Davis Historical Gold Medal from the United Daughters of the Confederacy and numerous other awards from various Southern Heritage organizations.

AL BENSON JR. was born in Rhode Island. Mr. Benson and his wife reside in Farmerville, Louisiana. Early in his life, Al's passion for history led him to understand that the whole truth about the "Civil War" was not being told. Al has spent the better part of his life writing articles and speaking to various historical and cultural groups correcting the false narrative about the War for Southern Independence. Al's articles can be found on several blog sites including the 'Copperhead Chronicles' and on New Oath_ Reminder at https://revisedhistory.wordpress.com/. Mr. Benson and Mr. Kennedy's first book exposing Lincoln and Marxism, Red Republicans and Lincoln's Marxist, iUniverse Press, is the foundation for the current work on this subject. Al is a member of the Confederate Society of America and the Capt. Thomas O. Benton Camp Sons of Confederate Veterans, Monroe, La.

Latest Releases & Best Sellers

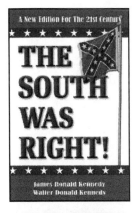
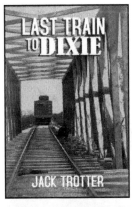

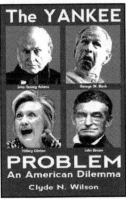

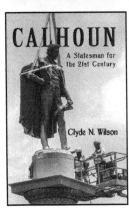
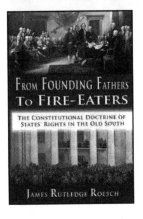

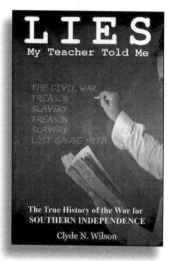

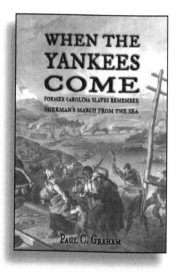

Made in the USA
Middletown, DE
10 November 2023

42377034R00181